gospelontheGO

God's Daily Direction for Your Life

Published by Blackstone Media Group, www.bmgcreative.com

ISBN-978-0-9825818-3-4

Printed in the United States of America.

Dedication

I dedicate this book to the three people who have impacted my life the most. First, I dedicate this book to my wife Daniele—a true Proverbs 31 woman. I am so grateful to the Lord for creating you and choosing you to be the love of my life. Our marriage and our ministry is an incredible joy because of you!

Second, I dedicate this book to my parents, Vlatko and Radmila Vuksic. I am so grateful to the Lord for allowing me the privilege to be called your son. I pray that my life can impact others in the same way that your lives have impacted me!

Topical Index

Acknowledgements

A writer needs good editors. For me, this statement is more than 100% true! I am so thankful to Sue Ann Sherwood, Jennifer Ryan, Michele Roberts, Maria Alfonso, Marko Jurin, Josie Moldenhauer, and Sonia Oliveira. Because of their efforts, these devotionals have been translated into four different languages! You are a true blessing to me. I also want to thank Blackstone Media Group for designing, proofing and printing this book.

Finally, and most importantly, I want to thank our great God. He is the true Author of these devotionals, for it is His Word, His power, and His daily direction that has allowed this book to be written. In other words, this book is all by God's grace, and therefore God deserves all the glory!

Forward

Many people have asked me how I came up with idea of writing a book of daily devotionals. Truth be told, I never, ever thought I would be writing a book on anything! For me, writing was something I was required to do for my seminary and doctorate classes. And writing for classes wasn't one of the highlights of my day!

However, God often seems to use our weaknesses for His glory. When God called my wife and me to start Gospel on the Go Ministries in September of 2007, I had no idea that God would eventually call me to start writing devotionals as well. However, when we moved to Croatia to plant a church in 2008, God started to tug at my heart to write daily devotionals for some of our friends back in the United States. I never expected that those "few friends" would turn into a huge group of people from all over the world who would be receiving the devotionals on a daily basis—in four different languages! And I never, ever expected that I would find such joy and excitement in writing the devotionals. Truth be told, I am having the time of my life!

"But he said to me, 'My grace is sufficient for you, for my power is made perfect in weakness.' Therefore I will boast all the more gladly about my weaknesses, so that Christ's power may rest on me." (2 Corinthians 12:9)

Tell me, is God right now tugging at your heart, looking to stretch you out of your comfort zone? Is He looking to take that which you consider a personal weakness and turn it to something great for His glory? If you're nodding your head in agreement (and maybe even disbelief!), then I truly believe that this book, God's Daily Direction for Your Life, will be a great blessing to you. A wise person once remarked that nothing encourages the people more than the Word of God. May you be encouraged and blessed as you daily digest the Word of God— remembering that the perfect Word of God will always direct you to the perfect will of God.

Celebrate that Christ Has Risen

(resurrection, God's provision)

"Very early on the first day of the week, just after sunrise, they were on their way to the tomb and they asked each other, 'Who will roll the stone away from the entrance of the tomb?'" (Mark 16:2-3)

1) Problem #1: How were these women going to roll away a stone that scholars estimate weighed anywhere between one to two tons?

"But when they looked up, they saw that the stone, which was very large, had been rolled away." (Mark 16:4)

2) Problem #2: The women must have been wondering why the stone was rolled away, and by whom. They also must have been wondering where the body of Jesus was. Did somebody steal it?

"As they entered the tomb, they saw a young man dressed in a white robe sitting on the right side, and they were alarmed." (Mark 16:5)

3) Problem #3: Can you imagine their shock when they saw this man who was an angel? What was he doing there? Was he going to hurt them?

"'Don't be alarmed,' he said. 'You are looking for Jesus the Nazarene, who was crucified. He has risen! He is not here. See the place where they laid him.'" (Mark 16:6)

4) Problems solved: The angel wasn't there to hurt the women; he was there to comfort the women. How? With the most incredible announcement ever, "He has risen!" A one-to-two ton stone couldn't stop Jesus from rising; human opposition couldn't stop Jesus from rising; even sin and death couldn't stop Jesus from rising. Why? Because Jesus is God, the second Person of the Trinity, and nothing is impossible for God!

"God raised him from the dead, freeing him from the agony of death, because it was impossible for death to keep its hold on him." (Acts 2:24)

Jesus Christ is risen, He is risen indeed! As Christians, we know that. Therefore, may our lives show that! May we celebrate this every day, for Jesus Christ is alive forever and ever!

A Channel of God's Peace

(relationships, prayer)

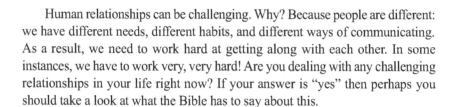

Human relationships can be challenging. Why? Because people are different: we have different needs, different habits, and different ways of communicating. As a result, we need to work hard at getting along with each other. In some instances, we have to work very, very hard! Are you dealing with any challenging relationships in your life right now? If your answer is "yes" then perhaps you should take a look at what the Bible has to say about this.

"Love must be sincere. Hate what is evil; cling to what is good. Be devoted to one another in brotherly love. Honor one another above yourselves. Never be lacking in zeal, but keep your spiritual fervor, serving the Lord. Be joyful in hope, patient in affliction, and faithful in prayer. Share with God's people who are in need. Practice hospitality." (Romans 12:9-13)

Love one another, be sincere and devoted to one another, honor each other, keep up your spiritual fervor, and be joyful and patient with each other. How is this all possible? How can we follow the teaching of these verses when we're in the midst of very challenging relationships? The key is found in the last three words of verse 12: "faithful in prayer." Through prayer we gain the proper perspective. Through prayer we're able to enjoy and appreciate the love of God, which in turn can lead to loving others. A great example of this is found in the prayer of Mother Teresa, a woman who is famous worldwide for her selfless love, "Lord, help me be a channel of your peace. That where there is hatred, I may bring love; that where there is wrong, I may bring the spirit of forgiveness; that where there is discord, I may bring harmony; that where there is error, I may bring truth; that where there is doubt, I may bring faith."

"If it is possible, as far as it depends on you, live at peace with everyone." (Romans 12:18)

Perhaps we should all take a few moments and reflect on how we're dealing with the various relationships in our lives right now. Are we doing everything we can to live at peace with those people? In other words, are we being "faithful in prayer"?

A Full-Hearted Sacrifice to the Lord

(gratitude, sacrifice)

In 2 Samuel 24:18-24, we see an incredible example of how King David wouldn't make a half-hearted sacrifice to the Lord. As David was looking for a place to make a sacrifice, he came upon a man named Araunah who offered to provide everything that was needed at no cost to David. In other words, David wouldn't have to do or worry about anything, for Araunah would incur all the costs out of respect to David. But take a look at David's response.

"The king replied to Araunah, 'No, I insist on paying you for it. For I will not sacrifice to the LORD my God something that costs me nothing.' " (2 Samuel 24:24)

David didn't want to offer anything to the Lord that didn't take any effort. He didn't want to offer anything half-heartedly. How about you and me? How is our attitude when it comes to making a full-hearted sacrifice to the Lord? When trials and temptations arise, are we willing to say, "I will not sacrifice to the LORD my God that which costs me nothing?" Do we take a look at the cost and say, "I need to offer to the Lord my God my very best, no matter how great the cost, no matter how great the sacrifice. Why? Because He gave His very best for me."

"So David bought the threshing floor and the oxen and paid fifty shekels of silver for them. David built an altar to the LORD there and sacrificed burnt offerings and fellowship offerings. Then the LORD answered prayer in behalf of the land, and the plague on Israel was stopped." (2 Samuel 24:24-25)

What an amazing example of how God honored the whole-hearted sacrifice of one man. The same awesome God can do the same in your life as well! May we be a people who live a life of gratitude and whole-hearted devotion to the Lord. May we offer our best to Him as an act of appreciation for who He is and for what He has done for us. May we be ever grateful and joyful when the Lord chooses to bless us in return!

God Leads Us and Protects Us

(protection, guidance)

"As for God, his way is perfect; the word of the LORD is flawless. He is a shield for all who take refuge in him." (2 Samuel 22:31)

1) The path of the Lord is perfect: The Lord has a perfect plan for your life. Your life matters! Your life has meaning and purpose! The Lord can perfectly guide you toward fulfilling that plan. How can we be so certain? Because the Lord's way is perfect.

2) The provision of the Lord is perfect: The Lord's Word perfectly provides all that we need to be able to live the life the Lord has for us. Do you need peace? The Word of the Lord provides that peace. Do you need wisdom? The Word of the Lord provides that wisdom. How can we be so certain? Because the Word of the Lord is flawless.

3) The protection of the Lord is perfect: The Lord is our perfect protector against all opposition. Therefore, if the Lord is for us, who or what can be against us! Are you feeling fear as you walk forward in faith? Don't give up or let yourself get discouraged. The Lord can keep you safe and strong. How can we be so certain? Because the Lord is a perfect shield for all who take refuge in Him.

"For who is God besides the LORD? And who is the Rock except our God? It is God who arms me with strength and makes my way perfect. He makes my feet like the feet of a deer; he enables me to stand on the heights." (2 Samuel 22:32-34)

As you go forward to face your day today, think about the One who is perfectly leading and protecting you. Christian, you are not alone today! With the Almighty Lord on your side, you are on the winning side!

The Lord Is Our Shepherd

(salvation, love)

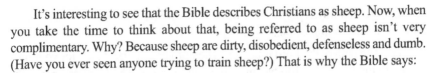

It's interesting to see that the Bible describes Christians as sheep. Now, when you take the time to think about that, being referred to as sheep isn't very complimentary. Why? Because sheep are dirty, disobedient, defenseless and dumb. (Have you ever seen anyone trying to train sheep?) That is why the Bible says:

"We all like sheep, have gone astray, each of us has turned to his own way." (Isaiah 53:6)

Not a very pretty picture of us! However, the Bible also tells us that in spite of our "sheep-ness," the Good Shepherd Jesus Christ was willing to be punished for us.

"The LORD (God the Father) has laid on him (God the Son) the iniquity of us all." (Isaiah 53:6)

Amazing, isn't it? But, there's more. Not only was Jesus willing to be punished in our place as our substitute; He was also willing to lay down His life for us so that we could have eternal life through Him.

" 'I am the good shepherd; I know my sheep and my sheep know me—just as the Father knows me and I know the Father—and I lay down my life for the sheep.' " (John 10:14-15)

Absolutely incredible! But, there's even more. Not only was Jesus willing to be punished as our substitute; and not only was Jesus willing to die the death that we deserved, but the Bible also tells us that Jesus came looking for us when we were lost and defenseless.

" 'I have other sheep that are not of this sheep pen [that was us!]. I must bring them also [Christian, He is talking about you and me!]. They too will listen to my voice, and there shall be one flock and one shepherd.' " (John 10:16)

To think: We were dirty, disobedient, dumb and defenseless. Yet Jesus, the Good Shepherd, was willing to go through all that He did so that we could be brought into the family of God. Who are we? What is our life that Jesus would actually lay down His life, so that we could have the free gift of eternal life? I guess that's why it's called amazing grace! May we all take the time today to thank our Good Shepherd that we have the unspeakable privilege of being called His sheep!

Keep Your Character in Christ

(character, relationships)

It has been said that you can't control your reputation, but you can control your character. In other words, you can't control what people think or say about you (that's your reputation), but you can control whether or not the things they think or say are true (that's your character).

In the Old Testament, we see a man named Daniel who courageously maintained his character in spite of repeated attempts to ruin his reputation. The Bible tells us that though his enemies tried to find anything they could to destroy Daniel they were unable to do so.

"At this, the administrators and the satraps tried to find grounds for charges against Daniel in his conduct of government affairs, but they were unable to do so. They could find no corruption in him, because he was trustworthy and neither corrupt nor negligent." (Daniel 6:5)

As you're preparing to begin your day today, are you resolved to keep your character in Christ regardless of the unfair attacks and false accusations you may face? More specifically, are you prepared to keep your character in Christ even if those attacks and accusations come from family, co-workers, or schoolmates today? Remember, you can't control what others will think or say about you today, but you can control whether or not those things they think or say are true. In other words, you can't stop people from making up rumors, or from trying to find charges against you, but you can live your life in such a way that you are trustworthy and neither corrupt nor negligent.

Give God All the Glory

(thankfulness)

From one end of the Bible to the other, we can see how God loves to bless His children. He graciously guides and provides for us in the most amazing of ways. However, the Bible also warns us that we should never forget that it is God, and not us, that deserves the credit for our blessings.

"Therefore, as it is written: Let him who boasts boast in the Lord." (1 Corinthians 1:31)

In the Old Testament, we see that the nation of Israel had received abundant blessings from God. He set them free from captivity in Egypt. He protected them and provided for them in their journey towards the Promised Land. He also granted them peace and blessings once they arrived in the Promised Land. However, God warned them to be careful not to get so overconfident in their blessing that they would forget the One who provided these blessings.

" 'You may say to yourself, "My power and the strength of my hands have produced this wealth for me" But remember the LORD your God, for it is he who gives you the ability to produce wealth, and so confirms his covenant, which he swore to your forefathers, as it is today.' " (Deuteronomy 8:17-18)

Have you been blessed by God lately? If so, are you giving Him the thanks and praise He deserves? Or, are you moving so fast that you're forgetting God and taking the credit for yourself? Be careful, for God gives us a very clear and sober warning:

"For my own sake, for my own sake, I do this. How can I let myself be defamed? I will not yield my glory to another." (Isaiah 48:11)

May we take the time today to thank God for all of His blessings. You'll be surprised at how much you can thank Him for! May we take every opportunity today to boast in the greatness of our God. You'll be surprised at how much you can boast about!

His Amazing Grace

(grace, salvation)

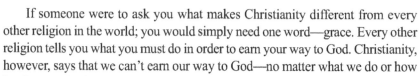

If someone were to ask you what makes Christianity different from every other religion in the world; you would simply need one word—grace. Every other religion tells you what you must do in order to earn your way to God. Christianity, however, says that we can't earn our way to God—no matter what we do or how hard we try. Rather, it is God who did for us that which we could not do. It's only because of His grace that we can be saved.

The Bible tells us: "For by grace you have been saved through faith; and that not of yourselves, it is the gift of God; not as a result of works, so that no one may boast." (Ephesians 2:8-9)

Grace is amazing because of what God did for us; it's also amazing because of how He did it. God the Father sent God the Son to this earth—that's called grace. God the Son, Jesus, allowed Himself to go to the cross for our sins—that's called grace. God the Father placed our sins on Jesus and punished Him in our place as our substitute—that's called grace. Jesus died and was entombed, but three days later He rose from the dead overcoming sin and death for us—that's called grace. Jesus offers forgiveness of sins and the free gift of eternal life to those who come to Him—that's called grace.

Have you trusted in this amazing grace? If so, are you rejoicing in this amazing grace? Just think . . . the God of this universe has extended His hand of grace to you. You are His through Jesus Christ. You have been brought into the family of God forever.

"Therefore, since we have been justified through faith, we have peace with God through our Lord Jesus Christ, through whom we have gained access by faith into this grace in which we now stand. And we rejoice in the hope of the glory of God." (Romans 5:1-2)

Our Problems Have A Purpose

(stress, trust)

The Apostle Paul faced many troubles in his life and ministry. He faced rejection and ridicule; he faced pressure and persecution; and he faced discouragement and difficulty. Yet, Paul understood that his problems had a purpose.

"Praise be to the God and Father of our Lord Jesus Christ, the Father of compassion and the God of all comfort, who comforts us in all our troubles, so that we can comfort those in any trouble with the comfort we ourselves have received." (2 Corinthians 1:3-4)

Paul understood that his troubles were an opportunity to receive God's comfort and compassion. He also understood that his troubles were an opportunity to help others with the help he himself received from God. It's interesting to note that the term "trouble" refers to crushing pressure. Reason being, that in Paul's life and ministry, he was always facing crushing pressures that tried to stop him from achieving God's plan for his life.

Are you feeling the crushing pressures of life right now? Are you feeling so weak that you're wondering how you're going to keep going forward? Don't quit. Instead, cry out to the God of all compassion and comfort, and watch how He will comfort you through those crushing pressures. Then, watch how He will use your experiences to help others who are also feeling the crushing pressures of life. Remember, your problems have a purpose. God will never waste what you're currently going through.

"For just as the sufferings of Christ flow over into our lives, so also through Christ our comfort overflows." (2 Corinthians 1:5)

God's Word Will Guide Us

(guidance, the Bible)

Do you have some difficult decisions that you need to make today? Are you struggling with whether or not you need to move forward on something? Well, in the confusion of our daily lives, we can find peace in knowing that the Bible is our perfect guide in this imperfect world. Through our daily Bible reading, we find that our souls are nourished, our faith is fortified and our vision is clarified.

"The unfolding of your words gives light; it gives understanding to the simple." (Psalm 119:130)

This means, each day as you open your Bible, you should look forward in excitement and anticipation to God's guidance and grace. Why? Because God wants to guide and direct you in the way you should go. Through His Word, He will lift you out of the fog of indecision and bring you into the wonderful light of His truth.

"Your word is a lamp to my feet and a light for my path." (Psalm 119:105)

Therefore, before you rush out today and make a decision that you may later regret, spend some time listening to the Lord through His Word. He promises that His Word will not fail and it will accomplish all that He intends. That includes giving you the guidance and wisdom you need for those difficult decisions!

"As the rain and snow come down from heaven, and do not return to it without watering the earth and making it bud and flourish, so that it yields seed for the sower and bread for the eater, so is my word that goes out from my mouth: It will not return to me empty, but will accomplish what I desire and achieve the purpose for which I sent it." (Isaiah 55:10-11)

Love One Another

(love, relationships)

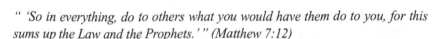

" 'So in everything, do to others what you would have them do to you, for this sums up the Law and the Prophets.' " (Matthew 7:12)

Jesus said these words as He was preaching His famous Sermon on the Mount. Can you imagine what the people back then must have been thinking when they heard those specific words? Probably the same thing many of us are thinking today when we hear those specific words, "This sounds nice, but in reality it's impossible!" True, we'll never perfectly obey these words on this side of heaven. However, don't you think Jesus knew that when He preached those words? Christian, we need to try our best and apply those words to our lives on a daily basis. Although we may not get it right each and every time, nevertheless we need to make the effort to bless others and bring glory to God.

"Jesus replied, ' "Love the Lord your God with all your heart and with all your soul and with all your mind." This is the first and greatest commandment. And the second is like it: "Love your neighbor as yourself." All the Law and the Prophets hang on these two commandments.' " (Matthew 22:37-40)

Love for others (and ourselves) flows from our love for the Lord. The proper perspective is Jesus first (J), others second (O), and you third (Y). The result is J-O-Y. However, when we change the order and put ourselves first, what does that spell? A mess! Christian, when we first show our love to the Lord, we're expressing gratitude to the Lord for the love He has shown us—and this then helps us have the proper attitude when it comes to doing to others as we would have them do to us.

"This is how God showed his love among us: He sent his one and only Son into the world that we might live through him. This is love: not that we loved God, but that he loved us and sent his Son as an atoning sacrifice for our sins." (1 John 4:9-10)

Christian, if God so loved us in this way, shouldn't we make the effort to love others? Although we may not get it right each and every time, nevertheless we need to make the effort to bless others and bring glory to God. Now that we know this, may our lives show this!

"Dear friends, since God so loved us, we also ought to love one another." (1 John 4:11)

The Love Challenge (Part 1)

(love, relationships)

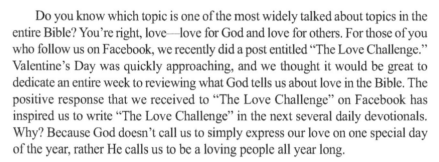

Do you know which topic is one of the most widely talked about topics in the entire Bible? You're right, love—love for God and love for others. For those of you who follow us on Facebook, we recently did a post entitled "The Love Challenge." Valentine's Day was quickly approaching, and we thought it would be great to dedicate an entire week to reviewing what God tells us about love in the Bible. The positive response that we received to "The Love Challenge" on Facebook has inspired us to write "The Love Challenge" in the next several daily devotionals. Why? Because God doesn't call us to simply express our love on one special day of the year, rather He calls us to be a loving people all year long.

The Love Challenge Day 1: Say it . . .

"Dear friends, let us love one another, for love comes from God. Everyone who loves has been born of God and knows God. Whoever does not love does not know God, because God is love." (1 John 4:7-8)

Today is a day where you can look for opportunities to tell someone that you love them. Spouses, maybe you can come up with a creative and romantic way for expressing how much you love each other. Think about how creative you were when you first fell in love. Think about how romantic you were when you first got married. Spouses, get creative! Parents, perhaps you can think of a creative way to tell your children how much you love them. Don't worry if they roll their eyes— get creative! Children, maybe you can come up with a special way to tell your parents how much you love them. Remember the love they've shown you throughout your lifetime. Finally, come up with a creative way to tell a friend or co-worker how much they matter to you. Make their day by telling them they're loved. Whoever it may be, and whatever way you decide to do it, make sure that you take the time today to tell someone that you love them.

"Hope does not disappoint us, because God has poured out his love into our hearts by the Holy Spirit, whom he has given us." (Romans 5:5)

God in His grace has poured His love into our hearts through His Spirit. God has done this so that He can constantly tell us how much He loves us. Think about it, if God is willing to graciously assure us of His love for us by telling us how much He loves us, shouldn't we do the same with others? After all, today's challenge only involves 3 simple words—"I love you."

The Love Challenge (Part 2)
(love)

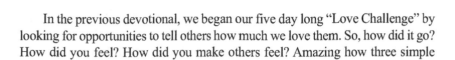

In the previous devotional, we began our five day long "Love Challenge" by looking for opportunities to tell others how much we love them. So, how did it go? How did you feel? How did you make others feel? Amazing how three simple words—"I love you"—can make such a meaningful difference.

The Love Challenge Day 2: Show it . . .

"Dear children, let us not love with words or tongue but with actions and in truth." (1 John 3:18)

Yesterday we were challenged to "Say it," while today we're challenged to "Show it." After reading this devotional, take some time to think of creative ways that you can show your love to someone today. It's amazing how loudly your actions will speak. Guys, flowers are great, but you can get even more creative. Ladies, food may be the best way to a man's heart, but try to get even more creative. Parents, slowing down and just listening to your children may be a great way to show your love today. This might mean setting aside your busy agenda (and the very busy agenda of your children), but giving them your undivided attention may be the challenge you need to fulfill. Children, just making the effort to creatively show your love to your parents may be all that you need! You will impact them in a great way!

"You see, at just the right time, when we were still powerless, Christ died for the ungodly. Very rarely will anyone die for a righteous man, though for a good man someone might possibly dare to die. But God demonstrates his own love for us in this: While we were still sinners, Christ died for us." (Romans 5:6-8)

God didn't just say that He loves us. God showed His love for us in the most visible and powerful way—He punished His beloved, sinless, and most holy Son in our place. Christians, the Scripture above doesn't mince words—we were ungodly sinners who were powerless to save ourselves. Yet, God in His grace demonstrated His love by providing the Perfect Substitute to save ungodly, powerless sinners like us. Jesus was punished for us and died for us—that's love. Jesus rose from the dead and thus demonstrated that He defeated sin and death for us—that's love. Jesus has granted us forgiveness of sins and life eternal as a free gift—that's love. Jesus has brought us into the family of God forever, where we have peace with God forever—that's love. If God considers it important enough to show His love to us, then perhaps we should consider it important as well. Wouldn't you agree? May today be the day where we rise to the challenge of creatively showing our love to others.

The Love Challenge (Part 3)

(love)

Let's continue our five day long "Love Challenge" by looking for opportunities to show others how much we love them. How creative did you get? Did you surprise someone? Did you surprise yourself by how well it worked and by how much you enjoyed it?

The Love Challenge Day 3: Model it . . .

"Follow my example, as I follow the example of Christ." (1 Corinthians 11:1)

Most experts agree that a wonderful teaching tool is when you model something for someone, then ask them to go out and do the same thing. Today your challenge is to have someone follow your love example as you follow the love example of Christ. We have learned over the past two days that we can express our love by either saying it or showing it. Now that you know it, go out and show it— so that someone else can repeat it.

"Finally, brothers, whatever is true, whatever is noble, whatever is right, whatever is pure, whatever is lovely, whatever is admirable—if anything is excellent or praiseworthy—think about such things. Whatever you have learned or received or heard from me, or seen in me—put into practice. And the God of peace will be with you." (Philippians 4:8-9)

Our challenge is to be able to model love in such a way today that others can see, learn, and put into practice that which they learned from us. I know that some of you may be thinking, "Man, that is hard!" Exactly! That's why it's called a "Love Challenge!" Several years ago I had two dogs which were three years apart in age. When I brought the younger puppy home, I remember thinking, "I wonder how long it's going to take me to house train this little guy?" You know what happened? The older dog did the house training for me! The young puppy simply followed the example of the older dog—and learned almost immediately that my house was not the place to go to the bathroom! Maybe today's "Love Challenge" of modeling love for others isn't as impossible as we thought, is it?

"I can do everything through him who gives me strength." (Philippians 4:13)

The Love Challenge (Part 4)

(love)

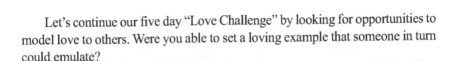

Let's continue our five day "Love Challenge" by looking for opportunities to model love to others. Were you able to set a loving example that someone in turn could emulate?

The Love Challenge Day 4: Encourage it . . .

"Let us hold unswervingly to the hope we profess, for he who promised is faithful. And let us consider how we may spur one another on toward love and good deeds." (Hebrews 10:23-24)

Love can be contagious—in a good and godly way. It can contagiously encourage those who are receiving your love to also go out and share that love. The result? More people are encouraged today with the love that started with you today. However, it takes effort. As the Scripture above reminds us, we need to spur people on towards love and good deeds. This means that we need to be proactive today in our effort to encourage love today. In other words, we need to be people builders—building up and blessing others so that they in turn can build up and bless others.

"Knowledge puffs up, but love builds up." (1 Corinthians 8:1)

Please understand, Scripture isn't discouraging knowledge. Throughout the Bible we see how God encourages us to use our minds for His glory. Rather, Scripture is discouraging arrogance, an arrogance that cares little about love and more about impressing others with our knowledge. Let us be the opposite—let us encourage love in a way that it spurs others towards love and good deeds. Think of some creative and proactive ways that you can do this today. Remember that love doesn't fail.

"Love is patient, love is kind. It does not envy, it does not boast, it is not proud. It is not rude, it is not self-seeking, it is not easily angered, it keeps no record of wrongs. Love does not delight in evil but rejoices with the truth. It always protects, always trusts, always hopes, always perseveres. Love never fails." (1 Corinthians 13:4-8)

The Love Challenge (Part 5)

(love, forgiveness)

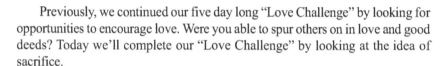

Previously, we continued our five day long "Love Challenge" by looking for opportunities to encourage love. Were you able to spur others on in love and good deeds? Today we'll complete our "Love Challenge" by looking at the idea of sacrifice.

The Love Challenge Day 5: Sacrifice it . . .

"This is how God showed his love among us: He sent his one and only Son into the world that we might live through him. This is love: Not that we loved God, but that he loved us and sent his Son as an atoning sacrifice for our sins. Dear friends, since God so loved us, we also ought to love one another." (1 John 4:9-11)

Sometimes love involves sacrifice. Sometimes it involves loving someone who maybe hasn't been very lovable to you—it even means being proactive and swallowing your pride (or bitterness!). Do you have any people in your life right now that you could extend that type of sacrificial love to? It won't be easy—that's why it's called a sacrifice. However, this type of love is the very love that Jesus displayed towards us. He loved us first, when we weren't loving towards Him. He sacrificed His life on the cross, for ungodly sinners like us. He was proactive in His love towards us; He made the first move. Also, as the Scripture above says, since He loved us in this way, we also ought to love others—even if it's a sacrifice for us.

"But the king replied to Araunah, "No I insist on paying you for it. I will not sacrifice to the LORD my God burnt offerings that cost me nothing." (2 Samuel 24:24)

King David lived with an attitude of gratitude. He felt so blessed to be loved by God, that he was willing to show his love to God—by offering a sacrifice, no matter the cost. Today we have the opportunity to show sacrificial love in a way that shows that we don't care about the cost to our pride or ego. Rather, we have an opportunity to please the Lord—the One who showed the ultimate sacrificial love. He paid the ultimate price for our souls!

"My command is this: Love each other as I have loved you. Greater love has no one than this, that he lay down his life for his friends. You are my friends if you do what I command." (John 15:12-14)

How Great Is Your God? (Part 1)

(God's greatness, God's name, trust)

How great is your God? The Old Testament reveals various different names for God. Each name is meant to give us a better understanding of who our God is, and to remind us of how great our God truly is.

Elohim: "His power and might"

"In the beginning God created the heavens and the earth." (Genesis 1:1)

"In the beginning God [Elohim] created the heavens and the earth." More specifically, Elohim created the heavens and the earth by His infinite power and might. How? Out of nothing—ex nihilo! Christian, do you know what kind of power we're talking about here? More specifically, do you know what kind of power is available to you each and every day? It's the same power that not only created the heavens and the earth; but, it's also the same power that Elohim displayed in parting the Red Sea and setting the Israelites free. It's the same awesome power that Elohim demonstrated by raising Jesus from the dead. In addition, it's the same amazing power that Elohim displayed by setting us free from the clutches of sin and eternal death—free indeed. Christian, do you think that Elohim has enough power and might to take care of those things that are worrying you right now?

"The heavens declare the glory of God; the skies proclaim the work of his hands. Day after day they pour forth speech; night after night they display knowledge." (Psalm 19:1-2)

I love this verse because it describes how consistently and joyfully creation brings forth praise to the awesome Creator (Elohim). In other words, God's incredible creation can't keep quiet—all it wants to do is bring glory to Elohim! How about you? Are you that excited to consistently and joyfully give glory to the awesome God who created and saved you by His infinite power and might? Are you excited to give glory to Elohim in your family today? How about at your job or school? God is mighty and powerful—nothing is impossible for Him. And since that's the case, it's safe to say that we can start to praise God even before He takes care of the things that are worrying us right now. After all, if Elohim can create the heavens and the earth out of nothing, He is more than able to turn our difficult problems into opportunities for praises! Wouldn't you agree?

How Great Is Your God?(Part 2)

(God's greatness, God's name, trust)

How great is your God? In the previous devotional, we saw that one of the names in the Old Testament for God is Elohim—for He is infinite in His power and might. Today we will take a look at another Old Testament name that reveals how great and awesome our God truly is.

El Roi: "The strong one who sees"

"She gave this name to the LORD who spoke to her: 'You are the God who sees me,' for she said, 'I have now seen the One who sees me.' That is why the well was called Beer Lahai Roi; it is still there, between Kadesh and Bered.." (Genesis 16:13-14)

Hagar was a woman who was in desperate need. She was abandoned and alone, she was expecting a child, and she had no one to help her. Suddenly, the angel of the Lord appeared and assured her that she was going to be fine. Although no human was there to help her in her desperate situation, the Lord saw her and promised to take care of her. Why? He is El Roi, the strong One who sees. Christian, have you been feeling alone and abandoned as of late? Have your problems so overwhelmed you that you're wondering if there's anyone who can help? Relax and remember, there is a strong One who sees you—He is called El Roi. Other people may not notice the burdens you're dealing with, but El Roi sees you. Certain people may not seem to care that you're struggling and they may not be offering you help in your time of need; but there is the strong One in heaven who cares for you and wants to help you in ways you can't imagine!

"So do not fear, for I am with you; do not be dismayed, for I am your God. I will strengthen you and help you; I will uphold you with my righteous right hand." (Isaiah 41:10)

How Great Is Your God? (Part 3)

(God's greatness, God's name, trust)

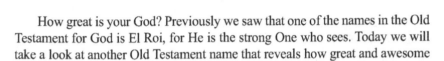

How great is your God? Previously we saw that one of the names in the Old Testament for God is El Roi, for He is the strong One who sees. Today we will take a look at another Old Testament name that reveals how great and awesome our God truly is.

Jehovah-Jireh: "The LORD will provide"

"Abraham looked up and there in a thicket he saw a ram caught by its horns. He went over and took the ram and sacrificed it as a burnt offering instead of his son. So Abraham called that place The LORD Will Provide. And to this day it is said, 'On the mountain of the LORD it will be provided.'" (Genesis 22:13-14)

Abraham passed one of the most grueling tests imaginable. He obediently built an altar to sacrifice his son Isaac. Can you imagine what he must have been thinking? He then reached out his hand and took the knife to kill his son. Once again, can you imagine what he must have been thinking? Suddenly, the angel of the Lord stopped him and redirected his attention to the ram that the Lord provided. This ram would be sacrificed and substituted in the place of Isaac. It was the Lord Himself who provided what was needed to accomplish what He required. Isn't this the same thing the Lord has done for us? He sacrificed His sinless Son as a substitute for sinners like us. Jesus was punished for our sins and He died our death. However, three days later He rose from the dead, overcoming sin and death for us. He also offers forgiveness of sins and eternal life as a free gift to those who place their faith and trust in Him alone. How could this be? The Lord, Jehovah-Jireh, provided what was needed to accomplish what was required!

"What, then, shall we say in response to this? If God is for us, who can be against us? He who did not spare his own Son, but gave him up for us all—how will he not also, along with him, graciously give us all things?" (Romans 8:31-32)

Christian, think about it: If Jehovah-Jireh could provide for us that which we could never provide for ourselves—eternal life through the Perfect Substitute—then doesn't it make sense that Jehovah-Jireh can also provide for everything we currently need to live the lives He saved us for? Remember, God's provision is perfect and plentiful!

"My God will meet all your needs according to his glorious riches in Christ Jesus." (Philippians 4:19)

How Great Is Your God? (Part 4)

(God's greatness, God's name, trust)

How great is your God? One of the names in the Old Testament for God is Jehovah-Jireh, for He is the Lord who provides. Today we will take a look at another Old Testament name that reveals how great and awesome our God truly is.

Jehovah-Shalom: "The LORD is Peace"

"But the LORD said to him, 'Peace! Do not be afraid. You are not going to die.' So Gideon built an altar to the LORD there and called it The LORD is Peace. To this day it stands in Ophrah of the Abiezrites." (Judges 6:23-24)

Gideon was called by God to accomplish great things for God. However, he needed a bit of coaxing to get going. Why? He was frozen in fear and doubt. Can you relate? However, the Angel of the Lord graciously assured Gideon that he wasn't alone. Jehovah-Shalom himself would be with him, providing amazing victory and perfect peace for Gideon. Christian, the Lord of Peace is also able to provide you amazing victories and perfect peace as you answer His call. He promises to be with you every step of the way. He also promises to go before you to handle all those obstacles that you're currently worried about!

"The LORD himself goes before you and will be with you; he will never leave you nor forsake you. Do not be afraid; do not be discouraged." (Deuteronomy 31:8)

Is the Lord right now asking you to trust Him and step forward in faith to answer His call? Are you feeling a bit like Gideon—overwhelmed and fearful of the unknown? Relax, Jehovah-Shalom Himself is your God, and He will provide you the perfect peace that will propel you forward to experience the amazing victories He has prepared for you!

"You will keep in perfect peace him whose mind is steadfast, because he trusts in you. Trust in the LORD forever, for the LORD, the LORD, is the Rock eternal." (Isaiah 26:3-4)

How Great Is Your God? (Part 5)

(God's greatness, God's name, trust)

How great is your God? In the previous devotional, we saw that one of the names in the Old Testament for God is Jehovah-Shalom, for He is our Lord of Peace. Today we will take a look at another Old Testament name that reveals how great and awesome our God truly is.

Jehovah-Shammah: "The LORD who is Present"

"And the name of the city from that time on will be: THE LORD IS THERE."
(Ezekiel 48:35)

Through the prophet Ezekiel, God assured His people that He hadn't forgotten or forsaken them. Although life got very difficult for them, God promised that He is Jehovah-Shammah: "The LORD who is Present" One of the awesome attributes of our awesome God is that He is omnipresent. This means that He is present everywhere. Christian, this also means that He is with you right now as you are reading this; He will be with you at work or school today; He will be with you in your highs and lows today; and He will be with you always.

"Where can I go from your Spirit? Where can I flee from your presence? If I go up to the heavens, you are there; if I make my bed in the depths, you are there. If I rise on the wings of the dawn, if I settle on the far side of the sea, even there your hand will guide me, your right hand will hold me fast." (Psalm 139:7-10)

The Psalmist was awestruck that, no matter where he went, the Lord was with him! Whether he was at the highest highs, or the lowest lows, Jehovah-Shammah was there. Christian, have you experienced some highly wonderful experiences in your life? The Lord was there. Have you experienced some lowly difficult experiences in your life? The Lord was there. Are you experiencing some lows in your life right now? Christian, the Lord is there. He is with you right now in the midst of your challenging circumstances. Therefore, you can rejoice—not in the difficulties—but in the fact that the Lord is with you and carrying you through those difficulties.

"Be joyful always; pray continually; give thanks in all circumstances, for this is God's will for you in Christ Jesus." (1 Thessalonians 5:16)

How Great Is Your God? (Part 6)

(God's greatness, God's names, trust)

How great is your God? One of the names in the Old Testament for God is Jehovah-Shammah, for He is our Lord who is always present with His people. Today we'll take a look at another Old Testament name that reveals how great and awesome our God truly is.

Adonai: "Lord, the Lordship of God"

"A son honors his father, and a servant his master. If I am a father, where is the honor due me? If I am master, where is the respect due me?" says the LORD Almighty. "It is you, O priests, who show contempt for my name. But you ask, 'How have we shown contempt for your name?'" (Malachi 1:6)

God's people failed to show honor and respect to the Lord. He is the Creator and Sustainer of the universe. He is the sovereign Ruler and Lord over all of His creation. Yet, the people failed to honor and respect Him for who He is: The Boss. Not a boss who is self-centered and unloving, like a dictator who cares nothing for his people; rather, a Boss who cares for His people, like a father for his children.

"Why do you call me, 'Lord, Lord,' and do not do what I say?" (Luke 6:46)

Just as in the time of the prophet Malachi, there were many people during the time of Jesus who called upon His name, yet they were simply playing a game. They called upon Him as Lord, yet they didn't listen to Him as their Lord. In other words, they didn't show Him the respect and honor that's due to One who is Lord over all. Unfortunately, this can be a problem during our time as well. Is Jesus truly the Adonai of your life? Do you look to Him as your Lord and Leader—desiring to obey Him and honor Him? None of us will be perfect in our obedience, however we should have a desire to do the best we can to submit to the Lordship of Jesus. After all, He is the One who showed His Lordship over sin and death for us. He is the One who showed His Lordship by forgiving our sins and granting us the free gift of eternal life. He is the One who rules and reigns from His heavenly throne, now and forever. He is the One who is truly Adonai—and every person in heaven and earth will one day acknowledge His Lordship. Have you acknowledged the Lordship of Jesus; is He the Boss of your life?

"Being found in appearance as a man, he humbled himself and became obedient to death—even death on a cross! Therefore God exalted him to the highest place and gave him the name that is above every name, that at the name of Jesus every knee should bow, in heaven and on earth and under the earth , and every tongue confess that Jesus Christ is Lord, to the glory of God the Father." (Philippians 2:8-11)

How Great Is Your God? (Part 7)

(God's greatness, God's names, trust)

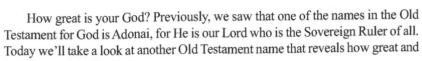

How great is your God? Previously, we saw that one of the names in the Old Testament for God is Adonai, for He is our Lord who is the Sovereign Ruler of all. Today we'll take a look at another Old Testament name that reveals how great and awesome our God truly is.

El-Shaddai: "God Almighty"

"When Abram was ninety-nine years old, the LORD appeared to him and said, 'I am God Almighty; walk before me and be blameless. I will confirm my covenant between me and you and will greatly increase your numbers.' " (Genesis 17:1-2)

Abraham had been walking with and serving God for approximately 25 years. From the beginning, God had promised to be with Abraham and bless him, making a covenant promise to grant Abraham land and descendants. However, Abraham and his wife Sarah were living in a foreign land and they had no children. Nevertheless, God assured Abraham that He would fulfill that which He had promised. Now, twenty-five years after the initial covenant promise, God once again appeared to Abraham to reaffirm His covenant of land and descendants. However, there was a problem. Abraham and Sarah were very old and far past child-bearing age. How could they have descendants if they couldn't even bear a child through whom those descendants could come? God then reminded Abraham who He really was—He was (and is) El–Shaddai. He is God Almighty; therefore, nothing is impossible for Him. It wasn't impossible for God Almighty to fulfill His promise of land and descendants for two very old people. It's not impossible for God Almighty to fulfill His promise and purposes in your life as well; in spite of what you may think are impossible circumstances in your life right now. Christian, think about it, do you believe that your challenges right now are all mighty, over God Almighty? Not a chance! He is above all and greater than all. Why? He is El–Shaddai. He cares for you and He can do whatever He promises. Why? He is El–Shaddai.

"He who dwells in the shelter of the Most High will rest in the shadow of the Almighty. I will say of the LORD, 'He is my refuge and my fortress, my God, in whom I trust.' " (Psalm 91:1-2)

The Greatness of Our Most Wonderful God!

(praising God, worship, thankfulness)

What will you do?

"Praise the LORD. I will extol the LORD with all my heart in the council of the upright and in the assembly." (Psalm 111:1)

Why?

"Great are the works of the LORD; they are pondered by all who delight in them. Glorious and majestic are his deeds, and his righteousness endures forever." (Psalm 111:2-3)

How have you been blessed by God?

"He has caused his wonders to be remembered; the LORD is gracious and compassionate. He provides food for those who fear him; he remembers his covenant forever." (Psalm 111:4-5)

How has God shown His faithfulness?

"He has shown his people the power of his works, giving them the lands of other nations. The works of his hands are faithful and just; all his precepts are trustworthy. They are steadfast for ever and ever, done in faithfulness and uprightness. He provided redemption for his people; he ordained his covenant forever—holy and awesome is his name." (Psalm 111:6-9)

Will you be faithful to the Lord?

"The fear of the LORD is the beginning of wisdom; all who follow his precepts have good understanding. To him belongs eternal praise." (Psalm 111:10)

Spend the next few days meditating on this Psalm. Ask the Lord to give you wisdom, insight and understanding. Then, go out and put your faith into action by praising the Lord—rejoicing in who He is and how He is. You will be amazed at how wonderful you feel as you praise the greatness of our most wonderful God!

Trust in God's Word

(the Bible, guidance)

How joyful are you for God's Word?

"Your statues are wonderful; therefore I obey them. The unfolding of your words gives light; it gives understanding to the simple." (Psalm 119:129-130)

How hungry are you for God's Word?

"I open my mouth and pant, longing for your commands." (Psalm 119:131)

How willing are you to submit to God's Word?

"Turn to me and have mercy on me, as you always do to those who love your name. Direct my footsteps according to your word; let no sin rule over me." (Psalm 119:132-133)

How trusting are you of God's Word?

"Redeem me from the oppression of men, that I may obey your precepts. Make your face shine upon your servant and teach me your decrees. Streams of tears flow from my eyes, for your law is not obeyed." (Psalm 119:134-136)

Spend the next few days meditating on this Psalm. Ask the Lord to give you wisdom, insight and understanding. Then, go out and put your faith into action by living according what you have been learning. In other words, let your walk with the Lord match the Word of the Lord. You will be amazed at how truly blessed you will be!

"Blessed is the man who does not walk in the counsel of the wicked or stand in the way of sinners or sit in the seat of mockers. But his delight is in the law of the LORD, and on his law he meditates day and night. He is like a tree planted by streams of water, which yields its fruit in season and whose leaf does not wither. Whatever he does prospers." (Psalm 1:1-3)

Christian, do you want to be blessed? How joyful and hungry are you for God's Word? Christian, do you want to experience a fruitful life? How willing are you to faithfully submit to and obediently trust in God's Word?

A Prayer for Protection

(prayer, trust)

"Lord, guard my life."

"O LORD, I call to you; come quickly to me. Hear my voice when I call to you. May my prayer be set before you like incense; may the lifting up of my hands be like the evening sacrifice." (Psalm 141:1-2)

"Lord, guard my mouth."

"Set a guard over my mouth, O LORD; keep watch over the door of my lips." (Psalm 141:3)

"Lord, guard my heart."

"Let not my heart be drawn to what is evil, to take part in wicked deeds with men who are evildoers, let me not eat of their delicacies." (Psalm 141:4)

"Lord, guard my character so that I do not return evil with evil."

"Let a righteous man strike me—it is a kindness; let him rebuke me—it is oil on my head. My head will not refuse it. Yet my prayer is ever against the deeds of evildoers; their rulers will be thrown down from the cliffs, and the wicked will learn that my words were well spoken. They will say, 'As one plows and breaks up the earth, so our bones have been scattered at the mouth of the grave.'" (Psalm 141:5-7)

"Lord, guard my eyes so that they faithfully look to You."

"But my eyes are fixed on you, O Sovereign LORD; in you I take refuge—do not give me over to death. Keep me from the snares they have laid for me, from traps set by evildoers. Let the wicked fall into their own nets, while I pass by in safety." (Psalm 141:8-10)

Spend the next few days meditating on this Psalm. Ask the Lord to give you wisdom, insight and understanding. Then, go out and fulfill God's plan for your life—trusting in His unlimited and unfailing protection and provision!

Glorify the Lord Today

(praising God, thankfulness)

How excited are you to praise God? That doesn't mean falsely manufacturing reasons to praise God. That also doesn't mean standing out in the streets and shouting praises in front of everyone. Rather, do you have any reasons in your life right now where you can honestly and joyfully praise God?

1)   Think about where you once were.

"But you are a chosen people, a royal priesthood, a holy nation, a people belonging to God, that you may declare the praises of him who called you out of darkness into his wonderful light. Once you were not a people, but now you are the people of God; once you had not received mercy, but now you have received mercy." (1 Peter 2:9-10)

2)   Think about Who is leading your life.

"I will proclaim the name of the LORD. Oh, praise the greatness of our God! He is the Rock, his works are perfect, and all his ways are just. A faithful God who does no wrong, upright and just is he." (Deuteronomy 32:3-4)

3)   Think about how much you are loved.

"I will praise you, O LORD my God, with all my heart; I will glorify your name forever. For great is your love toward me; you have delivered me from the depths of the grave." (Psalm 86:12-13)

Now that we've reviewed a few reasons to praise God, may we all take some time today to give Him the praise He is due. Our God is an awesome God—He saved us, He leads us, and He loves us. He is worthy of the praises of His people.

"I will extol the LORD at all times; his praise will always be on my lips. My soul will boast in the LORD; let the afflicted hear and rejoice. Glorify the LORD with me; let us exalt his name together." (Psalm 34:1-3)

The Glorious Fragrance of Christ

(thankfulness, salvation, love)

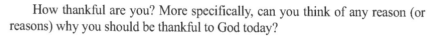

How thankful are you? More specifically, can you think of any reason (or reasons) why you should be thankful to God today?

"Don't you know that when you offer yourselves to someone to obey him as slaves, you are slaves to the one whom you obey—whether you are slaves to sin, which leads to death, or to obedience, which leads to righteousness? But thanks be to God that, though you used to be slaves to sin, you wholeheartedly obeyed the form of teaching to which you were entrusted. You have been set free from sin and have become slaves to righteousness." (Romans 6:16-18)

Christian, thank God that we're now serving a new Master, Jesus Christ. We're now servants of Christ because our lives have been purchased by Christ. Think about it—we used to be slaves and servants to sin, and we were being led straight to eternal damnation. However, now through God's amazing grace, we're slaves and servants to our Savior—and He is leading us straight to eternal life!

"Thanks be to God, who always leads us in triumphal procession in Christ and through us spreads everywhere the fragrance of the knowledge of him. For we are to God the aroma of Christ among those who are being saved and those who are perishing. To the one we are the smell of death; to the other, the fragrance of life. And who is equal to such a task?" (2 Corinthians 2:14-16)

Christian, thank God that we're not only saved, but we're saved to serve. By God's grace, we have the unspeakable privilege of being used by God to impact eternal destinies. Think about it, we actually are called by God and used by God to spread the glorious fragrance of Christ! To some, it may not be an appealing aroma. However, to others, it will be so appealing that they will become servants of Christ who have been purchased by Christ. No longer will they be slaves to sin, and no longer will they be led down the path of eternal damnation. Rather, they will become slaves and servants of Christ, and they will be forever on the path that is eternal salvation. Christian, there's nothing greater than to be used by God to impact eternal destinies—all by His grace and all for His glory!

"The sting of death is sin, and the power of sin is the law. But thanks be to God! He gives us the victory through our Lord Jesus Christ. Therefore, my dear brothers, stand firm, let nothing move you. Always give yourselves fully to the work of the Lord, because you know that your labor in the Lord is not in vain." (1 Corinthians 15:56-58)

A Prayer about Our Loving Lord

(prayer, trust)

Who is my Lord . . .

"The LORD is my light and my salvation—whom shall I fear? The LORD is the stronghold of my life—of whom shall I be afraid?" (Psalm 27:1)

The Lord is your light who enables you to see His perfect path and plan for your life. The Lord is the lover of your soul who has graciously reached down to save you from the clutches of sin and death. The Lord is your provider and protector, a stronghold of compassion and comfort. Who can possibly come against you when my Lord is for you?

"You were shown these things so that you might know that the LORD is God; besides him there is no other." (Deuteronomy 4:35)

The Lord is the one true God, and He is the One who is truly God. There is no one above Him and there is nothing that can overcome Him. He is the Lord who rules and reigns, He is the Lord who seeks and saves, He is the Lord who rescues and rewards. Who or what can possibly come against you when God is for you?

"Now choose life, so that you and your children may live and that you may love the LORD your God, listen to his voice, and hold fast to him. For the LORD is your life, and he will give you many years in the land he swore to give to your fathers, Abraham, Isaac and Jacob." (Deuteronomy 30:19-20)

The Lord is my life. He has specially created you and given you life, He has graciously recreated you in Christ and given you eternal life through Christ. Therefore, desire to love Him, listen to Him, and hold fast to Him. Trust Him to give you blessings beyond your hopes and dreams. Believe that He is the same awesome Lord who blessed Abraham, Isaac and Jacob beyond their hopes and dreams. Who or what can possibly come against you when God is for you?

"David also said to Solomon his son, 'Be strong and courageous, and do the work. Do not be afraid or discouraged, for the LORD God, my God, is with you.'" (1 Chronicles 28:20)

Your Spiritual Act of Worship
(worship, thankfulness)

God calls His people to live sacrificially. However, there is often much confusion as to what this really means. Some people say that sacrificial living is giving up all possessions and living a sacrificial life of poverty. Others say that sacrificial living is saying no to anything that makes you feel good. Although God may call some to live a life of poverty, not everybody is called to this type of sacrificial living. However, the Scriptures give us definition of sacrificial living that all Christ-followers are called to.

"Therefore, I urge you, brothers, in view of God's mercy, to offer your bodies as living sacrifices, holy and pleasing to God—this is your spiritual act of worship." (Romans 12:1)

In view of God's incredible mercy that He has displayed in saving sinners like us, all Christians are called to offer the totality of their lives as a living sacrifice—one that is pleasing to God. This should be our reasonable or rational act of worship to the One who has sacrificed His beloved Son in our place as our substitute. What should our spiritual act of worship look like?

"Do not conform any longer to the pattern of this world, but be transformed by the renewing of your mind. Then you will be able to test and approve what God's will is—his good, pleasing and perfect will." (Romans 12:2-3)

Sacrificial living is a daily discipline of saying "no" to the ways of the world and "yes" to the ways of God's Word. Sacrificial living means taking the time each day to read and meditate on God's Word of truth. Sacrificial living means that we take the time to set aside the hurry and busyness of our lives to allow God's Word to renew our minds. Sacrificial living means taking the time each day to allow God's Word to renew our minds so that we can submit to God's perfect, holy and pleasing will for our lives. Sacrificial living desires to follow God's will rather than the will of the world. Remember, doctrine and duty go hand in hand—our faith is demonstrated daily in our faithfulness to God's Word and His perfect will for our lives. Christian, how sacrificial has your life been as of late?

"For everything that was written in the past was written to teach us, so that through endurance and the encouragement of the Scriptures we might have hope." (Romans 15:4)

The Lord Is Our Vindicator and Defender

(conflict, forgiveness)

"Ruthless witnesses come forward; they question me on things I know nothing about. They repay me evil for good and leave my soul forlorn." (Psalm 35:11-12)

King David was being unfairly accused and unmercifully attacked by people who were jealous of him. Can you relate? However, what made these attacks and accusations even more painful is that they came from people whom he cared and prayed for. Again, can you relate?

"Yet when they were ill, I put on sackcloth and humbled myself with fasting. When my prayers returned to me unanswered, I went about mourning as though for my friend or brother. I bowed my head in grief as though weeping for my mother." (Psalm 35:13-14)

Have you ever persevered in prayer for somebody only to have them turn around and hurt you? Have you ever opened your heart and home to somebody only to have them turn around and stab you in the back? If so, you understand what King David was going through. Christian, this is not an easy thing to deal with. All kinds of thoughts start to run through our minds—thoughts of retaliation and revenge. Yet, we know this is not the way followers of Christ are to handle things. Instead, let's follow the example of King David and pray for the Lord to be our Vindicator.

"O LORD, you have seen this; be not silent. Do not be far from me, O Lord. Awake, and rise to my defense! Contend for me, my God and Lord. Vindicate me in your righteousness, O LORD my God; do not let them gloat over me. Do not let them think, 'Aha, just what we wanted!' or say, 'We have swallowed him up.'" (Psalm 35:22-25)

Christian, the Lord is the One who contends for us. He is the One who is our vindicator and defender. He is the One who contends, defends, and vindicates us in righteousness and justice. He is the One who can stop all gossipers and gloaters—He is our Mighty God!

Become Gamblers for God
(Part 1)
(finances)

Are you gambling for gold or are you gambling for God? Although the world economy is still struggling with numerous financial pressures, many gambling casinos and betting places are experiencing a financial boom. Why? People are lured by the promise of fast and easy money. They're tempted to gamble for gold, regardless of economic difficulties, and choosing to ignore the clear warnings the Bible gives us about the idea of fast and easy money.

"The plans of the diligent lead to profit as surely as haste leads to poverty." (Proverbs 21:5)

Scripture encourages us to be steady and consistent when it comes to making money. Those who follow this advice will discover that they have something to show for their diligence. However, Scripture also discourages us from trying to go for fast and easy money. Why? Fast money often will lead to fast losses . . . which inevitably leads to devastating debt . . . and slavery.

"The rich rule over the poor, and the borrower is servant to the lender." (Proverbs 22:7)

Watch the downward spiral: The lure of fast money can often lead to fast losses; fast losses usually lead to devastating debt; and devastating debt inevitably leads to slavery. What is the result of being under the slavery of debt? The weight of devastating debt creates such stress that people don't know what to do. Some try to take shortcuts to relieve the stress of debt. Instead, they find that they only create more debt. Others try to hide from the stress of devastating debt, only to find that when they wake up the debt is still there. Unfortunately, both approaches usually fail, resulting in all kinds of negative consequences: Families are negatively impacted, friendships are negatively impacted, physical health is negatively impacted, emotional health is negatively impacted, and spiritual health is negatively impacted.

"People who want to get rich fall into temptation and a trap and into many foolish and harmful desires that plunge men into ruin and destruction. For the love of money is a root of all kinds of evil. Some people, eager for money, have wandered

from the faith and pierced themselves with many griefs." (1 Timothy 6:9-10)

Initially, gambling for gold doesn't seem like it's very dangerous. Many people view it as a harmless way of relieving stress and having some fun. However, as we have seen today, gambling for gold is not as harmless as it may seem. May we all heed the warnings from Scripture, and may we instead be a people who become "gamblers" for God. Tomorrow we'll see what the Bible has to say about this type of "gambling."

Become Gamblers for God (Part 2)

(finances, God's kingdom)

Are you gambling for gold or are you gambling for God? Previously, we took a look at some of the potential pitfalls when it comes to gambling for money. Today we'll take a look at some of the potential blessings when it comes to gambling for God.

1)   Gambling for God will bring a return.

"The eyes of the LORD range throughout the earth to strengthen those whose hearts are fully committed to him." (2 Chronicles 16:9)

God is looking for people who are willing to honor Him and take a step of faith. God is looking to strengthen people with all they need to be able to do all God calls them to do. God is looking for people whose hearts are willing to commit to the greatest investment there is—the building of God's kingdom. Why is it such a great investment?

2)   Gambling for God will bring a guaranteed return.

" 'But the one who received the seed that fell on good soil is the man who hears the word and understands it. He produces a crop, yielding a hundred, sixty or thirty times what was sown.' " (Matthew 13:23)

Investing your life in the building of God's kingdom will produce a return. Actually, it will produce a guaranteed return. The Scripture above encourages us by saying that a person who is willing to take the things of God seriously will produce 30-60-100 times of what was invested—now that's a return that no stock market or gambling casino can ever guarantee! Not every Christian will have the same return on their investment, but every Christian will definitely have a return on their investment—a guaranteed return! How can such a gamble produce such a great guarantee?

3) Gambling for God is not a gamble.

"Therefore, since we are receiving a kingdom that cannot be shaken, let us be thankful, and so worship God acceptably with reverence and awe." (Hebrews 12:28)

Christian, God's kingdom can never be shaken or destroyed. It's a constantly growing kingdom that will last for all eternity. Therefore, gambling for God is actually not a gamble. It's a guaranteed return because you're investing in the safest and sturdiest investment there is. When you gamble in casinos, the house always wins. However, when you "gamble" for God, God's house always wins!

"Let us not become weary in doing good, for at the proper time we will reap a harvest if we do not give up." (Galatians 6:9)

Become Gamblers for God?
(Part 3)
(spiritual gifts, serving)

Are you gambling for gold or are you gambling for God? Earlier, we took a look at some of the potential blessings when it comes to gambling for God. We saw that gambling for God will bring a return, gambling for God will bring a guaranteed return, gambling for God is not a gamble. Today we'll take a look at the fact that, as Christians, God has given us everything we need to build His body and bring glory to His name.

God has given us spiritual gifts so that we can build His body and glorify His name.

"Each one should use whatever gift he has received to serve others, faithfully administrating God's grace in its various forms. If anyone speaks, he should

do it as one speaking the very words of God. If anyone serves, he should do it with the strength God provides, so that in all things God may be praised through Jesus Christ. To him be the glory and the power for ever and ever. Amen." (1 Peter 4:10-11)

Here's the good news: Christian, you have been given spiritual gifts. Here is the better news: Christian, you have been given different spiritual gifts than others have been given. Why is that good news? We can all use our various gifts in various ways to build the body of Christ and bring glory to Christ! Do you know what your spiritual gifts are? Are you using those spiritual gifts and "gambling" for God? Always remember, Jesus wants us to use our gifts and He expects us to use our gifts—He wants to see His body built and He expects us to do it in a way that His name is glorified.

"For we must all appear before the judgment seat of Christ, that each one may receive what is due him for the things done while in the body, whether good or bad." (2 Corinthians 5:10)

As Christians, we will all have to give an account to Jesus as to how we used our gifts that He entrusted to us. He will not accept excuses! Why? He has given us everything we need to succeed. Not only that, but His kingdom will bring a return; His kingdom will bring a guaranteed return—because His kingdom is not a gamble. May we as Christians spend our lives taking advantage of the indescribable privilege of building Christ's body and bringing glory to Christ's name.

Become Gamblers for God (Part 4)

(serving, opportunity)

Are you gambling for gold or are you gambling for God? Earlier we saw how God has graciously given us spiritual gifts so that we can build His body and glorify His name. Today we will see how God in His grace has given us even more!

God has given us opportunities so that we can build His body and glorify His name.

" 'Again, it will be like a man going on a journey, who called his servants and entrusted his property to them. To one he gave five talents of money, to another two talents, and to another one talent, each according to his ability. Then he went on his journey.' " (Matthew 25:14-15)

Talents are opportunities that the Lord provides us so that we can build His body and glorify His name. Here is the good news: Christian, you have been given opportunities. Here is the better news: Christian, you have been given different types of opportunities than others. Why is that good news? We can all use our various opportunities in various ways to build the body of Christ and bring glory to Christ! Have you been stepping through that door of opportunity? Are you using your spiritual gifts and taking advantage of those opportunities? In other words, are you "gambling" for God? Always remember, Jesus wants us to use our gifts and opportunities; He expects us to use our gifts and opportunities—He wants to see His body built and He expects us to do it in a way that His name is glorified.

" 'His master replied, "Well done, good and faithful servant! You have been faithful with a few things; I will put you in charge of many things. Come and share your master's happiness." ' " (Matthew 25:23)

Wouldn't it be wonderful to hear those very words said about you? Can you imagine the Lord looking you in the eyes and saying those very words as He welcomes you home to heaven? Christian, it's very simple—use the gifts the Lord has provided you and step through the doors of opportunity the Lord opens for you. Yes, it takes faith. No, it will not always be smooth sailing. However, the Lord promises that your labor for Him will never ever be in vain!

"Therefore, my dear brothers, stand firm. Let nothing move you. Always give yourselves fully to the work of the Lord, because you know that your labor in the Lord is not in vain." (1 Corinthians 15:58)

A Prayer for Forgiveness

(prayer, forgiveness)

Lord, I need Your mercy.

"Have mercy on me, O God, according to your unfailing love; according to your great compassion blot out my transgressions. Wash away all my inequity and cleanse me from my sin." (Psalm 51:1-2)

Lord, I admit that I messed up.

"For I know my transgressions, and my sin is always before me. Against you, you only, have I sinned and done what is evil in your sight, so that you are proved right when you speak and justified when you judge. Surely I was sinful at birth, sinful from the time my mother conceived me. Surely you desire truth in the inner parts; you teach me wisdom in the inmost place." (Psalm 51:3-6)

Lord, please cleanse me.

"Cleanse me with hyssop, and I will be clean; wash me, and I will be whiter than snow. Let me hear joy and gladness; let the bones you have crushed rejoice. Hide your face from my sins and blot out all my inequity." (Psalm 51:7-9)

Lord, please create in me a pure heart.

"Create in me a pure heart, O God, and renew a steadfast spirit within me. Do not cast me from your presence or take your Holy Spirit from me. Restore to me the joy of your salvation and grant me a willing spirit, to sustain me." (Psalm 51:10-12)

Lord, I want to tell others of Your marvelous mercy.

"Then I will teach transgressors your ways, and sinners will turn back to you. Save me from bloodguilt, O God, the God who saves me, and my tongue will sing of your righteousness." (Psalm 51:13-14)

Lord, I want to bring glory and honor to You because of Your marvelous mercy.

"O LORD, open my lips, and my mouth will declare your praise. You do not delight in sacrifice, or I would bring it; you do not take pleasure in burnt offerings. The sacrifices of God are a broken spirit; a broken and contrite heart, O God, you will not despise." (Psalm 51:15-17)

Lord, I am so grateful to You for Your marvelous mercy towards me, Amen.

Promise to Praise

(prayer, thankfulness)

Lord, I praise You with my lips.

"Shout for joy to the Lord, all the earth. Worship the Lord with gladness; come before him with joyful songs." (Psalm 100:1-2)

Lord, I praise You with my mind.

"Know that the LORD is God. It is he who made us, and we are his; we are his people, the sheep of his pasture." (Psalm 100:3)

Lord, I praise You with my walk.

"Enter his gates with thanksgiving and his courts with praise; give thanks to him and praise his name." (Psalm 100:4)

Lord, I praise You because of who You are and how You are.

"For the LORD is good and his love endures forever; his faithfulness continues through all generations." (Psalm 100:5)

Christian, how much time do you spend preparing to praise the Lord? Are you preparing your lips to praise the Lord? In other words, are you asking the Lord to cleanse your lips so that you can offer Him the praise He is due? Are you preparing your mind to praise the Lord? In other words, are you asking the Lord to fill you with thoughts about Him so that you can give Him the praise He is due? Are you preparing your walk to praise the Lord? In other words, are you offering the totality of your being to the Lord? Are you saying, "Lord, I desire that my walk and talk bring praise and pleasure to You." Finally, are you preparing to praise the Lord by focusing on who He is and how wonderful He is? Or, are you focused more on the things you need to accomplish throughout the rest of the day—turning your time of praise into a time of personal planning?

"Praise the LORD. Give thanks to the LORD, for he is good; his love endures forever. Who can proclaim the mighty acts of the LORD or fully declare his praise?" (Psalm 106:1-2)

Perfect Purpose Behind Your Problems

(suffering, trials)

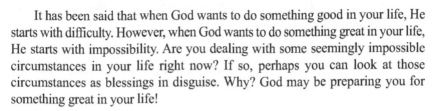

It has been said that when God wants to do something good in your life, He starts with difficulty. However, when God wants to do something great in your life, He starts with impossibility. Are you dealing with some seemingly impossible circumstances in your life right now? If so, perhaps you can look at those circumstances as blessings in disguise. Why? God may be preparing you for something great in your life!

"Consider it pure joy, my brothers, whenever you face trials of many kinds, because you know that the testing of your faith develops perseverance. Perseverance must finish its work, so that you may be mature and complete, not lacking in anything." (James 1:2-4)

It's not easy to go through difficult trials. It's not something that any of us look forward to. However, Scripture tells us that God has a purpose behind our problems. He is growing us and preparing us. Perhaps it may be for some special blessing that you have been fervently praying for. Or, perhaps it may be for some special blessing that you haven't even thought about. Whatever the purpose may be, do you believe that God is in full control of everything that is going on in your life right now—absolutely everything? Do you believe that He has a perfect purpose behind your particular problems, and that He is working it out for your good and His glory?

"We know that in all things God works for the good of those who love him, who have been called according to his purpose." (Romans 8:28)

Scripture tells us that God's children can be absolutely certain of something. What can we be certain of? We can be certain that our heavenly Father loves us and cares for us—and that He can turn our current problems into future praise; He can turn our current worry into future worship, and He can turn our current panic into future peace. In other words, when God wants to do something good in your life, He starts with difficulty. However, when God wants to do something great in your life, He starts with impossibility!

"Let us not become weary in doing good, for at the proper time we will reap a harvest if we do not give up." (Galatians 6:9)

A Prayer for Peace and Protection

(prayer, worry, peace)

O Lord, my thoughts trouble me.

"Listen to my prayer, O God, do not ignore my plea; hear me and answer me. My thoughts trouble me and I am distraught at the voice of the enemy, at the stares of the wicked; for they bring down suffering upon me and revile me in their anger." (Psalm 55:1-3)

O Lord, my heart troubles me.

"My heart is in anguish within me; the terrors of death assail me. Fear and trembling have beset me; horror has overwhelmed me. I said, 'Oh, that I had wings of a dove! I would fly away and be at rest—I would flee far away and stay in the desert; I would hurry to my place of shelter, far from the tempest and storm.'" (Psalm 55:4-8)

O Lord, my hope is in You.

"Confuse the wicked, O Lord, confound their speech, for I see violence and strife in the city. Day and night they prowl about on its walls; malice and abuse are within it." (Psalm 55:9-10)

O Lord, my trust is in You.

"But I call to God, and the LORD saves me. Evening, morning and noon I cry out in distress, and he hears my voice. He ransoms me unharmed from the battle waged against me, even though many oppose me." (Psalm 55:16-18)

O Lord, I cast all my cares on You.

"Cast your cares on the LORD and he will sustain you; he will never let the righteous fall. But you, O God, will bring down the wicked into the pit of corruption; bloodthirsty and deceitful men will not live out half their days. But as for me, I trust in you." (Psalm 55:22-23)

O Lord, thank You for the peace and protection You provide me. My thoughts and my heart are focused on You, for You are my great God in whom I place my hope and trust. O Lord, thank You that I can confidently cast all of my cares upon You, for I trust that You will sustain me against the difficult people and difficult circumstances I am currently facing. Amen.

What Is Your Purpose in Life?

(purpose)

How would you answer if someone asked, "What is your purpose in life?" Parents may answer by saying that raising their children is their primary purpose. Students may say that getting a good education is their primary purpose. Others may say that making money and living a comfortable life is their primary purpose.

" 'But seek first his kingdom and his righteousness, and all these things will be given to you as well.' " (Matthew 6:33)

Christian, our primary purpose is to glorify God and enjoy Him forever. We want to bring Him glory because of who He is—He is the perfect and holy Lord of the universe. We also want to bring Him glory because of what He has done for us—He is the perfect and holy Lord of the universe who has graciously granted us the free gift of salvation through Jesus Christ. We want to enjoy God because He is our loving Lord who wants to give us life to the fullest.

" 'The thief comes only to steal and kill and destroy; I have come that they may have life, and have it to the full.' " (John 10:10)

Christian, we once were being led and misled by the thief. Who is the thief? The devil, the one who tried to steal, kill and destroy us. However, our Savior came to give us life—life eternal and life in abundance. Our primary purpose is to worship our Lord and to live our lives in such a way that brings glory to our Lord. We do this with an attitude of gratitude for the One who gave His all for us. Therefore, parents look to raise their children in such a way that brings glory and honor to the Lord. In doing so, parents trust that their children will be blessed. Students seek to bring glory to the Lord as they pursue their educational goals. In doing so, they trust that their efforts will be blessed. Employers and employees look to bring glory and honor to the Lord in the workplace. They look at their desk as an altar that seeks to honor the name of the One whose name they bear. In doing so, they trust that their efforts will be blessed. Christian, are you fulfilling your primary purpose in life?

"Yet for us there is but one God, the Father, from whom all things came and for whom we live; and there is but one Lord, Jesus Christ, through whom all things came and through whom we live." (1 Corinthians 8:6)

A Prayer for Greater Faith

(prayer, faith)

O Lord, grant me the faith of Abraham.

"By faith Abraham, when called to go to a place he would later receive as his inheritance, obeyed and went, even though he did not know where he was going." (Hebrews 11:8)

O Lord, grant me the faith of Moses.

"By faith Moses, when he had grown up, refused to be known as the son of Pharaoh's daughter. He chose to be mistreated along with the people of God rather than to enjoy the pleasures of sin for a short time. He regarded disgrace for the sake of Christ as of greater value than the treasures of Egypt, because he was looking ahead to his reward." (Hebrews 11:24-26)

O Lord, grant me the faith to run the race You set for me.

"Therefore, since we are surrounded by such a great cloud of witnesses, let us throw off everything that hinders and the sin that so easily entangles, and let us run with perseverance the race marked out for us." (Hebrews 12:1)

O Lord, grant me the faith to stay focused on You.

"Let us fix our eyes on Jesus, the author and perfecter of our faith, who for the joy set before him endured the cross, scorning its shame, and sat down at the right hand of the throne of God. Consider him who endured such opposition from sinful men, so that you will not grow weary and lose heart." (Hebrews 12:2-3)

O Lord, grant me the faith to trust in Your discipline.

"Our fathers disciplined us for a little while as they thought best; but God disciplines us for our good, that we may share in his holiness. No discipline seems pleasant at the time, but painful. Later on, however, it produces a harvest of righteousness and peace for those who have been trained by it." (Hebrews 12:10-11)

O Lord, grant me the faith to please You.

"Without faith it is impossible to please God, because anyone who comes to him must believe that he exists and that he rewards those who earnestly seek him." (Hebrews 11:6)

A Prayer of Trust

(prayer, worry)

Dear Lord, I will not stress because I trust in Your protection.

"He who dwells in the shelter of the Most High will rest in the shadow of the Almighty. I will say of the LORD, 'He is my refuge and my fortress, my God, in whom I trust.' " (Psalm 91:1-2)

Dear Lord, I will not fear because I trust in Your faithfulness.

"Surely he will save you from the fowler's snare and from the deadly pestilence. He will cover you with his feathers, and under his wings you will find refuge; his faithfulness will be your shield and rampart. You will not fear the terror of night, nor the arrow that flies by day, nor the pestilence that stalks in the darkness, nor the plague that destroys at midday." (Psalm 91:4-6)

Dear Lord, I will not worry about the wicked because I trust in Your ways.

"A thousand may fall at your side, ten thousand at your right hand, but it will not come near you. You will only observe with your eyes and see the punishment of the wicked." (Psalm 91:7-8)

Dear Lord, I will not fear disaster because I trust in Your dwelling.

"If you make the Most High your dwelling—even the LORD, who is my refuge— then no harm will befall you, no disaster will come near your tent. For he will command his angels concerning you to guard you in all your ways; they will lift you up in their hands, so that you will not strike your foot against a stone. You will tread upon the lion and the cobra; you will trample the great lion and the serpent." (Psalm 91:9-13)

Dear Lord, I truly love you and I truly trust You.

"Because he loves me," says the LORD, "I will rescue him; I will protect him, for he acknowledges my name. He will call upon me, and I will answer him; I will be with him in trouble, I will deliver him and honor him. With long life will I satisfy him and show him my salvation." (Psalm 91:14-16)

A Prayer Regarding God's Word

(prayer, obedience)

Dear Lord, help me to obey Your Word.

"You have laid down precepts that are to be fully obeyed. Oh, that my ways were steadfast in obeying your decrees!" (Psalm 119:4-5)

Dear Lord, help me rejoice in obeying Your Word.

"I rejoice in following your statutes as one rejoices in great riches. I meditate on your precepts and consider your ways. I delight in your decrees; I will not neglect your word." (Psalm 119:14-16)

Dear Lord, help me to understand more of Your Word.

"Open my eyes that I may see wonderful things in your law. I am a stranger on earth; do not hide your commands from me. My soul is consumed with longing for your laws at all times." (Psalm 119:18-20)

Dear Lord, strengthen me through Your Word.

"My soul is weary with sorrow; strengthen me according to your word. Keep me from deceitful ways; be gracious to me through your law. I have chosen the way of truth; I have set my heart on your laws. I hold fast to your statutes, O LORD; do not let me be put to shame." (Psalm 119:28-32)

Dear Lord, protect me through Your Word.

"Turn my heart toward your statutes and not toward selfish gain. Turn my eyes away from worthless things; preserve my life according to your word. Fulfill your promise to your servant, so that you may be feared. Take away the disgrace I dread, for your laws are good. How I long for your precepts! Preserve my life in your righteousness." (Psalm 119:36-40)

Dear Lord, thank You for Your most wonderful Word.

"Your word, O LORD, is eternal; it stands firm in the heavens. Your faithfulness continues through all generations; you established the earth, and it endures. Your laws endure to this day, for all things serve you. If your law had not been my delight, I would have perished in my affliction. I will never forget your precepts, for by them you have preserved my life." (Psalm 119:89-93)

God Turns the Impossible Into Possible

(God's power, trust)

A wise man once said that we bring glory to God when we look to Him to accomplish the seemingly impossible for us. In other words, when we look to God by faith, trusting in Him by faith to accomplish something great, God is pleased and glorified.

"Without faith it is impossible to please God, because anyone who comes to him must believe that he exists and that he rewards those who earnestly seek him." (Hebrews 11:6)

Please understand, we are to not put God to the test by saying, "Okay, God, let's see if You are really as powerful as You say You are." Rather, we're to exercise faith and trust by saying, "God, I know that with You nothing is impossible. If it's Your will to accomplish this seemingly impossible thing in my life, then may Your perfect will be done and may it be done all for Your glory."

"The LORD detests the sacrifice of the wicked, but the prayer of the upright pleases him." (Proverbs 15:8)

Christian, God is pleased when we come to Him in faith. He is pleased when we seek His wisdom, power and guidance. He is pleased when we look to Him to accomplish great things in and through us—all for His glory. Is there something seemingly impossible you are facing in your life right now? Or, do you have some God-given goal that seems impossible to accomplish under your own power? Are you bringing glory and pleasure to God by looking to Him and trusting in Him to make the impossible possible?

"These are the words of him who is holy and true, who holds the key of David. What he opens no one can shut, and what he shuts no one can open. I know your deeds. See, I have placed before you an open door that no one can shut. I know that you have little strength, yet you have kept my word and have not denied my name." (Revelation 3:7-8)

Remember, Christian, if God calls you to it, He is more than able to bring you through it. God's work done God's way will never lack God's supply. Therefore, look to Him and trust in Him to turn the seemingly impossible into the possible—all for His glory!

Stay Humble and Look to the Lord for Strength

(humility, character)

The Bible tells us that God desires humility in His people. In fact, the Bible promises that God grants abundant grace to the humble. However, if truth be told, it's hard to be humble. Can anybody relate? The Bible gives us several reasons why humility is such a challenge for us:

Our sin nature.

"I know that nothing good lives in me, that is, in my sinful nature. For I have the desire to do what is good, but I cannot carry it out. For what I do is not the good I want to do; no, the evil I do not want to do—this I keep on doing." (Romans 7:18-19)

These words from the apostle Paul are the same words that so many of us Christians can relate to. We know that God desires humility in His people. We also know that God grants grace and blessings to the humble. However, our sin nature doesn't want us to be humble. Rather, it wants us to exalt ourselves and to be filled with pride. As Christians, the Spirit of Christ is with us and lives in us, and He wants us to live a life of humility that honors the Holy Trinity—God the Father, God the Son and God the Holy Spirit. However, the sin nature also resides in us and wants us to live a life of pride that exalts the "unholy trinity"—me, I and I. Once again, I ask, can you relate?

Our enemy the devil.

" 'You will not surely die,' the serpent said to the woman. 'For God knows that when you eat of it your eyes will be opened, and you will be like God, knowing good and evil.' " (Genesis 3:4-5)

The devil is a spirit being. He indwelled the serpent with the purpose of tempting Adam and Eve to disobey God. He told them that they didn't need to listen to God and humble themselves before him. Rather, he told them that they could do things their own way and be their own god. Interestingly, the devil still uses the same tempting tactic against us today. He still tempts us with the promise that if we ignore God and do things our own way, we will experience a life of freedom and success. Why? Because he persuades us to believe that we can be much better leaders of our lives than God. Is anybody experiencing that temptation right now?

The world.

"For everything in the world—the cravings of sinful man, the lust of his eyes and the boasting of what he has and does—comes not from the Father but from the world. The world and its desires pass away, but the man who does the will of God lives forever." (1 John 2:16-17)

The Bible often describes the world as a system that is in direct opposition to God and His commands. God's Word tells us to be meek and humble, trusting in God's grace and guidance for our lives. However, the world tells us to do anything and everything to succeed, trusting in our desires and appetites to guide our lives. Is anybody feeling the pull of the world on their lives right now? Are you finding it tough to stay humble when everything around you is tempting you to ignore God and do things your way?

"No, in all these things we are more than conquerors through him who loved us." (Romans 8:37)

Although it's hard to stay humble, it's not impossible. Yes, we are dealing with daily opposition that makes humility hard. However, God's grace is sufficient and His power is perfect in our weakness. The key is to recognize why it's challenging to stay humble, where the challenges come, and how the challenges come at us. Then, look to the Lord for His strength. Remember, He is much stronger than any of the challenges that come against you!

A Prayer for Wisdom

(wisdom, prayer)

Dear Lord, please make me wise in the use of my time.

"Be very careful, then, how you live—not as unwise but as wise, making the most of every opportunity, because the days are evil. Therefore, do not be foolish, but understand what the Lord's will is. Do not get drunk on wine, which leads to debauchery. Instead, be filled with the Spirit." (Ephesians 5:15-18)

Dear Lord, make me wise as a husband or a wife.

" 'For this reason a man will leave his father and mother and be united to his wife, and the two will become one flesh.' This is a profound mystery—but I am talking about Christ and the church. However, each one of you also must love his wife as he loves himself, and the wife must respect her husband." (Ephesians 5:31-33)

Dear Lord, make me wise as a son or daughter.

"Children, obey your parents in the Lord, for this is right. 'Honor your father and mother'—which is the first commandment with a promise—'that it may go well with you and that you may enjoy long life on the earth.' " (Ephesians 6:1-3)

Dear Lord, please make me wise as a father or mother.

"Fathers, do not exasperate your children; instead, bring them up in the training and instruction of the Lord." (Ephesians 6:4)

Dear Lord, make me wise at work.

"Serve wholeheartedly, as if you were serving the Lord, not men, because you know that the Lord will reward everyone for whatever good he does, whether he is slave or free." (Ephesians 6:7-8)

Dear Lord, make me wise in the daily spiritual battle.

"Finally, be strong in the Lord and in his mighty power. Put on the full armor of God so that you can take your stand against the devil's schemes. For our struggle is not against flesh and blood, but against the rulers, against the authorities, against the powers of this dark world and against the spiritual forces of evil in the heavenly realms." (Ephesians 6:10-12)

Dear Lord, make me wise in my daily use of prayer.

"Pray in the Spirit on all occasions with all kinds of prayers and requests. With this in mind, be alert and always keep on praying for all the saints." (Ephesians 6:18)

Do You Want Peace?

(peace, trials)

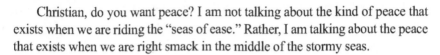

Christian, do you want peace? I am not talking about the kind of peace that exists when we are riding the "seas of ease." Rather, I am talking about the peace that exists when we are right smack in the middle of the stormy seas.

"Rejoice in the Lord always. I will say it again: Rejoice! Let your gentleness be evident to all. The Lord is near." (Philippians 4:4-5)

Christian, do you want peace? Rejoice and remember that the Lord is near. He is with you and will never forsake you. This means that He is with you right now in the middle of the stormy seas you are experiencing. He will never leave you nor forget you while you ride out those stormy seas. Christian, He is in full control of those stormy seas and He will safely navigate you to the other side. Rejoice, for the Lord is near.

"Do not be anxious about anything, but in everything, by prayer and petition, with thanksgiving, present your requests to God." (Philippians 4:6)

Christian, do you want peace? Present your anxieties to the Lord. He is near and He is the one who can turn your panic into peace. Remember, we all experience stormy seas, and therefore we all experience anxiety. That is called being human. However, we have a faithful Savior who knows our concerns and hears our cries. Therefore, we can rejoice and be thankful. We can be thankful that our God is Sovereign and All-Powerful over every stormy sea we experience!

"And the peace of God, which transcends all understanding, will guard your hearts and your minds in Christ Jesus." (Philippians 4:7)

Christian, do you want peace? God promises to grant us a type of peace that is literally unexplainable! It's a peace from God that guards our heart and minds in Christ Jesus. By the way, do you actually believe that any storm is too strong for Jesus? Of course not! Do you think that any high waves and stormy seas can prevent Jesus from guarding your life? Of course not! Then, relax and rejoice— for with Jesus on your side you're on the winning side. Talk about peace!

Have You Weighed Your Heart Lately?

(motives, relationships)

"All a man's ways seem right to him, but the LORD weighs the heart." *(Proverbs 21:2)*

Christian, have you weighed your heart lately? In other words, have you checked to see if your heart is right in the Lord's sight? The Scripture above tells us that it's very easy for us to rationalize our ways. It's very easy to fall into the trap of thinking that our ways are good and innocent—even if, in reality, they're not. The Scripture above also tells us that the Lord can see through our rationalizations and justifications. He can't be fooled, even when we try to fool ourselves and others.

"To do what is right and just is more acceptable to the LORD than sacrifice." *(Proverbs 21:3)*

Christian, have you weighed your actions lately? In other words, have you checked to see if you truly try to please the Lord instead of trying to put on a show in front of others? The Scripture above is not saying that God is opposed to sacrifices. Rather, God is opposed to sacrifices that are used to mask our true intentions. He wants actions that are honest and authentic, not sacrifices that are dishonest and hypocritical. Remember, the Lord can't be fooled, even when we try to fool ourselves or others.

"When a man's ways are pleasing to the LORD, he makes even his enemies live at peace with him." *(Proverbs 16:7)*

Christian, it's so easy to fall into the trap of being a people pleaser. This is especially true when it comes to trying to impress and please those people who are opposed to us. Can you relate? However, the Scripture above tells us that if we focus on pleasing the Lord, He can handle changing the heart of those who oppose us. This includes those challenging people or circumstances you are dealing with right now. The key is to live a life that is right in the sight of the Lord. May God in His grace grant us the desire and ability to live a life that is pleasing to Him, trusting that He can handle the hearts of those who oppose us.

"In the way of righteousness there is life; along that path is immortality." *(Proverbs 12:28)*

The Step of Faith that Honors God

(faith, trust)

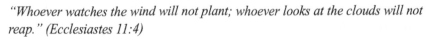

"Whoever watches the wind will not plant; whoever looks at the clouds will not reap." (Ecclesiastes 11:4)

This verse is basically saying that those who wait for the perfect conditions to do something are those who will never get anything done. Why? The perfect conditions never arrive. Therefore, we need to step forward in faith, trusting that God will guide and provide for us.

"Without faith it is impossible to please God, because anyone who comes to him must believe that he exists and that he rewards those who earnestly seek him." (Hebrews 11:6)

When we're looking for the perfect conditions, we're expressing faith in those conditions rather than in God. We shouldn't blindly barge forward and completely disregard all logical thinking. God has graciously given us a mind that He expects us to use in a sensible way. However, very often we can allow our "sensibility" to create all kinds of excuses for not taking the step of faith that honors God. Christian, has God placed something on your heart that He wants you to accomplish for Him? Have you been praying about it and studying the Scriptures to discern God's will on this? If so, have you been sensing a greater urgency and excitement to get started on what God has placed on your heart? Then take the step of faith, trusting that when God guides He always provides! Will your faith be tested? Of course it will, but take the step anyway. Will you meet with opposition that will challenge your vision? Of course you will, but take the step anyway. Will you meet with negativity that will question your sanity? Of course you will, but take the step anyway. Christian, you honor God when you show trust in God. Fulfill the purpose you have been created for and bring glory to God—you will not be disappointed!

"We are God's workmanship, created in Christ Jesus to do good works, which God prepared in advance for us to do." (Ephesians 2:10)

A Prayer When Discouraged and Downcast

(prayer, discouragement)

Dear Lord, I am so thirsty for You.

"As the deer pants for streams of water, so my soul pants for you, O God. My soul thirsts for God, for the living God. When can I go and meet with God?" (Psalm 42:1-2)

Dear Lord, I am so tired of crying.

"My tears have been my food day and night, while men say to me all day long, 'Where is your God?' These things I remember as I pour out my soul: How I used to go with the multitude, leading the procession to the house of God, with shouts of joy and thanksgiving among the festive throng." (Psalm 42:3-4)

Dear Lord, my soul is so downcast.

"Why are you downcast, O my soul? Why so disturbed within me? Put your hope in God, for I will yet praise him, my Savior and my God. My soul is downcast within me; therefore I will remember you from the land of the Jordan, the heights of Hermon—from Mount Mizar. Deep calls to deep in the roar of your waterfalls; all your waves and breakers have swept over me." (Psalm 42:5-7)

Dear Lord, my soul will trust in Your daily love.

"By day the LORD directs his love, at night his song is with me—a prayer to the God of my life." (Psalm 42:8)

Dear Lord, my soul will hope in You and praise You.

"Why are you so downcast, O my soul? Why so disturbed within me? Put your hope in God, for I will yet praise him, my Savior and my God." (Psalm 42:11)

A Message from Jesus

(stress, exhaustion)

Are you feeling tired and weary? Jesus says:

" *'Come to me, all you who are weary and burdened, and I will give you rest. Take my yoke upon you and learn from me, for I am gentle and humble in heart, and you will find rest for your souls. For my yoke is easy and my burden is light.'"* (Matthew 11:28-30)

Are you feeling weak and overwhelmed? Jesus says:

"My grace is sufficient for you, for my power is made perfect in weakness." (2 Corinthians 12:9)

Are you feeling busy and stressed? Jesus says:

"Come with me by yourselves to a quiet place and get some rest." (Mark 6:31)

Are you feeling hurt because of unfair criticism? Jesus says:

" *'A student is not above his teacher, nor a servant above his master. It is enough for the student to be like his teacher, and the servant like his master. If the head of the house has been called Beelzebub, how much more the members of his household!.'"* (Matthew 10:24-25)

Are you feeling like you want to lash out and criticize someone? Jesus says:

" *'Why do you look at the speck of sawdust in your brother's eye and pay no attention to the plank in your own eye? How can you say to your brother, 'Let me take the speck out of your eye,' when all the time there is a plank in your own eye? You hypocrite, first take the plank out of your own eye, and then you will see clearly to remove the speck from your brother's eye.'"* (Matthew 7:3-5)

Dear Jesus, please grant me the grace to trust You and obey You. Please grant me the grace to come to You daily for rest and recovery; and please allow me to rely on Your truly sufficient grace, no matter how difficult my challenges may be.

The Wisdom in God's Word

(wisdom, guidance)

How can a person walk in purity?

"How can a young man keep his way pure? By living according to your word. I seek you with all my heart; do not let me stray from your commands." (Psalm 119:9-10)

How can a person be protected from sinning?

"I have hidden your word in my heart that I might not sin against you. Praise be to you, O LORD; teach me your decrees." (Psalm 119:11-12)

How can a person overcome sorrow and guilt?

"My soul is weary with sorrow; strengthen me according to your word. Keep me from deceitful ways; be gracious to me through your law." (Psalm 119:28-29)

How can a person find blessings?

"Do good to your servant according to your word, O LORD. Teach me knowledge and good judgment, for I believe in your commands. Before I was afflicted I went astray, but now I obey your word. You are good, and what you do is good; teach me your decrees." (Psalm 119:65-68)

How can a person find safety and stability?

"Your word, O LORD, is eternal; it stands firm in the heavens. Your faithfulness continues through all generations; you established the earth, and it endures. Your laws endure to this day, for all things serve you. If your law had not been my delight, I would have perished in my affliction." (Psalm 119:89-92)

How can a person find guidance and wisdom?

"Your word is a lamp to my feet and a light for my path. I have taken an oath and confirmed it, that I will follow your righteous laws." (Psalm 119:105-106)

How can a person find compassion and comfort?

"Look upon my suffering and deliver me, for I have not forgotten your law. Defend my cause and redeem me; preserve my life according to your promise. Salvation is far from the wicked, for they do not seek out your decrees. Your compassion is great, O LORD; preserve my life according to your laws. Many are the foes who persecute me, but I have not turned from your statutes." (Psalm 119:153-157)

Praise the Lord

(worship, thankfulness)

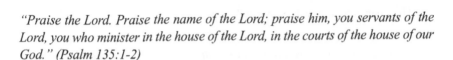

"Praise the Lord. Praise the name of the Lord; praise him, you servants of the Lord, you who minister in the house of the Lord, in the courts of the house of our God." (Psalm 135:1-2)

Are there times when you're moving so fast that you fail to take the time to praise the Lord for His goodness? With all that is happening in and around our lives, it's very easy to succumb to pressure rather than to take the time to praise.

"Praise the LORD, for the LORD is good; sing praise to his name, for that is pleasant." (Psalm 135:3)

A wise person once said that you can't wait until you feel like praising the Lord. Rather, start to praise the Lord and watch how you will feel like praising Him more and more. Christian, has the Lord done something good in your life over the past few days? Take some time to praise Him. Has the Lord protected you from something bad over the past few days? Take some time to praise Him.

"Praise the LORD. How good it is to sing praises to our God, how pleasant and fitting to praise him!" (Psalm 147:1)

Hurry leads to worry, but praise leads to peace. How do you want to live your life today? Do you want to trudge along in fear and worry, or do you want to dance in joy and praise? The Scripture above reminds us that it's good to sing praises to our great God, for it's fitting to praise our God of all grace and mercy. Christian, it's not difficult to find reasons to praise God—you don't have to search for reasons as though you were searching for eggs on an Easter egg hunt. You can praise God for who He is, and you can praise God for how He is. You can praise God for what He has done in your past, for what He is doing in your present, and for what He will do in your future. Christian, take some time today to praise the Lord—you will be very surprised at how much you can truly praise Him for!

"Praise the Lord. Praise God in his sanctuary; praise him in his mighty heavens. Praise him for his acts of power; praise him for his surpassing greatness." (Psalm 150:1-2)

Fulfilling God's Purpose for Your Life

(God's will, purpose)

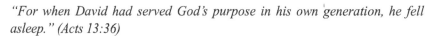

"For when David had served God's purpose in his own generation, he fell asleep." (Acts 13:36)

What an incredible verse. Once King David had fulfilled the purpose for which God created him, he then went home to be with the Lord. Talk about leaving a legacy! That would be such a wonderful truth to have written on your tombstone: "He fulfilled God's purpose in his generation."

"The eyes of the LORD range throughout the earth to strengthen those whose hearts are fully committed to him." (2 Chronicles 16:9)

How about you? Do you have a passion to fulfill God's purpose and bring glory to Him? In other words:

1) Do you want to leave a legacy?

2) Do you want to leave a mark?

3) Are you willing to make the sacrifice?

"As for you, be strong and do not give up, for your work will be rewarded." (2 Chronicles 15:7)

Christian, it may not always be easy to fulfill God's calling on your life. There may be times when you wonder if you are truly making a difference. But don't give up. Why? God has a special and unique purpose that He wants you to fulfill. God has a wonderful legacy that He wants you to leave; and God wants you to live a life for Him that is truly worth living! Take the step of faith and join in the most incredible adventure there is—living for God and bringing glory to His name!

"God is not unjust; he will not forget your work and the love you have shown him as you have helped his people and continue to help them." (Hebrews 6:10)

Jesus Is the Rock of Our Salvation

(stress, worry, trust)

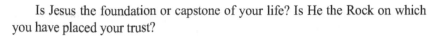

Is Jesus the foundation or capstone of your life? Is He the Rock on which you have placed your trust?

"The stone the builders rejected has become the capstone; the LORD has done this, and it is marvelous in our eyes." (Psalm 118:22-23)

Jesus is the Rock of our salvation, and He is the Rock who never rolls. In other words, He is our safety and security no matter what turbulent times we may encounter. Christian, are you dealing with some difficulty and stress in your life right now? Are you worried that things are spinning out of control? Try to relax and remember that our Rock of salvation is always in full control. Therefore, absolutely nothing is ever out of control—including those very things that you're dealing with right now!

"The salvation of the righteous comes from the LORD; he is their stronghold in time of trouble. The LORD helps them and delivers them; he delivers them from the wicked and saves them, because they take refuge in him." (Psalm 37:39-40)

Refuge in the Lord leads to rescue from the Lord. He is faithful and He is more than able to handle those difficult circumstances or difficult people you're dealing with right now. Even though it may be difficult, trust and wait for the Lord to act. Even though it may be tempting to run out and figure a way to handle things on your own, wait on the Lord and trust in the Lord. Even though it may seem like things are moving too slow for you right now, remember that the Lord is never late!

"Humble yourselves, therefore, under God's mighty hand, that he may lift you up in due time. Cast all your anxiety on him because he cares for you." (1 Peter 5:6-7)

Christian, God cares and God can. He has a perfect time (a due time) when He will lift you up out of your difficult circumstances. Cast your fears and worries upon the Rock who never rolls; place your feet solidly on the foundation of your salvation, and watch how the Lord will turn your fear into faith, your panic into peace, and your worry into worship!

The Lord's Grace Is Truly Sufficient

(prayer, righteous living, love)

O Lord, please help me to love others in a way that honors You.

"Love must be sincere. Hate what is evil; cling to what is good. Be devoted to one another in brotherly love. Honor one another above yourselves." (Romans 12:9-10)

O Lord, please help me to be joyful in a way that honors You.

"Never be lacking in zeal, but keep your spiritual fervor, serving the Lord. Be joyful in hope, patient in affliction, faithful in prayer." (Romans 12:11-12)

O Lord, please help me to share in a way that honors You.

"Share with God's people who are in need. Practice hospitality." (Romans 12:13)

O Lord, please help me to seek harmony with others in a way that honors You.

"Bless those who persecute you; bless and do not curse. Rejoice with those who rejoice; mourn with those who mourn. Live in harmony with one another. Do not be proud, but be willing to associate with people of low position. Do not be conceited." (Romans 12:14-16)

O Lord, please help me to handle difficult people in a way that honors You.

"Do not repay anyone evil for evil. Be careful to do what is right in the eyes of everybody. If it is possible, as far as it depends on you, live at peace with everyone. Do not take revenge, my friends, but leave room for God's wrath, for it is written: 'It is mine to avenge; I will repay,' says the LORD. On the contrary: 'If your enemy is hungry, feed him; if he is thirsty, give him something to drink. In doing this, you will heap burning coals on his head.' Do not be overcome by evil, but overcome evil with good." (Romans 12:17-21)

Dear Lord, thank You for the grace to be able to live my life in a way that blesses others and honors You. Your grace is truly sufficient!

The Gift of God (Part 1)

(salvation, forgiveness)

"As for you, you were dead in your transgressions and sins, in which you used to live when you followed the ways of this world and of the ruler of the kingdom of the air, the spirit who is now at work in those who are disobedient. All of us also lived among them at one time, gratifying the cravings of our sinful nature and following its desires and thoughts. Like the rest, we were by nature objects of wrath." (Ephesians 2:1-3)

The bad news is that we all have come into this world physically alive, but spiritually dead (spiritually disconnected) to God. This is because of what happened with Adam and Eve back in the Garden of Eden. Since Adam and Eve disobeyed God by eating the forbidden fruit, God punished them with the punishment of death—spiritual death, physical death, and eternal death/damnation. The Bible tells us that what Adam and Eve did contaminated the entire human race. So, we're all born into this world as sinners in God's sight; sinners who are facing God's eternal judgment. Do you really believe this? Do you really believe that what Adam and Eve did was passed down to us and there is absolutely nothing we can do through our own efforts to change this situation? In other words, do you really believe the bad news is really, really bad?

"As it is written, 'There is no one righteous, not even one; there is no one who understands, no one who seeks God. All have turned away, they have together become worthless; there is no one who does good, not even one.'" (Romans 3:10-12)

Who are you counting on to save you from your sins? Are you counting on yourself, or are you counting on a Savior? Don't rush into your day today without first taking time to think through your answers. Why is this so important? Your answers to these questions carry the weight of your eternal destiny.

"The wages of sin is death, but the gift of God is eternal life in Christ Jesus our Lord." (Romans 6:23)

The Gift of God (Part 2)
(salvation, forgiveness)

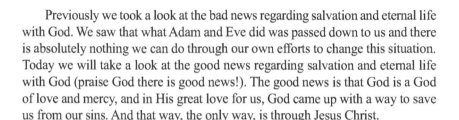

Previously we took a look at the bad news regarding salvation and eternal life with God. We saw that what Adam and Eve did was passed down to us and there is absolutely nothing we can do through our own efforts to change this situation. Today we will take a look at the good news regarding salvation and eternal life with God (praise God there is good news!). The good news is that God is a God of love and mercy, and in His great love for us, God came up with a way to save us from our sins. And that way, the only way, is through Jesus Christ.

"The wages of sin is death, but the gift of God is eternal life in Christ Jesus our Lord." (Romans 6:23)

Jesus is God, God the Son, the Second person of the Trinity. Two thousand years ago, Jesus left His Heavenly throne and He came to this earth on a mission—a mission to save people like us. Jesus was born without a sin nature, He lived a perfect life, and He never sinned once—even though He was tempted in every way, as we are. Yet, in spite of His perfection, Jesus allowed Himself to be killed on a cross in order to pay for our sins. It was there, while Jesus was on that cross that God the Father took our sins—even the ones we're most ashamed of. He placed our sins on Jesus and punished Jesus in our place, as our substitute. Jesus bore our sins, He assumed our guilt, and He died our death. Do you see how much God loves us?

"God made him who had no sin to be sin for us, so that in him we might become the righteousness of God." (2 Corinthians 5:21)

After He died, Jesus was entombed, but three days later Jesus rose from the dead! He conquered sin and death—for us! He offers forgiveness of sins—to us! He offers to us the free gift of eternal life. That's why it's called grace—we can't earn eternal life, we don't deserve eternal life, but Jesus offers eternal life—as a gift! Again, do you see how much God loves us? This is the good news of salvation. Have you embraced God's grace? It's amazing grace that God would do for us that which we could never do on our own—He forgives us of our sins and brings us into His family forever through that which Jesus did on our behalf. Amazing, absolutely amazing!

"It is by grace you have been saved, through faith—and this not from yourselves, it is the gift of God—not by works, so that no one can boast." (Ephesians 2:8-9)

Give Thanks in All Circumstances

(thankfulness)

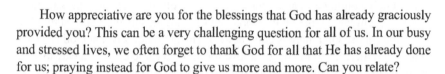

How appreciative are you for the blessings that God has already graciously provided you? This can be a very challenging question for all of us. In our busy and stressed lives, we often forget to thank God for all that He has already done for us; praying instead for God to give us more and more. Can you relate?

"Now on his way to Jerusalem, Jesus traveled along the border between Samaria and Galilee. As he was going into a village, ten men who had leprosy met him. They stood at a distance and called out in a loud voice, 'Jesus, Master, have pity on us!' When he saw them, he said, 'Go, show yourselves to the priests.' And as they went, they were cleansed." (Luke 17:11-14)

Ten men came to Jesus looking for help. They were all suffering from leprosy, and they all begged Jesus for mercy and healing. In His grace, Jesus heard their requests and healed their bodies. All ten men received mercy and compassion from Jesus. You would expect all ten men to be thankful and forever grateful—right?

"One of them, when he saw he was healed, came back, praising God in a loud voice. He threw himself at Jesus' feet and thanked him—and he was a Samaritan. Jesus asked, 'Were not all ten cleansed? Where are the other nine? Was no one found to return and give praise to God except this foreigner?' Then he said to him, 'Rise and go; your faith has made you well.' " (Luke 17:15-19)

Ten men came to Jesus looking for help. All ten men received mercy and healing from Jesus. However, only one man came back to thank Jesus for His help and healing. Which group of healed men would you say characterizes your attitude when it comes to gratitude as of late?

"Be joyful always; pray continually; give thanks in all circumstances, for this is God's will for you in Christ Jesus." (1 Thessalonians 5:16-18)

The Lord's Gift of Contentment

(finances, contentment)

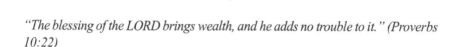

"The blessing of the LORD brings wealth, and he adds no trouble to it." (Proverbs 10:22)

Christian, would you rather have a ton of wealth that does not come from the Lord, or would you rather have less in your bank account knowing that what you have is from the Lord? Think of this question the next time you open your checkbook.

"Better a little with the fear of the LORD than great wealth with turmoil." (Proverbs 15:16)

Christian, would you rather honor the Lord with your finances, or would you rather accumulate as much as you can, as fast as you can, regardless of the turmoil that may come along with it? Think of this question the next time you are at your place of employment.

"Moreover, when God gives any man wealth and possessions, and enables him to enjoy them, to accept his lot and be happy in his work—this is a gift of God. He seldom reflects on the days of his life, because God keeps him occupied with gladness of heart." (Ecclesiastes 5:19-20)

Christian, would you rather experience the gift of contentment that comes from the Lord, or would you rather try to find joy and peace on your own through the unhealthy drive for more wealth and possessions? Remember, when the Lord provides blessings, He also provides contentment to accept and enjoy those blessings. However, when we lust for wealth and possessions through our own efforts, we experience all kinds of turmoil and traps that cause ulcers and heart attacks. What do you want to expose your heart to: Joy and contentment or stress and fear? Ask the Lord for the gift to be able to recognize and enjoy all that He has given you. In other words, ask Him to make you a person of peace and contentment.

"Godliness with contentment is great gain. For we brought nothing into the world, and we can take nothing out of it. But if we have food and clothing, we will be content with that." (1 Timothy 6:6-8)

Hope in the Lord and Renew Your Strength

(guidance, God's provision)

"As the eyes of slaves look to the hand of their master, as the eyes of a maid look to the hand of her mistress, so our eyes look to the LORD our God, till he shows us his mercy." (Psalm 123:2)

What a wonderful picture of faith! In addition, what a wonderful example of commitment, trust and patience to wait on the Lord. The slave is completely dependent on the master for guidance and provision. The maidservant is also completely dependent on the head mistress of the household for guidance and provision. As Christians, we are completely dependent on the guidance and provision of our Lord and Master, Jesus Christ. Are you in need of the Lord's mercy and guidance? Stay focused on Him and faithful to Him until He reveals Himself to you. Are you in need of the Lord's provision and protection? Stay focused on Him and faithful to Him, trusting that when the Lord guides he also provides.

"My God will meet all your needs according to his glorious riches in Christ Jesus." (Philippians 4:19)

Christian, do you not know that your needs will be met because the Lord has all that you need? Have you not heard that your plans will succeed because you have committed yourself to the plans of the Lord? Do you not know that you will be guided in the proper direction because you are trusting the Lord to work out His perfect plans in and through your life? Have you not heard that your plans will succeed because you are waiting on the Lord's perfect timing to be revealed in and through your life?

"Do you not know? Have you not heard? The LORD is the everlasting God, the Creator of the ends of the earth. He will not grow tired or weary, and his understanding no one can fathom. He gives strength to the weary and increases the power of the weak. Even youths grow tired and weary, and young men stumble and fall; but those who hope in the LORD will renew their strength. They will soar on wings like eagles; they will run and not grow weary, they will walk and not be faint." (Isaiah 40:28-31)

Build Up and Bless One Another
(relationships)

As Christians, we're called to be our brother's keeper. In other words, we're called to bless and build up the body of Christ. Sometimes a form of blessing can actually be in the form of a rebuke and tough love. However, the Bible tells us that we need to be careful so as to not become "constantly-critical" Christians.

"You my brothers, were called to be free. But do not use your freedom to indulge the sinful nature; rather, serve one another in love. The entire law is summed up in a single command: 'Love your neighbor as yourself.' If you keep on biting and devouring each other, watch out or you will be destroyed by each other." (Galatians 5:13-15)

Love builds up, but backbiting and constant criticism devours and destroys. While we shouldn't ignore and condone sinful behavior from those who claim to be followers of Christ, we need to make sure that our motives are pure and our methods are meant to help and not hurt. As Christians we're called to be free; and to use our freedom in a conducive and God-glorifying way. Christian, each day you are faced with the opportunity to build up and bless—or to backbite and devour. Which one will you choose?

"As charcoal to embers and as wood to fire, so is a quarrelsome man for kindling strife." (Proverbs 26:21)

Constant criticism of others can be a type of charcoal that ignites a fire among people. Bitterness and backbiting can also do the same. A quarrelsome attitude often inflames such bitter strife that the best of relationships can suddenly be destroyed. Are you currently involved in creating some "forest fires" in your home, school, or work place? Open your heart to the Lord and ask Him to show you the true intentions of your heart. Ask Him to purify your motives so that you can truly be your brother's keeper.

"Get rid of all bitterness, rage and anger, brawling and slander, along with every form of malice. Be kind and compassionate to one another, forgiving each other, just as in Christ God forgave you." (Ephesians 4:31-32)

Hearts that Delight the Lord

(integrity, Christlike)

"The LORD abhors dishonest scales, but accurate weights are his delight."
(Proverbs 11:1)

Honesty honors the Lord, but dishonesty dishonors the Lord. Although none of us can be perfect and blameless in the Lord's sight; we'd all like to have hearts that are a delight to the Lord, not hearts that are detestable to Him. Are you honoring the Lord with honesty in your family, workplace and school? Or, are you dishonoring Him with dishonesty?

"The LORD detests men of perverse heart but he delights in those whose ways are blameless." (Proverbs 11:20)

Christian, do you want to be blessed? Do you want the favor of the Lord on your work, school and family? Then strive to honor the Lord in your words, your work and in your walk. When we seek to honor the Lord by living a life of integrity and honesty in His sight, we then bring delight to the Lord. Moreover, when the Lord is pleased with our ways, He pours out blessings in ways that we can't even imagine. Do you want to experience blessings from the Lord? Then live a life that brings pleasure and delight to Him.

"He whose walk is blameless is kept safe, but he whose ways are perverse will suddenly fall." (Proverbs 28:18)

Take some time right now and ask the Lord to give you a heart and hands that strive for honesty and humility. Ask the Lord to grant you the grace to live a life that shows awe and reverence for His holy name. Christian, there is no greater privilege and honor then to bless the heart of our lovely Lord. Think about how often He brings delight to you. Now ask Him to lead you today in His path of righteousness to help you live a life that brings delight to Him.

A Prayer for Wisdom

(wisdom, anger, words)

Dear Lord, please help me to be wise and not a mocker.

"Mockers stir up a city, but wise men turn away anger." (Proverbs 29:8)

Dear Lord, please help me to be wise and not vent my anger.

"A fool gives full vent to his anger, but a wise man keeps himself under control." (Proverbs 29:11)

Dear Lord, please help me to be wise and not stir up dissension.

"An angry man stirs up dissension, and a hot-tempered one commits many sins." (Proverbs 29:22)

Dear Lord, please help me to be wise and not get involved in gossip.

"The words of a gossip are like choice morsels; they go down to a man's inmost parts." (Proverbs 26:22)

Dear Lord, please help me to be wise and not get involved in the arguments of others.

"Like one who seizes a dog by the ears is a passer-by who meddles in a quarrel not his own." (Proverbs 26:17)

Dear Lord, please help me to be wise and not gloat over the problems of those who oppose me.

"Do not gloat when your enemy falls; when he stumbles, do not let your heart rejoice, or the LORD will see and disapprove and turn his wrath away from him." (Proverbs 24:17-18)

Dear Lord, please help me to be wise and not lust after riches.

"Do not wear yourself out to get rich; have the wisdom to show restraint. Cast but a glance at riches, and they are gone, for they will surely sprout wings and fly off to the sky like an eagle." (Proverbs 23:4-5)

Dear Lord, please help me to be wise and not despise Your ways.

"The fear of the LORD is the beginning of knowledge, but fools despise wisdom and discipline." (Proverbs 1:7)

How Have You Been Dressing Lately? (Part 1)
(obedience, serving, relationships)

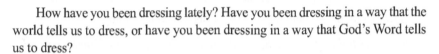

How have you been dressing lately? Have you been dressing in a way that the world tells us to dress, or have you been dressing in a way that God's Word tells us to dress?

"Therefore, as God's chosen people, holy and dearly loved, clothe yourselves with compassion, kindness, humility, gentleness and patience. Bear with each other and forgive whatever grievances you may have against one another. Forgive as the Lord forgave you. And over all these virtues put on love, which binds them all together in perfect unity." (Colossians 3:12-14)

God's Word tells us to clothe ourselves in compassion and patience. The world often tells us to clothe ourselves in such a way so as to look out only for ourselves and go for what we want, no matter how many people we hurt along the way. Christian, how have you been dressing lately? God's Word tells us to clothe ourselves with forgiveness and love, just as we have been granted forgiveness and love by our Lord. However, the world often tells us to hurt those who have hurt us, to get back and to get even. Christian, how have you been dressing lately?

"Let the peace of Christ rule in your hearts, since as members of one body you were called to peace. And be thankful. Let the word of Christ dwell in you richly as you teach and admonish one another with all wisdom, and as you sing psalms, hymns and spiritual songs with gratitude in your hearts to God." (Colossians 3:15)

God's Word tells us to be people of peace, since we have been granted peace with God through Jesus Christ. God's Word also tells us to be a people who are grateful to God for His free gift of salvation through Jesus Christ. In addition we are to encourage and uplift each other with God's wonderful truth. Christian, how have you been dressing lately?

"Whatever you do, whether in word or deed, do it all in the name of the Lord Jesus, giving thanks to God the Father through him." (Colossians 3:17)

How Have You Been Dressing Lately? (Part 2)

(obedience, serving, relationships)

How have you been dressing lately? Previously we took a look at the difference between dressing in a way that the world tells us to dress and dressing in a way that God's Word tells us to dress. Today we'll continue to look at this idea of dressing God's way for God's glory.

"Put to death, therefore, whatever belongs to your earthly nature: sexual immorality, impurity, lust, evil desires and greed, which is idolatry. Because of these, the wrath of God is coming. You used to walk in these ways, in the life you once lived." (Colossians 3:5-7)

Do you still wear the same clothes you used to wear as a child? Of course not, because it doesn't make sense. Do you still think and act the same way you did as a child? Of course not, you're a different person now. God's Word tells us the same thing: As Christians we no longer wear the same sinful and dirty "clothes" we once did, nor do we act in the same sinful and dirty "ways" we once did when we followed the ways of the world. As Christians, we're new creations in Christ Jesus; and we're called to dress and live in this new kind of life. Although we can't achieve perfection on this side of Heaven, nevertheless we're called to live a new life according to the standards of God's ways, found in God's Word.

"Now you must rid yourselves of all such things as these: anger, rage, malice, slander, and filthy language from your lips. Do not lie to each other, since you have taken off your old self with its practices and have put on the new self, which is being renewed in knowledge in the image of its Creator." (Colossians 3:8-10)

Christian, how have you been dressing and living lately? Have you been following the ways of the world; or have you been following the ways of God's Word? Remember, a huge price was paid for our salvation—the least we can do is give our best to live a life in honor of the One who gave His all to clothe us in His righteousness. Don't you agree?

"Therefore, as God's chosen people, holy and dearly loved, clothe yourselves with compassion, kindness, humility, gentleness and patience. Bear with each other and forgive whatever grievances you may have against one another. Forgive as the Lord forgave you. And over all these virtues put on love, which binds them all together in perfect unity." (Colossians 3:12-14)

God's Treasure Chest of Wisdom

(wisdom, trust)

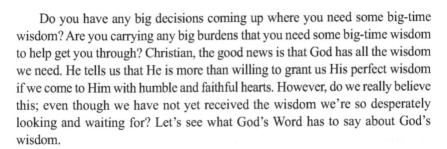

Do you have any big decisions coming up where you need some big-time wisdom? Are you carrying any big burdens that you need some big-time wisdom to help get you through? Christian, the good news is that God has all the wisdom we need. He tells us that He is more than willing to grant us His perfect wisdom if we come to Him with humble and faithful hearts. However, do we really believe this; even though we have not yet received the wisdom we're so desperately looking and waiting for? Let's see what God's Word has to say about God's wisdom.

1) Christ has the treasure chest of wisdom.

"My purpose is that they may be encouraged in heart and united in love, so that they may have the full riches of complete understanding, in order that they may know the mystery of God, namely, Christ, in whom are hidden all the treasures of wisdom and knowledge." (Colossians 2:2-3)

2) Christ has a treasure chest of wisdom because He is God.

"For in Christ all the fullness of the Deity lives in bodily form, and you have been given fullness in Christ, who is the head over every power and authority." (Colossians 2:9-10)

3) Christ invites you to ask Him for wisdom from his treasure chest.

"If any of you lacks wisdom, he should ask God, who gives generously to all without finding fault, and it will be given to him." (James 1:5)

4) Christian, will you trust or doubt in the wisdom of Christ?

"But when he asks, he must believe and not doubt, because he who doubts is like a wave of the sea, blown and tossed by the wind." (James 1:6)

Once again: Do you have any big decisions coming up where you need some big-time wisdom? Are you carrying any big burdens that you need some big-time wisdom to help get you through? Meditate on these verses from today, tuck them into your heart, and trust in the wonderful wisdom Christ has for you—a treasure chest of wisdom that can perfectly get you through any big decision or any big burden you are dealing with!

Extend Grace to Others

(giving, God's will, trust)

We all want to gain more when it comes to blessings. However, how many of us are willing to give more when it comes to blessings?

"One man gives freely, yet gains even more; another withholds unduly, but comes to poverty." (Proverbs 11:24)

Christian, be honest with yourself—do you think that maybe you can give more when it comes to blessing others? We're not just talking about finances. Giving can take on many forms. The key is to be willing to extend grace where it's needed, trusting that God can more than make up that which we have given. Please understand that we should not give because we expect that God must automatically give us more in return; that's not the type of giving that honors God. Rather, we give because we want to bless others and show gratitude to God for that which He has ALREADY given us in our lives—eternal life through the selfless sacrificial act, Jesus our Savior. So, let's rephrase the original question and ask it this way: Do you feel you can show more gratitude to God by extending more grace to others?

"A generous man will prosper; he who refreshes others will himself be refreshed." (Proverbs 11:25)

In God's economy, giving from an attitude of gratitude usually ends up refreshing and blessing us even more than those we have given to! Here's a phrase that perfectly summarizes this very truth: "You can't out-give God." You can probably think of times in your life where this has been a very real occurrence. Do you remember how amazed you were at how you felt? Do you remember how content you were and how appreciative you were to God? Do you remember the burst of joy you felt as you realized that God used you to bless others and bring glory to His great name?

"Blessings crown the head of the righteous, but violence overwhelms the mouth of the wicked." (Proverbs 10:6)

Very often we can talk ourselves out of taking a forward step of faith. Can you relate? We often come up with various good reasons as to why we need to sit back and wait. Maybe we decide the timing is not right, or the circumstances are not ideal—or that the weather isn't good! Whatever the reasons may be, are you in the position right now where you are literally talking yourself out of taking a forward step of faith and trusting in God's plans for you?

"As you do not know the path of the wind, or how the body is formed in a mother's womb, so you cannot understand the work of God, the Maker of all things." (Ecclesiastes 11:5)

As Christians, we have the Spirit of God in us and the Word of God to guide us. However, nowhere in the Bible does it say that we can completely understand the ways of God. Our finite minds cannot fully comprehend the infinite wisdom and perfect timing of God. Therefore, our attempts to "wrap our arms" around the plans and timing of God is futile. Christian, is God asking you to take a step forward on something, and are you trying to first "wrap your arms" around everything before you take that step of faith? In other words, are you saying, "God, show me first and then I'll step?" Be careful, for we see throughout the Bible that God says to His people, "Step first in obedience and then I will show you."

"Sow your seed in the morning, and at evening let not your hands be idle, for you do not know which will succeed, whether this or that, or whether both will do equally well." (Ecclesiastes 11:6)

If you have spent time seeking the Lord's wisdom in prayer, and if you have spent time seeking His guidance in His Word, you can then feel confident to take the forward step of faith. Don't worry about making a perfect decision, and don't look for the perfect scenario before you decide to step. If you have spent time with the Lord, and if you believe that you are hearing from the Lord, take the step of faith and trust in the Lord—He will not let you down!

"Without faith it is impossible to please God, because anyone who comes to him must believe that he exists and that he rewards those who earnestly seek him." (Hebrews 11:6)

Do You Give God the Proper Thanks for All You Have?

(thankfulness, giving)

"Wealth and honor come from you; you are the ruler of all things. In your hands are strength and power to exalt and give strength to all. Now, our God, we give you thanks, and praise your glorious name." (1 Chronicles 29:12-13)

King David clearly understood that all he was and all he had was all because of God. How about us? Do we have that same perspective and praise God the way King David did? Christian, how many times over the past week did you give God thanks for the strength and power you have? How many times over the past week did you give God thanks for the wealth and honor that you have?

"But who am I, and who are my people, that we should be able to give as generously as this? Everything comes from you, and we have given you only what comes from your hand." (1 Chronicles 29:14)

King David clearly understood that all he was giving back to the Lord was all that originally came from the Lord. Talk about having a God-centered and God-honoring perspective! David was praising God. Why? He was praising God for the ability to give back to God. What was he giving back? He was giving back that which God had given to him! How many of us give that same type of praise to God when we are giving to the building of His kingdom. In other words, how many of us take the time to praise and appreciate God as we write that check or as we give that cash for the building of God's kingdom. Do we simply fulfill our "Christian duty" and give a bit of money without even thinking where it came from and for whom it is going?

" 'O LORD our God, as for all this abundance that we have provided for building you a temple for your Holy Name, it comes from your hand, and all of it belongs to you. I know, my God, that you test the heart and are pleased with integrity. All these things have I given willingly and with honest intent. And now I have seen with joy how willingly your people who are here have given to you.' " (1 Chronicles 29:16-17)

May all of us learn from the example of King David. May we realize that all we have is from God, and all that we have belongs to God. In addition, may we have hearts of integrity and humility as we joyfully give back to the One who has given His all for us!

We Are Saved to Serve

(serving, love)

"It is by grace you have been saved, through faith—and this not from yourselves, it is the gift of God—not by works, so that no one can boast. For we are God's workmanship, created in Christ Jesus to do good works, which God prepared in advance for us to do." (Ephesians 2:8-10)

As Christians, we understand that we are saved by grace, not by works. However, we are saved to do good works that God planned in advance for us to do. We are saved to serve, and our mission in life is very clear: To bring glory to God and blessings to others. The result of doing these two things is that we are blessed in ways that are immeasurably greater than we can imagine.

"I want you to stress these things, so that those who have trusted in God may be careful to devote themselves to doing what is good. These things are excellent and profitable for everyone." (Titus 3:8)

Christian, do you want to experience joy and a sense of satisfaction in your life? Stand up and serve in a way that brings glory to God and blessings to others. Do you want to fulfill your purpose and find meaning for your life? Stand up and serve in a way that brings glory to God and blessing to others. Do you want to experience adventure and excitement in your life? Stand up and serve in a way that brings glory to God and blessings to others. Christian, you are a unique and wonderful creation of God. You have been granted gifts from God to be able to bring glory to God and blessings to his people. May we all be a people who are eager to do what is good—all by God's grace and all for His glory!

"God is not unjust; he will not forget your work and the love you have shown him as you have helped his people and continue to help them." (Hebrews 6:10)

Seek to Please the Lord

(character, peer pressure, priorities)

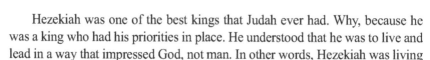

Hezekiah was one of the best kings that Judah ever had. Why, because he was a king who had his priorities in place. He understood that he was to live and lead in a way that impressed God, not man. In other words, Hezekiah was living for the praises of God rather than the praises of man.

"This is what Hezekiah did throughout Judah, doing what is good and right and faithful before the Lord His God. In everything that he undertook in the service of God's temple and in obedience to the law and the commands, He sought his God and worked wholeheartedly. And so he prospered." (2 Chronicles 31:20-21)

As you live and lead, who will you be looking to impress? Will you seek to be a Christ-pleaser or will you seek to be a crowd-pleaser? Be careful, for Scripture warns us that:

"Fear of man will prove to be a snare, but whoever trusts in the Lord is kept safe." (Proverbs 29:25)

It's natural to want to be accepted by others. It's normal to want to be appreciated by others. However, make sure that like Hezekiah you have your priorities in place. Resolve that today you will seek to do what is good, right and faithful before the Lord. Trust that as you seek to please Him, He will handle how you are perceived by others.

God Is Our Faithful Protector

(trust, encouragement, stress)

My wife and I live near a lake filled with numerous beautiful white swans. These swans are very friendly and often will eat food right out of our hands. However, these swans are also very protective of their little ones. This fact became very clear to me recently as I witnessed how truly protective the mother swan can be.

One day as I was walking near the lake, I noticed a dog suddenly pull loose from his master and run straight to the area where the little swans were. All I remember thinking was, this dog is going to rip these defenseless little swans apart. There was no way for them to protect themselves. However, as the dog got closer and closer, the mother swan suddenly swam in front of them. She quickly spread out her wings so that the little ones could hide behind her. When the attacking dog saw the mother swan with her wings spread out, he suddenly stopped and no longer pursued the little swans. Why? Because he saw they were safely sheltered behind the wings of their mother.

In like manner, the Bible tells us that God is our faithful protector against the sudden, unexpected attacks that come our way.

"He will cover you with his feathers, and under his wings you will find refuge; his faithfulness will be your shield and refuge." (Psalm 91:4)

We serve an awesome God who is faithful to protect His little ones. May today be the day that we "joyfully swim" in that lake of assurance!

Are You Setting a Godly Example?

(character, integrity)

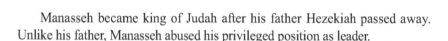

Manasseh became king of Judah after his father Hezekiah passed away. Unlike his father, Manasseh abused his privileged position as leader.

"But Manasseh led Judah and the people of Jerusalem astray, so that they did more evil than the nations the Lord had destroyed before the Israelites." (2 Chronicles 33:9)

Although Manasseh eventually seemed to have repented, the spiritual damage was already done. Not only were the people misled, but Manasseh's own son Amon was also negatively influenced by his father.

"He did evil in the eyes of the Lord, as His father Manasseh had done. Amon worshipped and offered sacrifices to all the idols Manasseh had made." (2 Chronicles 33:22)

It has been said, with privilege comes responsibility. Although you may not be a king responsible for leading a nation, nevertheless, we all are in a position to influence others for good or for evil. The question is: "Will your influence draw others closer to God or will your influence lead them away from God?"

Every day you are being watched by someone. Perhaps it's your children, your co-workers, or your classmates. Every day you have the opportunity to set a godly example before them. Your example will not only influence them in the present, but also impact them for the future. Don't follow the example of Manasseh who misled the people and his son into ungodliness. Instead, continuously pray to the Lord that He will give you the wisdom and grace to influence others for good, all for His glory.

God Has Everything Under Control

(trust, stress, trials)

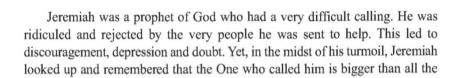

Jeremiah was a prophet of God who had a very difficult calling. He was ridiculed and rejected by the very people he was sent to help. This led to discouragement, depression and doubt. Yet, in the midst of his turmoil, Jeremiah looked up and remembered that the One who called him is bigger than all the seemingly impossible challenges he was facing.

"Ah, Sovereign Lord, you have made the heavens and the earth by your great power and outstretched hand. Nothing is too hard for you." (Jeremiah 32:17)

Are you standing in the midst of some seemingly impossible challenge right now? The question is, "Where are you looking?" Are you looking around at all the difficulties and getting stressed? Are you looking within at your weaknesses and getting depressed? Perhaps, like Jeremiah, you should try to look up at the sovereign Creator of the universe and start to feel blessed!

You see, when we take our eyes off our problems and instead focus our eyes on the One who is in full control of all of our problems, the One who has all power over our problems, an amazing thing begins to occur. We replace our panic with His peace. We replace our turmoil with trust. We replace our worry with worship. How does this happen? When we look up, we are reminded that God is still on the throne, and therefore no circumstance is impossible for Him!

"Then the word of the Lord came to Jeremiah, 'I am the Lord, the God of all mankind, is anything too hard for me?' " (Jeremiah 32:26-27)

Are You an Ambassador for Christ?

(evangelism)

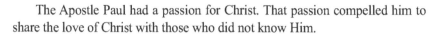

The Apostle Paul had a passion for Christ. That passion compelled him to share the love of Christ with those who did not know Him.

"For Christ's love compels us, because we are convinced that one died for all, and therefore all died." (2 Corinthians 5:14)

Because Paul experienced the incredible love of Christ, he was just bursting to share that love with others. How about you? Have you experienced the love of Christ? In other words, have you experienced the freedom of forgiveness through Christ, and have you experienced the joy of knowing that you're a child of God through Christ? If so, are you feeling like the Apostle Paul? Are you just bursting to share that love, that forgiveness and that joy with others?

It has been said that most Christians feel fear and inadequacy when it comes to sharing their faith. Perhaps you can relate to those feelings. However, the key to overcoming these feelings is to remember two things:

You're sharing, not selling. Just like you probably have no problem sharing the joy and blessings of being in love with another human being (i.e. your spouse, boyfriend or girlfriend), in the same way, simply relax and share the joy of your love relationship with Jesus. Share what He has done and continues to do in your life. Always remember, it's pretty hard for others to argue with your changed life.

You're an ambassador and you're not alone. God is working in you and through you to bring people to Himself.

"We are therefore Christ's ambassadors, as though God were making his appeal through us. We implore you on Christ's behalf: Be reconciled to God." (2 Corinthians 5: 20)

Because God is actively involved, you can relax and remember that as you're sharing, God is saving!

Do Your Words Honor God?

(words, character)

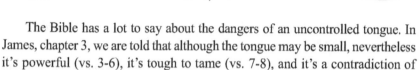

The Bible has a lot to say about the dangers of an uncontrolled tongue. In James, chapter 3, we are told that although the tongue may be small, nevertheless it's powerful (vs. 3-6), it's tough to tame (vs. 7-8), and it's a contradiction of blessings towards God and curses towards man (vs. 9-12). Because of this, each day our tongues have the potential to release words that can either build up or tear down others.

As you face your day today, have you put in place the necessary "tongue control precautions" that will be needed for you to speak in a way that honors God and blesses others? For example, have you thought about how you will handle the inevitable hurtful and harmful words that will come your way today? Will you respond in anger, using your tongue as a weapon of vengeance and retribution? Or, will you follow the wisdom of the Bible that counsels us by stating:

"My dear brothers, take note of this: Everyone should be quick to listen, slow to speak and slow to become angry." (James 1:19)

Quick—Slow—Slow as the Scripture states, we should be quick to listen, slow to speak, and slow to anger. As we take the time to listen first, we then have the time to think and pray before we respond. As we take the time to think and pray before we respond, we then have the time to bring our anger under control. The result is a tongue that honors God and blesses others. We can then experience the joy of a calm and controlled life. May we all be quick, slow and slow today!

The All-Powerful Hand of the Lord

(trust, peace, trials)

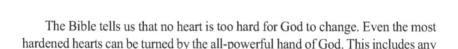

The Bible tells us that no heart is too hard for God to change. Even the most hardened hearts can be turned by the all-powerful hand of God. This includes any person in any powerful position of life.

"The king's heart is in the hand of the Lord; he directs it like a watercourse wherever he pleases." (Proverbs 21:1)

This verse tells us that even the heart of a powerful king is in the hand of the Lord; and that He directs it to bring about His perfect purposes. This also means that those hardhearted people in your life right now are in the all-powerful hand of the Lord; and that He is directing them to bring about His perfect purposes.

Therefore, you can relax and rejoice that those in your life who right now seem farthest from God are actually like water in the hand of the Lord. Water is not hard to move, especially for the Lord! So, don't get stressed with those who are making your life difficult. They are like water in the hand of the Lord. Don't get frustrated with those who ridicule your faith. They are like water in the hand of the Lord. Don't get upset with those who are trying to stop God's plan in your life. They are like water in the hand of the Lord.

God's Amazing Work
in You

(character, humility)

The apostle Paul kept the proper perspective.

"By the grace of God I am what I am, and his grace to me was not without effect. No, I worked harder than all of them—yet not I, but the grace of God that was with me." (1 Corinthians 15:10)

Notice how much the apostle Paul recognized and rejoiced in God's grace:

Paul knew who he was by God's grace—"But by the grace of God I am what I am"—that's called humility.

Paul knew that God's grace was not in vain—"And his grace to me was not without effect"—that's called appreciation.

Paul knew that God's grace was not an excuse to be lazy—" No, I worked harder than all of them"—that's called perspective.

Paul knew that God's grace was the reason for his success—"Yet not I, but the grace of God that was with me"—that's called praise.

How are you responding to God's work in your life right now? Are you filled with humility, appreciation, perspective, and praise? Or, are you filled with pride, lack of appreciation, excuses, and complaints? Take the time today to pray for the proper perspective when it comes to what God is doing in your life. Watch how your day will be filled with abundant joy and peace, as you realize that God is doing an amazing work in and through you!

Our Heavenly Father Provides Perfect Justice

(justice, trust, trials)

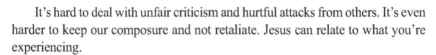

It's hard to deal with unfair criticism and hurtful attacks from others. It's even harder to keep our composure and not retaliate. Jesus can relate to what you're experiencing.

"When they hurled insults at him, he did not retaliate; when he suffered, he made no threats. Instead, he entrusted himself to him who judges justly." (1 Peter 2:23)

Rather than retaliating with His mouth and losing focus on His mission, Jesus instead trusted that God the Father (the just Judge) would handle all wrongs. How about you? Are you facing some unfair criticism and unjust attacks right now? If so, are you following the example of Jesus and entrusting your heavenly Father to bring about justice? It's funny, but very often God will allow challenging people to come our way so as to bring us closer to Him.

"For it is commendable if a man bears up under the pain of unjust suffering because he is conscious of God." (1 Peter 2:19)

This means that the very people who are giving you the most problems right now may actually be great blessings in your life. How? Their attacks are taking you to your knees in prayer and causing you to draw closer to God!

Make a commitment today to follow the example of Jesus. Don't retaliate, stay focused on your mission and trust your loving heavenly Father to right all wrongs, in His perfect timing. If you start to feel impatient and wonder why you have to deal with these unfair attacks, just remember the words of Scripture.

"To this you were called, because Christ suffered for you, leaving you an example, that you should follow in his steps." (1 Peter 2:21)

Don't Let the Devil Steal Your Joy

(joy, trust)

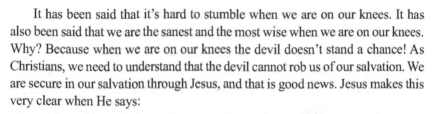

It has been said that it's hard to stumble when we are on our knees. It has also been said that we are the sanest and the most wise when we are on our knees. Why? Because when we are on our knees the devil doesn't stand a chance! As Christians, we need to understand that the devil cannot rob us of our salvation. We are secure in our salvation through Jesus, and that is good news. Jesus makes this very clear when He says:

" 'My sheep listen to my voice; I know them, and they follow me. I give them eternal life, and they shall never perish; no one can snatch them out of my hand.' " (John 10:27-28)

However, we also need to understand that though the devil cannot rob us of our salvation, he will try to rob us of the "joy" of our salvation. In other words, although we are secure in our salvation through Jesus, we are not always so joyful in that salvation. If today you're feeling a bit joyless, don't despair. Drop to your knees and remember who you are because of whose you are.

"You, dear children, are from God and have overcome them, because the one who is in you [the Spirit of Christ] is greater than the one who is in the world [the devil]." (1 John 4:4)

With Christ on your side, you're on the winning side. Therefore, you don't have to go through this day feeling like a victim. Instead, you can dance joyfully through this day, recognizing that through Christ you're a victor! Once you start to realize who you are because of whose you are; then you will begin to start to realize what the apostle Paul meant when he joyfully said:

"What, then, shall we say in response to this? If God is for us, who can be against us? He who did not spare his own Son, but gave him up for us all—how will he not also, along with him, graciously give us all things." (Romans 8:31-32)

The Lord Is Our Strength

(trust, stress, trials)

In the Old Testament, the prophet Habakkuk was dealing with doubt and depression. Why? He couldn't understand why God was using the hated Babylonians to discipline his own people. Although Habakkuk understood that God was perfect in all of His ways, nevertheless, the prophet was struggling with understanding God's methods. Have you ever felt that way? Perhaps you're feeling that way today. Perhaps you're wondering why God is allowing certain challenges to come your way right now. Possibly, like Habakkuk, you're facing this day with some doubt and depression.

Rather than letting your circumstances take control of your emotions, look to the Lord and be reminded that He is in control of your circumstances. (Including those difficult circumstances you're facing today!). That is exactly what Habakkuk did. Take a look at how his doubt and depression turned to joy and confidence.

"Though the fig tree does not bud and there are no grapes on the vines, though the olive crop fails and the fields produce no food, though there are no sheep in the pen and no cattle in the stalls, yet I will rejoice in the Lord, I will be joyful in God my Savior." (Habakkuk 3:17-18)

Though Habakkuk didn't like to see some of the difficult circumstances he was facing, he could rejoice in the Lord, because the prophet knew with certainty, that the Lord was in full control of everything. Even though he felt weak, Habakkuk knew where his strength would come from.

"The Sovereign Lord is my strength; he makes my feet like the feet of a deer, he enables me to go on the heights." (Habakkuk 3:19)

May today be the day where you look at your circumstances and realize; though they may be difficult, you have an awesome God who can carry you through and to new heights!

Seeking God's Wisdom During Troubled Times

(trust, trials, wisdom)

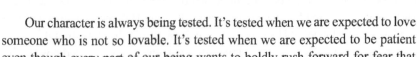

Our character is always being tested. It's tested when we are expected to love someone who is not so lovable. It's tested when we are expected to be patient even though every part of our being wants to boldly rush forward for fear that time is running out. It's tested when we are expected to walk by faith even though we have no idea where we are going.

"Consider it pure joy, my brothers, whenever you face trials of many kinds." (James 1:2)

Is your character being tested right now? Do you have some challenging people in your life right now who are testing your love and patience? Are you struggling with some challenging circumstances in your life right now that are testing your patience and faith? The Bible tells us to consider it pure joy. Why?

"Because you know that the testing of your faith develops perseverance. Perseverance must finish its work so that you may be mature and complete, not lacking anything." (James 1:3-4)

In other words, the testing of your character right now is meant to grow you up, not to beat you down. God is making you better, so don't be bitter! The best way to keep this perspective and to keep persevering through this time of testing is to seek the wisdom of God.

"If any of you lacks wisdom, he should ask God, who gives generously to all without finding fault, and it will be given him." (James 1:5)

Reaping A Full Harvest

(actions, character)

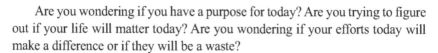

Are you wondering if you have a purpose for today? Are you trying to figure out if your life will matter today? Are you wondering if your efforts today will make a difference or if they will be a waste?

"Therefore, my brothers, stand firm. Let nothing move you. Always give yourselves fully to the work of the Lord, because you know that your labor in the Lord is not in vain." (1 Corinthians 15:58)

"Stand firm."

We must be grounded in the supremacy of God's Word and the sufficiency of Christ's sacrifice. In other words, we need to stand firm on God's Word as our source of all truth. We need to stand firm on the sacrifice of Jesus Christ as the source of our salvation.

"Let nothing move you."

We must expect the storms of life to try to throw us off balance. Therefore, we must actively pursue the spiritual disciplines of prayer and studying the Bible so as to strengthen and brace ourselves for these inevitable storms.

"Always give yourselves fully to the work of the Lord."

As Christians we must seek to serve our "Chief Executive Officer," Jesus Christ. We need to remember that we are saved to serve. We bring glory to Christ when we reach out in love to serve others in the name of Jesus.

"Because you know that your labor in the Lord is not in vain."

Our efforts to serve others in the name of Jesus are not a waste! No matter how challenging, we must remember that He will bring about His perfect purpose for His glory and the good of others (including us!).

"Let us not become weary in doing good, for at the proper time we will reap a harvest if we do not give up." (Galatians 6:9)

Lift Your Eyes to the Lord

(stress, trials, trust)

When in doubt, where are you looking for your answers? It's really simple. You can look around at all of your circumstances and feel stressed, or you can look up to the Lord and feel blessed.

"I lift up my eyes to the hills—where does my help come from? My help comes from the Lord, the maker of heaven and earth." (Psalm 121:1-2)

Are you feeling that God is too busy to pay attention to you and your problems? Are you wondering if God is watching over you right now?

"He will not let your foot slip—he who watches over you will not slumber; indeed, he who watches over Israel will neither slumber nor sleep." (Psalm 121:3-4)

Do you trust God to protect you? Do you trust God to provide for you?

"The Lord watches over you—the Lord is your shade at your right hand; the sun will not harm you by day, nor the moon by night. The Lord will keep you from all harm—He will watch over your life; the Lord will watch over your coming and going both now and forevermore." (Psalm 121:5-8)

What should our response be to all of this? What should we be saying as we reflect on God's faithfulness and compassion? It's really simple: Our God is an amazing God!

Bless Others with Your Words

(words, character)

Our words have the power to build up and bless others.

"Pleasant words are a honeycomb, sweet to the soul and healing to the bones." (Proverbs 16:24)

This means that our words today can be sweet tasting and provide emotional, as well as spiritual, healing to someone's life. What an honor!

However, our words also have the power to tear down and cause chaos to others.

"A perverse man stirs up dissension, and a gossip separates close friends." (Proverbs 16:28)

This means that our words today can be bitter tasting and provide emotional, as well as spiritual, damage to someone's life. What a warning!

The best way to protect the words that come out of our mouths is to make sure of the words that we take into our mouths. This means, as we take in the sweet words of God's truth, we will then be able to share those sweet words with others.

"How sweet are your words to my taste, sweeter than honey to my mouth! I gain understanding from your precepts; therefore I hate every wrong path." (Psalm 119:103-104)

Let today be the day that you digest the pleasant words of God's truth. Let today be the day that you take those sweet tasting words and use them to build up and bless others.

Let it be so Lord! AMEN!

Seek Him with All Your Heart

(the Bible, wisdom)

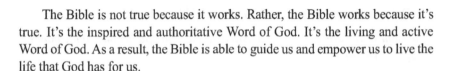

The Bible is not true because it works. Rather, the Bible works because it's true. It's the inspired and authoritative Word of God. It's the living and active Word of God. As a result, the Bible is able to guide us and empower us to live the life that God has for us.

"All Scripture is God-breathed and is useful for teaching, rebuking, correcting and training in righteousness, so that the man of God may be thoroughly equipped for every good work." (2 Timothy 3:16-17)

Do you need wisdom when it comes to managing your family? Then spend time reading the Bible. Why? Because the Bible will teach you, train you, and equip you to be able to lead your family God's way for God's glory. Do you need wisdom when it comes to managing your work and finances? Then spend time reading the Bible. Why? Because there is no greater book to teach you how to manage your money God's way for God's glory. Do you need wisdom when it comes to making some tough decisions? Read the Bible. Why? Because there is no greater guidebook to counsel us in making decisions that will not only guide us in the present, but will also protect us for the future.

"Your statutes are my delight; they are my counselors." (Psalm 119:24)

It has been said that the more we get into the Bible, the more the Bible will get into us. The more that the Bible starts to get into us; the more we are able to live the life that God has for us . . . a life that brings blessings to us, blessings to others, and glory to our gracious God.

"Blessed are they whose walk is blameless, who walk according to the law of the Lord. Blessed are they who keep his statutes and seek him with all their heart." (Psalm 119:1-2)

Time Is a Gift from God

(time management, prayer)

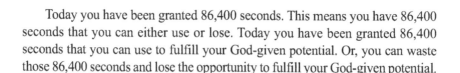

Today you have been granted 86,400 seconds. This means you have 86,400 seconds that you can either use or lose. Today you have been granted 86,400 seconds that you can use to fulfill your God-given potential. Or, you can waste those 86,400 seconds and lose the opportunity to fulfill your God-given potential.

"Be very careful, then, how you live—not as unwise but as wise, making the most of every opportunity, because the days are evil." (Ephesians 5:15-16)

As you prepare to face your day today, take some time to pray to God. Ask Him to guide you in a way that you can fulfill His purposes for His glory. Ask Him to help you to use those 86,400 seconds in a way that can bless others and bless God. Ask Him to organize your thoughts and actions in such a way, so that you make the most of every opportunity that God graciously gives you today.

Remember, those 86,400 seconds are a gift to you today. You can either make the most of those seconds, or you can waste them. Which way will you go today?

"For we are God's workmanship, created in Christ Jesus to do good works, which God prepared in advance for us to do." (Ephesians 2:10)

Is Your Guilt Separating You from God?

(guilt, sin)

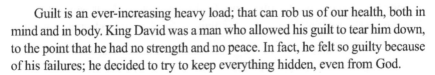

Guilt is an ever-increasing heavy load; that can rob us of our health, both in mind and in body. King David was a man who allowed his guilt to tear him down, to the point that he had no strength and no peace. In fact, he felt so guilty because of his failures; he decided to try to keep everything hidden, even from God.

"When I kept silent, my bones wasted away through my groaning all day long. For day and night your hand was heavy upon me; my strength was sapped as in the heat of the summer." (Psalm 32:3-4)

However, in spite of David's attempt to keep things hidden, God in His grace moved David to confess and come clean about his sins. As a result, King David's guilt was replaced with God's forgiving grace and mercy.

"Then I acknowledged my sin to you and did not cover my inequity. I said, 'I will confess my transgressions to the Lord' and you forgave the guilt of my sin." (Psalm 32:5)

Are you holding on to some guilt right now? Do you feel that your failures are so bad that you don't even want to talk to God about them? Are you feeling like King David? Are you feeling as if your bones are wasting away right now? Don't stay silent, and don't try to carry the ever-increasing burden of your guilt. Instead, get alone with the God of all compassion and comfort, and confess your transgressions to the Lord. He will forgive you and replace your guilt with His amazing grace!

"Blessed is he whose transgressions are forgiven, whose sins are covered. Blessed is the man whose sin the Lord does not count against him and in whose spirit is no deceit." (Psalm 32:1-2)

Offer Your Plans Up to the Lord

(future, trust, integrity)

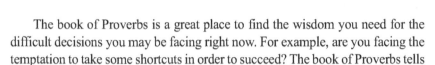

The book of Proverbs is a great place to find the wisdom you need for the difficult decisions you may be facing right now. For example, are you facing the temptation to take some shortcuts in order to succeed? The book of Proverbs tells us:

"Better a little with righteousness than much gain with injustice." (Proverbs 16:8)

In other words, it's better to have less from the Lord (but to have the peace and contentment that comes with it), than to have much without the Lord (and to have the turmoil and worry that also comes with it).

Shortcuts often lead to lead to hurry and worry. Trying to climb the ladder of success without wisdom from the Lord can often lead to a difficult fall. Therefore, make a commitment today to offer your plans to the Lord. Trust Him to help you climb that ladder in the right way and at the right pace. Why? Look at what the book of Proverbs tells us:

"Commit to the Lord whatever you do, and your plans will succeed." (Proverbs 16:3)

Doesn't it make sense to seek guidance and wisdom from the only One who is perfect in wisdom and guidance? Of course it does! Also, doesn't it make sense to trust in the only One who is perfect to protect us and provide for us? Of course it does! That's why the book of Proverbs tells us:

"Trust in the Lord with all your heart and lean not on your own understanding; in all your ways acknowledge him, and He will make straight your paths." (Proverbs 3:5-6)

Walk by Faith

(faith, trust, encouragement)

Fear immobilizes our faith and causes us to live in a state of panic and stress. Faith immobilizes our fear and causes us to live in a state of calm and peace. As you face your day today, are you walking by fear or are you walking by faith?

"The Lord himself goes before you and will be with you; he will never leave you nor forsake you. Do not be afraid; do not be discouraged." (Deuteronomy 31:8)

"The Lord himself goes before you"—the Lord is out in front of you today. He is already handling those very things that are worrying you.

"And will be with you"—the Lord is also with you at this very moment. He is giving you the faith and strength to walk forward to face this day.

"He will never leave you nor forsake you"—the Lord is with you every step of the way. He is faithful to guide your steps today.

"Do not be afraid; do not be discouraged"—if God is with us, who or what can be against us?

Our God is an awesome God! Make today the day that you walk and talk to God. Watch how He can replace your fear with faith!

Who Is in Control of Your Emotions?

(thankfulness)

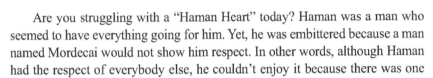

Are you struggling with a "Haman Heart" today? Haman was a man who seemed to have everything going for him. Yet, he was embittered because a man named Mordecai would not show him respect. In other words, although Haman had the respect of everybody else, he couldn't enjoy it because there was one person out there who wouldn't bow to him.

"All the royal officials at the king's gate knelt down and paid honor to Haman, for the king had commanded this concerning him. But Mordecai would not kneel down or pay him honor. . . . When he saw that Mordecai would not kneel down or pay him honor, he was enraged." (Esther 3:2, 5)

Perhaps you have someone in your life right now that isn't showing you the respect you feel you deserve. Although you have many other people who are currently treating you with respect and honor, nevertheless, you're struggling because one or two people out there are mistreating you. As a result, you're becoming so fixated with those few who are disrespecting you, that you cannot enjoy the many who are respecting you. In other words, your anger and rage is giving you a "Haman Heart" today.

Don't let the actions of someone else rob you of enjoying the many blessings that you currently have. Don't let someone else control your emotions to the point that you become embittered and full of rage. Instead, thank the Lord for all that He has given you (you will be amazed at how much He has given you!), and make sure that your heart is right in His sight. Why?

"When a man's ways are pleasing to the Lord, he makes even his enemies live at peace with him." (Proverbs 16:7)

Are We Obedient Children of God?

(character, obedience)

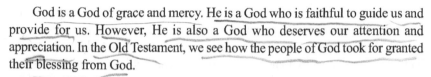

God is a God of grace and mercy. He is a God who is faithful to guide us and provide for us. However, He is also a God who deserves our attention and appreciation. In the Old Testament, we see how the people of God took for granted their blessing from God.

"Hear, O Heavens! Listen, O earth! For the Lord has spoken: I reared children and brought them up, but they have rebelled against me." (Isaiah 1:2)

As Christians, we too are God's children who have been raised by God. Through our relationship with Jesus Christ, God has raised us from the dead spiritually. Through our relationship with Jesus Christ, God has blessed us with the privilege of having Him provide for us and protect us as His children. Through our relationship with Jesus Christ, God grants us grace in abundance and mercy beyond our imagination. However, how are we responding to God's love and God's care for us?

"The ox knows his master, the donkey his owner's manger, but Israel does not know, my people do not understand." (Isaiah 1:3)

God chose two dumb and disobedient animals as an example to show God's people how far they had fallen from their knowledge and obedience to God. Perhaps today we should look at their example as a humbling reminder for us as well. God deserves our attention and our appreciation. Why? Because of who He is and because of how He is. God deserves our obedience and our continual desire to know more of Him. Why? Because of who He is and because of how He is. Our God is an awesome God and we are so blessed to be called His children. May it never be said of us that the ox and donkey are more loyal and obedient than we are!

Do You Feel You Can Earn God's Favor and Forgiveness?

(salvation, grace)

How does a person enter into a saving relationship with God? More specifically, how do you believe that you can enter into a saving relationship with God? Do you believe that God will accept you because of your good works? In other words, do you feel that you can earn God's favor and forgiveness? Or, do you believe that God will accept you because of His grace, love and mercy? In other words, do you believe that you cannot earn God's favor and forgiveness, but that God's favor and forgiveness has been earned for you through what Jesus Christ accomplished for you?

"When the kindness and love of God our Savior appeared, he saved us, not because of righteous things we had done, but because of his mercy. He saved us through the washing of rebirth and renewal by the Holy Spirit, whom he poured out on us generously through Jesus Christ our Savior, so that, having been justified by his grace, we might become heirs having the hope of eternal life." (Titus 3:4-7)

One of the reasons we want to be able to earn God's favor and forgiveness is that we want to be able to take some credit for God's favor and forgiveness. This is because we all have a sin nature that wants to exalt self. Self wants to get some credit, self wants to boast in what we have accomplished, and self wants to say to God, "See what we have done!" However, Scripture is very clear; the only One who gets credit for God's favor and forgiveness is our Savior Jesus Christ . . . not our self-seeking, self-glorifying sin nature. Take a look at the verses above and notice that God's favor and God's forgiveness is all from God . . . He sent His Son, He saved us because of His mercy, He generously poured out His Spirit, He justified us by His grace, He has made us heirs.

"What then shall we say that Abraham, our forefather, discovered in this matter? If, in fact, Abraham was justified by works, he had something to boast about—but not before God. What does the Scripture say? 'Abraham believed God, and it was credited to him as righteousness.' Now when a man works, his wages are not credited to him as a gift, but as an obligation. However, to the man who does not

work but trusts God who justifies the wicked, his faith is credited as righteousness." *(Romans 4:1-5)*

Abraham was an Old Testament hero who understood that salvation is a gift of grace based on what Christ would do for him on the cross. He understood that he could not earn God's favor or forgiveness, rather he trusted in God and his promises. However, he wasn't the only Old Testament hero who understood this wonderful truth. Take a look at what King David said:

"David says the same thing when he speaks of the blessedness of the man to whom God credits righteousness apart from works: 'Blessed are they whose transgressions are forgiven, whose sins are covered. Blessed is the man whose sin the Lord will never count against him.'" (Romans 4:6-8)

Do you still believe that God will accept you because of your good works? Do you still feel that you can earn God's favor and forgiveness? Or, do you now understand that God will accept you solely because of His grace, love and mercy? Do you now understand that you cannot earn God's favor and forgiveness, but that God's favor and forgiveness has been earned for you through what Jesus Christ accomplished for you? If so, have you placed your complete faith and trust in Jesus as your personal Lord and Savior?

"The words 'it was credited to him' were written not for him alone, but also for us, to whom God will credit righteousness—for us who believe in him who raised Jesus our Lord from the dead. He was delivered over to death for our sins and was raised to life for our justification." (Romans 4:23-25)

110

Who's Approval Are You Seeking?

(identity, peer pressure)

only god

Who are you trying to impress today? Are you looking for the applause of God or are you looking for the applause of man? Please understand, there is nothing wrong with trying to do good and bring pleasure to others. However, we must be careful not to allow ourselves to find our significance and satisfaction in the approval or disapproval of others. Why? We will end up becoming consumed by the opinions of others; kind of like Olympic athletes who base their success or failure on what scores the judges choose to give.

"Am I now trying to win the approval of men, or of God? Or am I trying to please men? If I were still trying to please men, I would not be a servant of Christ." *(Galatians 1:10)*

As Christians, our significance and satisfaction is to be found first and foremost in the Lord. And the only scores that matter are the ones provided by the true Judge, the Lord Jesus Christ. Famous Christian writer, John Bunyan once said: "If my life is fruitless, it doesn't matter who praises me. And if my life is fruitful, it doesn't matter who criticizes me." This is a man who clearly understood that his goal in life was to live for the praises of God, not to live for the praises of people.

"Now it is required that those who have been given a trust must prove faithful. I care very little if I am judged by you or by any human court; indeed, I do not even judge myself." (1 Corinthians 4:2-3)

Lord I pray I will always be able to stand before you. Worthy of being your daughter. Thank you for loving me!

Are You A Good Representative of God?

(character, integrity, evangelism)

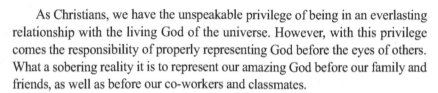

As Christians, we have the unspeakable privilege of being in an everlasting relationship with the living God of the universe. However, with this privilege comes the responsibility of properly representing God before the eyes of others. What a sobering reality it is to represent our amazing God before our family and friends, as well as before our co-workers and classmates.

"May those who hope in you not be disgraced because of me, O Lord, the Lord Almighty; may those who seek you not be put to shame because of me, O God of Israel." (Psalm 69:6)

King David was the person who said those words. He understood, that with the privilege of being in a relationship with the Lord Almighty, came the responsibility of representing Him before others. How about you? As you face your day today are you thinking about how your life will bring glory to the Lord Almighty? Are you thinking about what your life will say to others about the living God of the universe?

"But thanks be to God, who always leads us in triumphal procession in Christ and through us spreads everywhere the fragrance of the knowledge of him." (2 Corinthians 2:14)

Pray to the Lord and ask Him to make your life today a sweet aroma, pleasing to Him and to others. Ask the Lord Almighty to grant you the grace to live a life that represents Him and causes others to be attracted to Him.

Submitting to God's Control

(sin, humility)

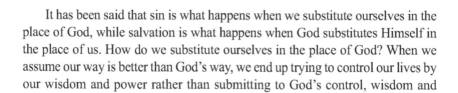

It has been said that sin is what happens when we substitute ourselves in the place of God, while salvation is what happens when God substitutes Himself in the place of us. How do we substitute ourselves in the place of God? When we assume our way is better than God's way, we end up trying to control our lives by our wisdom and power rather than submitting to God's control, wisdom and power.

"Everyone who sins breaks the law; in fact, sin is lawlessness." (1 John 3:4)

How does God substitute Himself in the place of us? Two thousand years ago God the Son, Jesus Christ, allowed Himself to be hung on the cross for our sins. It was there on the cross that He allowed Himself to be punished in our place as our substitute.

"God made him [Jesus] who had no sin to be sin for us, so that in him we [the sinners!] might become the righteousness of God." (2 Corinthians 5:21)

As you face your day today, who is in control? Jesus, the One who substituted Himself for you and your salvation, or are you substituting yourself in the place of Jesus by trusting in your wisdom and power? Take some time right now to pray to the Lord. Ask Him to give you a Heart that is willing to submit to His plans for you today. You will be glad that you did!

"Blessed is the man who fears [reverent submission] the Lord, but he who hardens his heart falls into trouble." (Proverbs 28:14)

Take Delight in His Word

(the Bible)

"Blessed is the man who does not walk in the counsel of the wicked or stand in the way of sinners or sit in the seat of mockers." (Psalm 1:1)

Do you want to be blessed by God? Then, watch where you walk and watch how you talk, including those people with whom you walk and talk. By the way, notice the downward spiral into sin: The walk with the wrong people turns into standing with the wrong people, which then turns into sitting with the wrong people. This inevitably turns into living a life that will not be blessed by God.

"But his delight is in the law of the Lord, and on his law he meditates day and night." (Psalm 1:2)

Do you want to be blessed by God? Then spend some time listening to the Lord through His Word. By the way, notice the increased enjoyment from God's Word: Delighting in God's Word leads to reading God's Word, which in turn leads to meditating on God's Word day and night. And what is the result?

"He is like a tree planted by streams of water, which yields its fruit in due season and whose leaf does not wither. Whatever he does prospers." (Psalm 1:3)

Do you want to be blessed by God? Look at the life of the person who not only watches his walk and talk; but also spends quality time with the Lord reading and meditating on His perfect Word. This person yields all kinds of Godly fruit: In the family, workplace and school. Talk about being blessed by God!

Take some time to read and meditate on Psalm 1 today. Ask the Lord to give you a delight for His Word, and also ask Him to reveal to you those things that you may have to change about your walk and talk. Do you want to be blessed by God?

God Provides Rest for Our Souls

(rest, peace)

Are you feeling burdened and stressed? Are you tired of carrying the heavy burdens of life? Take a look at what the Bible says:

"Humble yourselves, therefore, under God's mighty hand, that he may lift you up in due time. Cast all your anxiety on him because he cares for you." (1 Peter 5:6-7)

Is today one of those days where you're feeling anxious and worried? Is today one of those days where you would rather stay in bed than face the burdens of the day? Take a look at what the Bible says:

"Praise be to the Lord, to God our Savior, who daily bears our burdens." (Psalm 68:19)

Are you looking for some rest from all your weariness? Are you simply tired of being tired? Take a look at what Jesus says:

"Come to me, all you who are weary and burdened, and I will give you rest. Take my yoke upon you and learn from me, for I am gentle and humble in heart, and you will find rest for your souls. For my yoke is easy and my burden is light." (Matthew 11:28-30)

The Lord says that we can cast all of our burdens upon Him; He will carry all of them for us today and He will give us rest for our souls. What an incredible God we serve! And what a faithful God He is! Take some time right now to meditate on those three verses. Don't just simply read the verses, meditate on them. Think about what they are saying to you and to your situation right now. In doing this, watch how your weariness will turn to worship, and how your feelings of burden will turn to feelings of blessings.

Do You Judge Others?

(justice, character)

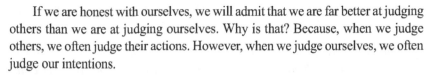

If we are honest with ourselves, we will admit that we are far better at judging others than we are at judging ourselves. Why is that? Because, when we judge others, we often judge their actions. However, when we judge ourselves, we often judge our intentions.

" 'Why do you look at the speck in your brother's eye and pay no attention to the plank in your own eye?' " (Matthew 7:3)

Why do we judge the actions of others? Actions are very clear cut and obvious. Certain actions are good, while others are wrong. However, when it comes to judging ourselves, why do we feel more comfortable judging our intentions rather our actions? Because, when we judge our intentions we can then justify our actions, even if those actions are not very good. In other words, we can rationalize our actions under the umbrella of this line of thinking: "At least my intentions were good."

" 'How can you say to your brother, "Let me take the speck out of your eye," when all the time there is a plank in your own eye? You hypocrite, first take the plank out of your own eye, and then you will see clearly to remove the speck from your brother's eye.' " (Matthew 7:4-5)

Take some time to pray to the Lord about this topic. Ask Him to reveal to you the motives of your heart when it comes to judging others. Ask Him to also reveal to you the motives of your heart when it comes to judging yourself.

"All a man's ways seem innocent to him, but motives are weighed by the Lord." (Proverbs 16:2)

God's Perfect Purpose Prevails

(future, trust)

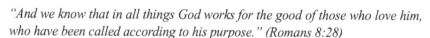

"And we know that in all things God works for the good of those who love him, who have been called according to his purpose." (Romans 8:28)

The Bible gives us example after example of how God can turn bad into good. Think of some of the women in the Bible: Tamar seduced her father-in-law; Rahab was a prostitute; Ruth was a non-Jew who broke God's law by marrying a Jew; and Bathsheba committed adultery with King David. Yet, Scripture clearly shows us how God turned all that bad into good and for His glory. Those four women are listed in the genealogy of Jesus Christ (see Matthew: 1). Talk about turning bad into good!

But it's not just in the women of the Bible that we see God working out His perfect purposes in spite of all their problems. Think of some of the men in the Bible: Abraham was a liar, Jacob was a deceiver, Judah let himself get seduced by his daughter-in-law; and King David committed adultery and murder. Yet, Scripture once again clearly shows us how God turned all that bad into good and for His glory. These men are also listed in the genealogy of Jesus Christ (see Matthew 1). Talk about turning bad into good!

" 'For my thoughts are not your thoughts, neither are your ways my ways,' declares the Lord. 'As the heavens are higher than the earth, so are my ways higher than your ways and my thoughts than your thoughts.' " (Isaiah 55:8-9)

The point of all this is not to justify sin and say that God doesn't mind when we disobey Him. Scripture is very clear that we must always seek to honor and obey God. Rather, the point of all this is to show how God's perfect purposes prevail—in spite of all of our problems, pain, and even our sinfulness. Perhaps lately, you have been feeling as though you have made so many mistakes that you have messed up God's plan for your life. My friend, nothing could be further from the truth. Our great God can turn any bad for good and for His glory!

"We know that in all things God works for the good of those who love him, who have been called according to his purpose." (Romans 8:28)

Fulfill Your Divine Purpose and Potential

(purpose, future)

A certain species of bird has an amazing way of getting its baby birds to fly. The baby birds are initially reluctant to fly and would rather stay in the safety of their nest. Why? The nest is warm, comfortable, and the place where the baby birds feel most secure. However, the baby birds were not created to stay in the nest; they were created to fly. Therefore, in order to get her baby birds to fly, the mother bird will slowly start removing the branches of the nest to the point that the baby birds have no choice but to flap their wings and start flying. Does this sound cruel? No, because the mother bird in her love for her babies is doing what she has to do in order to get her babies to fulfill their purpose and potential—to fly.

In same way, we as humans were not created to sit in the "safety nest" of our lives. Rather, we were created "to fly" for God! Just like the mother bird, God will often start to pull "the branches" from our safety nest in order to get us to fulfill our purpose and potential.

"Those who hope in the Lord will renew their strength. They will soar on wings like eagles; they will run and not grow weary, they will walk and not be faint." (Isaiah 40:31)

Do you feel God moving you out of the comfort and security of your life right now? Are you wondering how you're going "to fly" for God? Do not fear, just flap your wings! God is faithful to catch you if you fall, and He is faithful to lead you to fulfill your purpose and potential. Just start flapping by faith.

"In a desert land he [God] found him, in a barren and howling waste. He shielded him and cared for him; he guarded him as the apple of his eye, like an eagle that stirs up its nest and hovers over its young, that spreads its wings to catch them and carries them on its pinions." (Deuteronomy 32:10-11)

God Is Our Leader and Our Guide

(trust, future, faith)

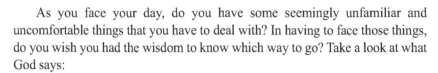

As you face your day, do you have some seemingly unfamiliar and uncomfortable things that you have to deal with? In having to face those things, do you wish you had the wisdom to know which way to go? Take a look at what God says:

"I will lead the blind by ways they have not known, along unfamiliar paths I will guide them; I will turn the darkness into light before them and make the rough places smooth. These are the things I will do; I will not forsake them." (Isaiah 42:16)

When it comes to the uncertainty of our situations, God says in that verse, "I will lead . . . I will guide . . . I will turn . . . I will make . . . I will do." What incredible promises from our most incredible God! Remember, God is not limited by our limitations!

Are you unfamiliar with a path you should take today? Look to God, for He will lead and guide you. Are you feeling like you're walking in the dark on some important decision that you have to make? Look to God, for He will enlighten your darkness and show you the proper decision to make. Do you feel like you may be facing some rough things today? Look to God, for He will make those rough places smooth. Finally, do you wish you had enough faith to be able trust that God will do all of these things? Look to God and rejoice, for He says that He will do these things and that He will not forsake them (or you!).

Where Is Your Devotion?

(finances, character, priorities)

It's amazing to read how much the Bible talks about money. In fact, Jesus Himself talked about money as much as He talked about prayer, heaven and hell. Are you surprised? You shouldn't be. Money has always played an important role in the lives of people. It has been used for good and it has been abused for bad.

" 'No one can serve two masters. Either he will hate the one and love the other, or he will be devoted to the one and despise the other. You cannot serve God and money.' " (Matthew 6:24)

Notice that Jesus did not say that you cannot "have" God and money in your life. He said that you could not "serve" God and money in your life. Why? No one can serve two masters. Either we will live to serve and worship the One who blesses us (our great God), or we will live to serve and honor the blessings (money). Who are we living to serve and honor today? Where is our devotion?

The Bible is filled with examples of people who were blessed by God and who in turn used those blessings to help others. In other words, they did not serve the money. They used the money to serve God and others. How we handle money often reflects our attitude and gratitude (or lack of gratitude) towards God. By grace, God not only gives us what we need to live our lives for Him today—if we look really closely we will notice that He has also given us enough to help someone else as well.

" 'Give generously to him and do so without a grudging heart; then because of this the Lord God will bless you in all your work and in everything you put your hand to. There will always be poor people in the land. Therefore I command you to be openhanded toward your brothers and toward the poor and needy in your land.' " (Deuteronomy 15:10-11)

Exalt the Lord Your God

(trust, faith)

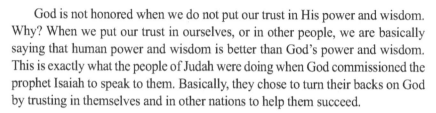

God is not honored when we do not put our trust in His power and wisdom. Why? When we put our trust in ourselves, or in other people, we are basically saying that human power and wisdom is better than God's power and wisdom. This is exactly what the people of Judah were doing when God commissioned the prophet Isaiah to speak to them. Basically, they chose to turn their backs on God by trusting in themselves and in other nations to help them succeed.

"Stop trusting in man, who has but a breath in his nostrils. Of what account is he?" (Isaiah 2:22)

Through the prophet Isaiah, God told the people that they were foolish to put their trust in fallible and finite humans. Instead, they needed to put their trust in the infallible and infinite God of the universe; who created all humans and who controls each breath that is taken. The same message applies to all of us today as well. God is not saying that we need to avoid all human friendship and fellowship. Rather, God is saying that we need to avoid exalting humans (ourselves or others) to the point that we place our complete trust in human wisdom and power. Why?

"The arrogance of man will be brought low and the pride of men will be humbled; the Lord alone will be exalted in that day, and the idols will totally disappear." (Isaiah 2:17-18)

Think about where you're placing your hope and trust today. Think about from where you're seeking power and wisdom today. Is it from your husband or wife? Is it from your boyfriend or girlfriend? Is it from your boss or co-worker? Or, is it from the all-powerful and all-knowing God of this universe?

Sunday 2016   YES AMEN

Lord every thing is in your hands, and you time it all under control.

God Can Turn Your Bitterness Into Blessings!

(trials, stress, trust)

Job was a godly man who seemed to have everything going for him. He was blessed with a wonderful family. He was blessed with health and wealth. He was also blessed to have a wonderful relationship with God. But suddenly, Job's life took a tragic turn for the worse. He lost everything. Yet, Job held on to his integrity and would not curse God for his tragedies.

"His wife said to him, 'Are you still holding on to your integrity? Curse God and die!' He replied, 'You're talking like a foolish woman. Shall we accept good from God, and not trouble?' In all this, Job did not sin in what he said." (Job 2:9-10)

Shall we only accept good from God, not trouble? This is a very, very challenging question. So often we act as though we are entitled to only blessings from God. We act as if He has no right to bring difficulties into our lives. Then, when the difficulties do come, we come very close to taking the advice of Job's wife by letting go of our integrity and cursing God.

Perhaps lately you have been struggling with all the difficulties in your life. Perhaps you have been getting angry with God and wondering why your life is turning out the way it is. My friend, don't give up, for God has not given up on you! Read the rest of the book of Job and see how God honored and restored Job in the most amazing ways. The God who did that for Job is the same God who can turn your bitterness into blessings!

"Naked I came from my mother's womb, and naked I will depart. The Lord gave and the Lord has taken away; may the name of the Lord be praised." (Job 1:21)

The Lord Disciplines Those He Loves

(discipline, trials)

One of the ways we as Christians experience God's love is through God's discipline. Although that may sound a bit strange, the Bible makes it very clear that one of the ways God shows His love for us is by disciplining us.

"And have you forgotten the word of encouragement that addresses you as sons: My son do not make light of the Lord's discipline, and do not lose heart when he rebukes you, because the Lord disciplines those he loves and he punishes everyone he accepts as a son." (Hebrews 12:5-6)

Are you experiencing God's loving discipline in your life right now? If so, are you despising that discipline? Are you resenting His rebuke? Although it can be challenging, you and I must learn to relax and remember, God is demonstrating His love to us and He is disciplining us for our good.

"Our fathers disciplined us for a little while as they thought best; but God disciplines us for our good, that we may share in His holiness." (Hebrews 12:10)

God has a purpose in His discipline for us. God never wastes His purpose! God wants to grow us. God wants to prepare us for the plans He has for us. God wants to produce wonderful blessings in and through our lives. Even though it may be difficult to maintain this perspective as we are experiencing discipline; nevertheless, we need to focus on the fact that God is producing something wonderful in us.

"No discipline seems pleasant at the time, but painful. Later on, however, it produces a harvest of righteousness and peace for those who have been trained by it." (Hebrews 12:11)

Spiritual Gifts

(spiritual gifts, identity, purpose)

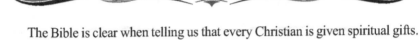

The Bible is clear when telling us that every Christian is given spiritual gifts. The Bible is also clear that our spiritual gifts are given for the purpose of building up of the body of Christ. In other words, our gifts are not for self-edification, but for the edification of others.

"Now to each one the manifestation of the Spirit is given for the common good." (1 Corinthians 12:7)

Are you using your gifts to build up the body of Christ? Do you even know what your spiritual gifts are? Perhaps you should take a look at the four passages that describe the various gifts that God grants Christians (see Romans 12, 1 Corinthians 12, Ephesians 4, and 1 Peter 4). The good news is that as we use our gifts to build up others, we are built up as well. In other words, if you want to grow as a Christian, then grow the body of Christ.

"There are different kinds of gifts, but the same Spirit. There are different kinds of service, but the same Lord. There are different kinds of working, but the same God works all of them in all men." (1 Corinthians 12:4-6)

Think of a sponge under a running faucet. Initially, the sponge can absorb the oncoming water. However, after a while the sponge can no longer absorb anymore of the water. Why? Because it's too full. You need to ring out the sponge in order for it to absorb more water. In like manner, we as Christians often become so filled with God's Word we find it difficult to absorb anymore. What must we do? We need "to ring out" and build up others with what we have already absorbed of God's Word. Then we will be able to absorb more. Remember, if you want to grow as a Christian, you need to grow the body of Christ.

"So it is with you. Since you are eager to have spiritual gifts, try to excel in gifts that build up the church." (1 Corinthians 14:12)

Humbly Submit to the Lord Your God

(humility, submission, trust)

Obedience to the Lord Jesus shows that we are truly in a saving relationship with the Lord Jesus. In other words, if Jesus is to be our Lord that means that He is to be the leader and director of our lives. He is the Boss who is to be obeyed.

"'Why do you call me, "Lord, Lord," and do not do what I say?'" (Luke 6:46)

It's easy to look to Jesus as our Savior who can get us into heaven. After all, it's much better than the alternative! But it's also expected that we humbly submit to Him as our Lord as well. The Bible is clear that we are saved by grace alone, through faith alone, in Jesus alone. This means that none of our good works, including our good efforts of obedience, get us into heaven. However, obedience should be the natural result of someone who has been saved through the amazing grace of Jesus. Once we understand who Jesus is and what He has done for us; we should have the desire to obey Him. Why? Out of immense gratitude for who He is and what He has done for us! Although we will never be perfect in our obedience to Jesus down here on earth; nevertheless, we should have an ever-increasing desire to please Him and obey Him.

"Therefore, I urge you, brothers, in view of God's mercy, to offer your bodies as living sacrifices, holy and pleasing to God—this is your spiritual act of worship." (Romans 12:1)

As Christians, in view of God's incredible mercy through Jesus Christ, our reasonable or rational act of worship is to offer the totality of our being to the Lord. This means that we are to come to the Lord each morning and offer our lives to Him in a way that is holy and pleasing to Him. Meaning, we are to look to Him to be the Lord and Leader of our day—to be the Boss of our families, of our work, of our school, of our dreams and of our desires. How do we find out what is holy and pleasing to the Lord? Simply look to His holy and pleasing Word. He has graciously given His Word to us to show us how to live a life of gratitude for His amazing grace.

"Do not conform any longer to the pattern of this world, but be transformed by the renewing of your mind. Then you will be able to test and approve what God's will is—his good, pleasing and perfect will." (Romans 12:2)

The Lord Looks at Your Heart

(character, integrity)

Society has always focused on the outer appearance. Outward beauty is considered the benchmark of success and prestige. If a person looks good to others, that person will often be treated well by others. However, the Bible has something very different to say about this.

"The Lord said to Samuel, 'Do not consider his appearance or his height, for I have rejected him. The Lord does not look at the things that man looks at. Man looks at the outward appearance, but the Lord looks at the heart.'" (1 Samuel 16:7)

This is not to say that God wants us to forsake our outer appearance and simply let our bodies and minds waste away. The Bible is very clear about how we are to honor God with our bodies.

"Do you not know that your body is a temple of the Holy Spirit, who is in you, whom you have received from God? You are not your own; you were bought at a price. Therefore, honor God with your body." (1 Corinthians 6:19-20)

It's okay to go to the gym, watch what you eat, and try to have a nice outer appearance. However, those things should not become our obsession. We need to be more focused on training our inner self, so as to grow more and more into the character and likeness of Christ.

"For physical training is of some value, but godliness has value for all things, holding promise for both the present life and the life to come." (1 Timothy 4:8)

How is your training program going to be today? Is it going to be balanced, working on both your inner and outer self? Are you going to make time to go to the "spiritual gym" today; where you can spend that time working on your heart and growing in godliness? Remember, your spiritual workout will not only impact you for today. It will also impact you for all of eternity as well!

The Lord Is Our Helper

(fear, trials, stress)

As you face your day today, are you full of fear and anguish? Are you feeling overwhelmed and outnumbered?

"In my anguish I cried to the Lord, and he answered by setting me free. The Lord is with me; I will not be afraid. What can man do to me?" (Psalm 118:5-6)

Do you feel resentment because somebody has lied to you and let you down? Are you wondering who you can trust?

"The Lord is with me; he is my helper. I will look in triumph on my enemies. It is better to take refuge in the Lord than to trust in man. It is better to take refuge in the Lord than to trust in princes." (Psalm 118:7-9)

Do you feel surrounded by all of your problems? Do you feel like you're about to fall and fail?

"I was pushed back and about to fall, but the Lord helped me. The Lord is my strength and my song; he has become my salvation." (Psalm 118:13-14)

Isn't it amazing how the Bible can provide comfort and peace in our most challenging moments? Isn't it also amazing how the Bible gives us the perfect reminder (at the perfect time!). The Lord is with us and He is an ever-present help in our time of need?

"Shouts of joy and victory resound in the tents of the righteous: 'The Lord's hand has done mighty things! The Lord's right hand is lifted high; the Lord's right hand has done mighty things!'" (Psalm 118:15-16)

Freedom in Christ

(purpose, faith, trust)

What does freedom mean to you? More specifically, what does freedom in Christ mean to you? Do you believe that Jesus was punished for your sins; that He died the death you deserve, and that three days later He rose from the dead paying for your sins in full? If so, do you believe that when Jesus sets you free (from eternal condemnation) that you're free indeed?

Freedom in Christ means peace with your past:

"Jesus replied, 'I tell you the truth, everyone who sins is a slave to sin. Now a slave has no permanent place in the family, but a son belongs to it forever. So if the Son sets you free, you will be free indeed.'" (John 8:34-36)

Freedom in Christ means a purpose in your present:

"It's for freedom that Christ has set us free. Stand firm, then, and do not let yourselves be burdened again by a yoke of slavery." (Galatians 5:1)

Freedom in Christ means a glorious guarantee for your future:

"Now the Lord is the Spirit, and where the Spirit of the Lord is, there is freedom. And we, who with unveiled faces all reflect the Lord's glory, are being transformed into His likeness with ever-increasing glory, which comes from the Lord, who is the Spirit." (2 Corinthians 3:17-18)

Isn't it amazing to see, as Christians, how free we truly are? Our response should be:

"To him who is able to keep you from falling and to present you before his glorious presence without fault and with great joy—to the only God our Savior be glory, majesty, power and authority, through Jesus Christ our Lord, before all ages, now and forevermore! Amen." (Jude 24-25)

God's Will for Our Lives

(God's will, prayer, future)

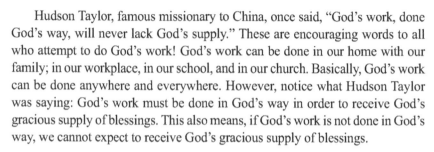

Hudson Taylor, famous missionary to China, once said, "God's work, done God's way, will never lack God's supply." These are encouraging words to all who attempt to do God's work! God's work can be done in our home with our family; in our workplace, in our school, and in our church. Basically, God's work can be done anywhere and everywhere. However, notice what Hudson Taylor was saying: God's work must be done in God's way in order to receive God's gracious supply of blessings. This also means, if God's work is not done in God's way, we cannot expect to receive God's gracious supply of blessings.

"Unless the Lord builds the house, its builders labor in vain. Unless the Lord watches over the city, the watchmen stand guard in vain. In vain you rise early and stay up late, toiling for food to eat—for he grants sleep to those he loves." (Psalm 127:1-2)

As you face your day today, are you attempting to do God's work? If so, are you looking to do it God's way or your way? The best way to make sure that you're following God's plan is to spend time in prayer, asking Him to establish the work you're to do.

"May the favor of the Lord our God rest upon us; establish the work of our hands for us—yes, establish the work of our hands." (Psalm 90:17)

God Stretches Our Faith

(faith, trials)

How is your faith today? Is it strong, or are you struggling? It has been said that faith believes that something is so, even though it's not yet so. In other words, faith believes and trusts today what God has planned for you tomorrow.

"Now faith is being sure of what we hope for and certain of what we do not see. This is what the ancients were commended for." (Hebrews 11:1-2)

Faith in God is something that honors God. When we exercise faith in God's purpose for our lives, we are trusting God to guide and provide for us. We are trusting that God's way is the best way, and that God is worthy to be believed. This is pleasing to God.

"Without faith it's impossible to please God, because anyone who comes to him must believe that he exists and that he rewards those who earnestly seek him." (Hebrews 11:6)

Is there something in your life right now that is stretching your faith to the point that you're struggling? Are you trying to trust today that God will take care of what you're concerned about tomorrow? Remember, even the great heroes of faith in the Bible had their faith stretched to the point that they had no idea how things would turn out. You're in good company!

"By faith Abraham, when called to go to a place he would later receive as his inheritance, obeyed and went, even though he did not know where he was going." (Hebrews 11:8)

The Lord Rewards Integrity

(integrity, character)

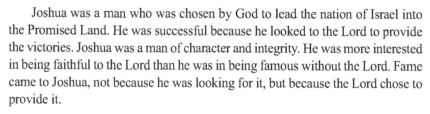

Joshua was a man who was chosen by God to lead the nation of Israel into the Promised Land. He was successful because he looked to the Lord to provide the victories. Joshua was a man of character and integrity. He was more interested in being faithful to the Lord than he was in being famous without the Lord. Fame came to Joshua, not because he was looking for it, but because the Lord chose to provide it.

"So the Lord was with Joshua, and His fame spread throughout the land." (Joshua 6:27)

As you face your day today, are you looking to be faithful or are you looking to be famous? In other words, do you trust in the Lord to grant you your victories? Or, are you looking to win on your own—even if you have to sin in order to win? Be careful, for the Bible warns us that self-centered shortcuts will be exposed by the Lord.

" 'But if you fail to do this, you will be sinning against the Lord; and you may be sure that your sin will find you out.' " (Numbers 32:23)

As we face the challenges of a difficult world economy, the temptation is there to do whatever it takes to succeed. After all, times are tough and waiting on the Lord may seem like a waste of time. However, the Lord rewards integrity and honesty. The Lord is pleased with those who faithfully wait upon Him. The Lord is with those who obediently look to Him for the victories.

"The man of integrity walks securely, but he who takes crooked paths will be found out." (Proverbs 10:9)

"The wicked man earns deceptive wages, but he who sows righteousness reaps a sure reward." (Proverbs 11:18)

Keep A Heavenly Perspective

(future, perspective)

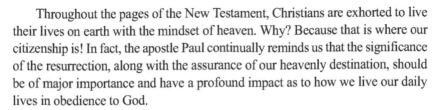

Throughout the pages of the New Testament, Christians are exhorted to live their lives on earth with the mindset of heaven. Why? Because that is where our citizenship is! In fact, the apostle Paul continually reminds us that the significance of the resurrection, along with the assurance of our heavenly destination, should be of major importance and have a profound impact as to how we live our daily lives in obedience to God.

"Our citizenship is in heaven. And, we eagerly await a savior from there, the Lord Jesus Christ." (Philippians 3:20)

In urging us to keep a heavenly perspective, Paul is not telling us to ignore the fact that we live in the world, to shirk our responsibilities, or to walk around with our heads in the clouds. Rather, he tells us to live our lives in light of eternity, with the assurance of the promise of heaven. It's because Christ was raised from the dead that we too shall be raised from the dead. This also means that we should continue faithfully and steadfastly in the Lord's work.

"Therefore, my dear brothers, stand firm. Let nothing move you. Always give yourself fully to the work of the Lord, because you know that your labor in the Lord is not in vain." (1 Corinthians 15:58)

Be steadfast, immovable, always abounding in the work of the Lord. Why? Because as Christians we know something very, very special—we are citizens of heaven, we are ambassadors for the true King Jesus Christ, and we are part of a kingdom that can never be destroyed. Therefore, we know that our labor in the Lord is not in vain! Christian, your day today has purpose and meaning—so go live it and make a mark that will last forever!

"Therefore, since we are receiving a kingdom that cannot be shaken, let us be thankful, and so worship God acceptably with reverence and awe." (Hebrews 12:28)

Take some time and thank the Lord for the fact that you're His. Also, thank Him for the fact that you have a home with Him in heaven! Then go out and represent your King and His kingdom—you will be amazed at how glorious your day will be.

How Do You Respond When You're Surprised?

(trials, trust)

How do you respond when you're surprised? More specifically, how do you respond when you're surprised by bad news? Perhaps it's the surprise of bad news in regards to work or school. Or, maybe it's the surprise of bad news when it comes to your family or your health. Whatever it may be, being surprised by bad news is a very real, yet very difficult part of life. We are not ready for bad news; it drains us and devastates us to the point that we have no strength.

"When David and his men came to Ziklag, they found it destroyed by fire and their wives and sons and daughters taken captive. So, David and his men wept aloud until they had no strength left to weep." (1 Samuel 30:3-4)

One day King David and his soldiers came to the town of Ziklag. Ziklag was the temporary headquarters for David and his army. It was also the place where David's family and the families of his soldiers were staying. Can you imagine the shock they experienced when they came to the city and couldn't find their families? However, things got even worse for David.

"David was greatly distressed because the men were talking of stoning him; each one was bitter in spirit because of his sons and daughters." (1 Samuel 30:6 a)

David was a king and military leader who was greatly used by God to lead the people of God. He had experienced many great victories because of the grace of God. He was faithful in his service to God, and was considered a man after God's own heart. Yet, look at all the bad news he suddenly had to deal with:

The city was destroyed by his enemies.

His family and the families of his soldiers were taken captive by his enemies.

His soldiers blamed him—to the point that they were thinking of killing him!

"But David found strength in the Lord his God." (1 Samuel 30:6)

Surprised by the sudden onslaught of bad news, David lost all of his strength. He was devastated by what he saw and he was distressed by what might happen to him. In fact, the Scriptures tell us that he wept so loud and so long that he finally ran out of strength to weep. That's how David reacted to the surprise of bad news. How about you? How do you handle the sudden onslaught of bad news? David was a real man who was experiencing real pain, and he dealt with it in a real way. He didn't bottle up his emotions, acting as though he was a rock of strength. Nor did he try to cope with his emotions in an unhealthy and ungodly way. He poured his heart out to the Lord, and eventually he found his strength in the Lord. Are you being real with your emotions right now? More specifically, are you being real before the Lord with your emotions right now? Are you opening up and being honest about your feelings? Or, are you acting as though you have everything under control and that the bad news you're dealing with is "simply a part of life?" Be careful, eventually those emotions are going to have to be dealt with. Better to pour your heart out to the Lord—(even weeping so long and so loud that you lose all of your strength)—than to ignore your pain or numb the pain in some unhealthy vice. In other words, being open and honest with the Lord is the prescribed path to finding your strength from the Lord.

"But he said to me, 'My grace is sufficient for you, for my power is made perfect in weakness.'" (2 Corinthians 12:9)

Do Not Envy Wicked Men

(character, relationships)

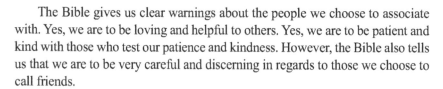

The Bible gives us clear warnings about the people we choose to associate with. Yes, we are to be loving and helpful to others. Yes, we are to be patient and kind with those who test our patience and kindness. However, the Bible also tells us that we are to be very careful and discerning in regards to those we choose to call friends.

"Do not make friends with a hot-tempered man, do not associate with one easily angered, or you may learn his ways and get yourself ensnared." (Proverbs 22:24-25)

Have you been careful in choosing those people with whom you're currently associating with? Or, have you been haphazard in making those choices; to the point that you're actually starting to mirror their behaviors? In other words, are you getting ensnared in the very activities and attitudes that you once had disdain for?

"Do not be misled: 'Bad company corrupts good character.' " (1 Corinthians 15:33)

Take some time to evaluate those relationships that you're involved in right now. Are these people inspiring you to grow closer to God or are they pulling you away from God? Remember, you can't control how others act, but you can control if their actions inspire you for good or bad. As Christians we are called to live to a higher standard. Let us make sure that we are careful not to compromise that standard for the sake of other people.

"Do not envy wicked men, do not desire their company; for their hearts plot violence, and their lips talk about making trouble." (Proverbs 24:1-2)

The Salt of the Earth

(relationships, character)

How is your saltiness? As Christians, we have a very clear mandate from Jesus Himself to make sure that we stay salty. How? Just as salt is used to prevent meat from decaying, we too are to live our lives in such a way (both verbally and visually) that we prevent the decay of this world. This also means that we have to be careful to not let our "salty lives" get contaminated with outside worldly influences.

"You are the salt of the earth. But if the salt loses its saltiness, how can it be made salty again? It is no longer good for anything, except to be thrown out and trampled by men." (Matthew 5:13)

How is your light shining? As Christians, we also have a clear mandate from Jesus to make sure that the light of Christ continues to shine in and through us. How? Just as light is used to dispel darkness, in like manner, we are to live our lives in such a way (both verbally and visually) that the light of Christ shines clearly into the darkness of others' lives. In doing this, and through God's grace, hearts and eyes will be opened to the glory of Christ and our heavenly Father will be praised.

"You are the light of the world. A city on a hill cannot be hidden. Neither do people light a lamp and put it under a bowl. Instead they put it on its stand, and it gives light to everyone in the house. In the same way, let your light shine before men, that they may see your good deeds and praise your Father in heaven." (Matthew 5:15-16)

As you start your day today, ask the Lord to help you be a salt-filled Christian. Ask the Lord to help you to be a light-shining Christian, so that those around you will be eternally impacted by your life. Give glory to the great God of heaven and earth.

Dealing with Criticism in a God-Glorifying Way

(character, trials)

How are you at handling criticism? Are you surprised when you're criticized, or do you expect it and deal with it in a God-glorifying way?

"However, I consider my life worth nothing to me, if only I may finish the race and complete the task the Lord Jesus has given me—the task of testifying to the gospel of God's grace." (Acts 20:24)

The apostle Paul had a calling from God and he wouldn't let anything or anybody stop him from fulfilling his calling—including criticism. He understood that criticism was inevitable. He wasn't afraid to keep moving forward regardless of what people thought or said.

"The fear of the Lord teaches a man wisdom and humility comes before honor." (Proverbs 15:33)

Criticism can be a good coach, in that, it can keep us humble. Perhaps we can find a kernel of truth in the criticism that can help us grow and succeed. Criticism can also be a good coach, in that; it reminds us that we are to seek the approval of God (who is always faithful) rather than the approval of man (who can be fickle).

It's important to understand that criticism is inevitable and we cannot avoid it. Therefore, we must not hide from it, but learn to deal it and overcome it. Otherwise, we may fall into the trap that Greek philosopher Aristotle warned against when he said: "Criticism is something that you can avoid easily—by saying nothing, doing nothing, and being nothing."

Opening a Door For God's Message

(evangelism, character)

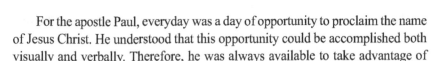

For the apostle Paul, everyday was a day of opportunity to proclaim the name of Jesus Christ. He understood that this opportunity could be accomplished both visually and verbally. Therefore, he was always available to take advantage of this opportunity, no matter how challenging the opposition.

"And pray for us, too, that God may open a door for our message, so that we proclaim the mystery of Christ, for which I am in chains. Pray that I may proclaim it clearly, as I should." (Colossians 4:3-4)

How about you? Are you prepared to take advantage of the opportunities to proclaim the name of the Lord Jesus Christ today? Are you prepared to proclaim the name of Jesus visually and verbally?

"Be wise in the way you act toward outsiders; make the most of every opportunity." (Colossians 4:5)

Today is a day where you can be wise in how you act towards those who are not in a saving relationship with Jesus. People are looking for hope, and they are looking for peace. Through your actions today, especially in how you handle challenging situations, people can see the true Source of your hope and peace. They can see that Jesus is alive and that He is active in and through your life. What an amazing privilege and honor!

"Let your conversation be always full of grace, seasoned with salt, so that you may know how to answer everyone." (Colossians 4:6)

Today is also a day where your words about Jesus can make an eternal difference in someone's life. Therefore, let your conversation be full of the wonderful news of God's saving grace through Jesus Christ. Remember, you don't have to sound like a preacher on the pulpit, you can be yourself. Simply explain: 1) Who Jesus is, 2) What Jesus has done for us on the cross, and 3) Why Jesus is the only way to eternal life. Who, What, and Why—simple, isn't it? Through your words today, eternal destinies can be impacted and the name of Jesus will be glorified. What an amazing privilege and honor!

Have You Forsaken Your First Love?

(love, relationship with God)

How is your love life? More specifically, how is your love life when it comes to Jesus? In Revelation 2, we see that the Christians in the church of Ephesus were phenomenal when it came to all the works they were doing. In fact, if there were ever a group of Christians that you would want to look upon as role models and to try to emulate, it seems it would be the group from Ephesus. They were busy in their service, they were patient in their sufferings, and they were orthodox in their beliefs (Revelation 2: 2-3). What more could possibly have been asked of them?

"Yet I hold this against you: You have forsaken your first love." (Revelation 2:4)

Despite all of their wonderful works, their hearts for Jesus had grown cold. Their earlier heights of love and devotion for Jesus had descended down to the depths of the mundane and the mediocre. They no longer had that fervent love for Jesus that they once had. Notice that Jesus did not say that they had lost their first love. He said that they had forsaken their first love. Meaning, they once were fervent in their love for Jesus, enjoying a relationship of holy intimacy with Jesus. But, over time they slowly turned their backs as it were and ended up taking their relationship with Jesus for granted, forsaking their first love. How did it happen? The external activity, the works for Jesus, ended up becoming much more important than the internal relationship, love for Jesus. In other words, duty ended up superseding devotion. This same problem can happen to us today as well. Perhaps we should all take a few moments and meditate on the following verses.

"I pray that out of his glorious riches he may strengthen you with power in your inner being, so that Christ may dwell in your hearts through faith. And I pray that you, being rooted and established in love, may have power, together with all the saints, to grasp how wide and long and high and deep is the love of Christ, and to know this love that surpasses knowledge—that you may be filled to the measure of all the fullness of God." (Ephesians 3:16-19)

Too Blessed to Be Stressed

(stress, thankfulness)

The Apostle Paul opens His letter to the Christians in Ephesus with one of the most amazing statements in all of Scripture.

"Praise be to the God and Father of our Lord Jesus Christ, who has blessed us in the heavenly realms with every spiritual blessing in Christ." (Ephesians 1:3)

What Paul was saying to them, and to us as well, is that every blessing of the Holy Spirit has been graciously given to us by God the Father because we are in Jesus, God the Son. No spiritual blessing has been withheld. Meaning, that as a Christian, everything that you need to become all that God wants you to be has already been placed on deposit in your heavenly bank account, with your name on it. All you have to do is draw on those blessings that are already on deposit in the account.

This is an amazing statement—and the apostle Paul thought so too. For as he sat there and thought about his heavenly bank account and all those spiritual blessings that God had graciously deposited in Paul's account; Paul realized that by God's grace, he was a spiritual millionaire. Now here's the interesting twist about all of this: Do you know where Paul was when he was focusing on his heavenly bank account, praising God and thanking him for making him a spiritual millionaire? Paul was a prisoner in Rome, under house arrest, handcuffed to a Roman soldier. Yet, despite Paul's stressful situation, his heart and mind was focused on heaven. His heart and mind was focused on his heavenly bank account and all of those spiritual blessings that God had deposited in his bank account. Spiritual blessings, that no doubt, Paul was drawing on that not only enabled him to patiently and faithfully persevere his prison experience; but spiritual blessings that Paul was drawing on that also enabled him to send this letter to the Christians in Ephesus. In this letter Paul's words literally were shouting, "Hey, don't worry about me! I'm in Christ—I'm too blessed to be stressed!"

Can you imagine what the Christians in Ephesus (knowing where Paul was) were thinking as they read this opening section of Paul's letter? How about the Roman soldier who was guarding Paul? Can you only imagine what he must have been thinking as he was listening to Paul praising God for blessing him so much? Can you only imagine if you and I shared in Paul's thinking—if you and I shared in Paul's Heavenly perspective? No doubt that you and I would also share in Paul's praise, right? No doubt that you and I would also realize that as Christians we are truly blessed. Too blessed to be stressed!

Live Your Life for the Lord

(relationships, forgiveness)

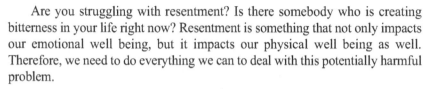

Are you struggling with resentment? Is there somebody who is creating bitterness in your life right now? Resentment is something that not only impacts our emotional well being, but it impacts our physical well being as well. Therefore, we need to do everything we can to deal with this potentially harmful problem.

"Get rid of all bitterness, rage and anger, brawling and slander, along with every form of malice. Be kind and compassionate to one another, forgiving each other, just as in Christ God forgave you." (Ephesians 4:31-32)

Scripture is clear that we need to let go of resentment and live a life of gratitude for the forgiveness we have received through Christ. As Christians we understand this, but how can we do this in a practical way?

Admit: The first step towards healing is to admit that we have resentment towards somebody else. We need to admit it to God, we need to admit it to ourselves and we may even need to admit it to others whom we trust. We must be open and honest about our struggle, recognizing that we are powerless to overcome our feelings of resentment on our own.

Release: The second step towards healing is to release the person with whom we are struggling. We need to release them to the point that we no longer will let them take up space in our minds. We need to release them to the point that we no longer will let them control our emotions. We also need to release them to the point that we no longer will try to impress them, finally recognizing that we will never be able to impress them anyway. Therefore, don't waste your time!

Refocus: The final step towards healing is to change our focus and start living to impress God. We need to remember that we answer to Him, not to others (this includes those with whom you were having those private mental and emotional battles!). Once you start to refocus on God's plan and purpose for your life; you will then start to get so busy living your life for the Lord that you won't have time to think about that other person. So start getting busy listening to and living for the Lord—He has plans for you!

"For we are God's workmanship [in the original Greek this means "masterpiece"], created in Christ Jesus to do good works, which God prepared in advance for us to do." (Ephesians 2:10)

The Ultimate in Wisdom

(wisdom, trust)

In difficult times like these, we need to be very wise in the decisions we make. We need to be wise when it comes to family decisions; we need to be wise when it comes to financial decisions, and we need to be wise when it comes to future decisions. Where do we find this type of wisdom; to be able to handle such a wide variety of important decisions? The apostle Paul tells us to look no further than to Jesus Christ.

"My purpose is that they may be encouraged in heart and united in love, so that they may have the full riches of complete understanding, in order that they may know the mystery of God, namely, Christ, in whom are hidden all treasures of wisdom and knowledge." (Colossians 2:2-3)

The apostle Paul tells us that in Jesus, there is a treasure box filled with all the wisdom we will ever need. Paul says that he wants us to understand this truth and approach Jesus with confidence that He will grant us the wisdom we need for any and every decision. But how can Paul be so confident?

"For in Christ all the fullness of the Deity lives in bodily form." (Colossians 2:9)

Jesus possesses the fullness of wisdom because He possesses the fullness of Deity. In other Words, Jesus is God. Therefore, He knows all, He sees all, and He has all the treasures of wisdom and understanding when it comes to our family, finances, and future!

"For by him all things were created: Things in heaven and on earth, visible and invisible, Whether thrones or powers or rulers or authorities; all things were created by him and for him. He is before all things, and in him all things hold together." (Colossians 1:16-17)

Seems like we should all start looking to Jesus and listening to Him when it comes to making wise decisions in these difficult times, doesn't it? As you start out your day today, rather than first turning on the TV or reading the newspaper, perhaps it makes more sense to spend some time talking to and listening to the only One who has all the answers that you will ever need. After all, Jesus will never lead you where His grace and wisdom cannot sustain you!

Having a Heart of Compassion

(compassion, character)

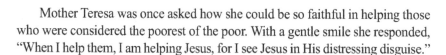

Mother Teresa was once asked how she could be so faithful in helping those who were considered the poorest of the poor. With a gentle smile she responded, "When I help them, I am helping Jesus, for I see Jesus in His distressing disguise."

"Then the righteous will answer him, 'Lord, when did we see you hungry and feed you, or thirsty and give you something to drink? When did we see you as a stranger and invite you in, or needing clothes and clothe you? When did we see you sick or in prison and go visit you?' The King will reply, 'I tell you the truth, whatever you did for one of the least of these brothers of mine, you did for me.'" (Matthew 25:37-40)

As Christians, we are called to Help those who are considered the least, the last, and the lost. In doing so, Jesus tells us that we are doing it for Him—we are helping Jesus in His "distressing disguise." As you prepare to face your day today, are you asking the Lord to help you see His face in those who need help? Are you asking the Lord to give you His heart of compassion for those who are hurting? Are you asking the Lord to give you His passion when it comes to doing something to bless another life?

"They will also answer, 'Lord, when did we see you hungry or thirsty or a stranger or needing clothes or sick or in prison, and did not help you?'" He will reply, 'I tell you the truth, whatever you did not do for one of the least of these, you did not do for me.'" (Matthew 25:44-45)

Like Mother Teresa, when you're asked today how you could be so faithful in helping those who are hurting; simply smile and say, "When I help them, I am helping Jesus, for I see Jesus in His distressing disguise."

Strength Through Weakness

(trials, trust, stress)

It's hard to walk in weakness, isn't it? Yet, it's through our weakness, God's grace is shown in and through our lives. In fact, people will often be impacted more by seeing God's grace through our weaknesses than they will be when we look like we are strong and seemingly have things together.

"That is why, for Christ's sake, I delight in weaknesses, in insults, in hardships, in persecutions, in difficulties. For when I am weak, then I am strong." (2 Corinthians 12:10)

The apostle Paul understood the paradox of strength through weakness. He also understood that his weakness didn't disqualify him from being used by God. Rather, his weakness was essential for him to be used by God. How did he come to that conclusion?

"But he [Jesus] said to me, 'My grace is sufficient for you, for my power is made perfect in weakness.' Therefore I will boast all the more gladly about my weaknesses, so that Christ's power may rest on me." (2 Corinthians 12:9-10)

Like the apostle Paul, our weakness is the perfect opportunity for Christ's perfect grace and His perfect power to strengthen us. Yes, it's difficult to always maintain this heavenly perspective. However, doesn't it make sense to be emptied of our strength and filled with the infinite strength of Christ? Doesn't it make sense to be emptied of our self-sufficiency and filled with the infinite grace of Christ that He tells us is sufficient for any and all circumstances? Perhaps strength through weakness isn't so bad after all!

"For our light and momentary troubles are achieving for us an eternal glory that far outweighs them all." (2 Corinthians 4:17)

Seek Help from the Lord

(stress, trust)

Are you feeling surrounded and overwhelmed by problems and pressures? Is it a struggle to figure out which course of action you should take today? If you're answering "Yes" to these questions, then you can certainly relate to a man named Jehoshaphat.

"O our God, will you not judge them? For we have no power to face this vast army that is attacking us. We do not know what to do, but our eyes are on you." (2 Chronicles 20:12)

Jehoshaphat was the king of Judah during a time when the people were being attacked from all sides by the enemy army. He felt overwhelmed and outnumbered, yet he led the people in the wisest thing they could do.

"Alarmed, Jehoshaphat resolved to inquire of the Lord, and He proclaimed a fast for all of Judah. The people of Judah came together to seek help from the Lord; indeed, they came from every town in Judah to seek him." (2 Chronicles 20:3-4)

As you're facing your problems and pressures, are you resolved to inquire of the Lord and to seek help from the Lord; or are you letting your panic cause you to make your own decisions apart from the Lord? Be careful, for we must remember that ultimately our battle is the Lord's battle, therefore we need to look to our Divine Warrior for comfort and clarity.

He said: "Listen, King Jehoshaphat and all who live in Judah and Jerusalem! This is what the Lord says to you: 'Do not be afraid or discouraged because of this vast army. For the battle is not yours, but God's.'" (2 Chronicles 20:15)

What incredible words of comfort and confidence! These words gave Jehoshaphat the faith to march forward trusting that the Lord would give him victory. The Lord gave him incredible victory over seemingly impossible odds (read 2 Chronicles 20 to see what happened!). These same words should also fortify our faith to march forward trusting that our God is able to overcome any and all challenges that we are facing. Inquire of the Lord, seek help from the Lord, walk forward by faith in the Lord, and remember that the battle is not ours, but the Lord's!

God Deserves Our All

(relationship with God, worship, God's will)

In the book of Deuteronomy, we find Moses giving his last speeches to the nation of Israel. As he is about to turn over the leadership reins to Joshua, Moses reminds them that their God is the true living God who reigns over heaven and earth. As a result, Moses explains to them that God deserves more than a passing nod from time to time. He deserves their attention and affection. He deserves their hearts and minds. God deserves their all.

" 'And now, O Israel, what does the Lord your God ask of you but to fear the Lord your God, to walk in all his ways, to love him, to serve him with all your heart and with all your soul, and to observe the Lord's commands and decrees that I am giving you today for your own good.' " (Deuteronomy 10:12-13)

God's people were to worship, love, obey and serve God. They were to do these things for God's honor as well as for their own good. A right attitude towards God would translate into a right way of living for the people. The same message applies to us today. When we strive to honor God in all that we say and do; God honors us by blessing our lives in ways that we can't imagine. However, we need to make sure that we do not strive to honor God simply because we want Him to bless us. No, the primary motivation for honoring God is because of Who He is and how He is.

"He is your praise; he is your God, who performed for you those great and awesome wonders you saw with your own eyes." (Deuteronomy 10:21)

When you start to think about all the awesome things God has done for you (especially to secure your salvation!), then you can't help but want to worship Him—to love Him, obey Him, and serve Him. You want to do this with your all. Why? Because God is your praise, He is your God!

Under His Perfect Control

(stress, trials, trust)

God knows your fears, your frustrations and your future. Did you hear that? God is in full control (He is sovereign) and God knows everything (He is omniscient). However, when it comes to your fears, your frustrations and your future, do you truly believe that?

"Remember the former things, those of long ago; I am God, and there is no other; I am God, and there is none like me. I make known the end from the beginning, from ancient times, what is still to come. I say: My purpose will stand, and I will do all that I please." (Isaiah 46:10)

This powerful verse shows several things about the greatness of God:

Nothing is equal with God: God does not share His position with anyone or anything. He is the only true living God of the universe. He is God, there is no other.

Nothing is confusing to God: God knows the end from the beginning. This means that He knows everything today that will happen in your tomorrow. This also means that absolutely nothing catches Him by surprise (even if it surprises us).

Nothing can change God's purposes: God has a perfect plan and purpose for your life. There is absolutely nothing (or no one) that can change God's plans for you. What God pleases, He will bring to pass.

Take some time right now to meditate on what God's sovereignty and God's omniscience means to your day today. Then, take some time to rejoice in this amazing truth: The awesome God of this universe has your fears, your frustrations and your future under His perfect control. Once you do that, then go enjoy this day that God has perfectly prepared for you!

Put On the Full Armor of God

(spiritual warfare, Satan)

The Bible tells us that there is someone who specializes in firing flaming darts of doubt at us. This someone is much more skilled than anyone we will ever face. The Bible describes him as a slanderer, an accuser, and opposer of God's people. In fact, Jesus Himself tells us that he is the biggest liar there is.

" 'When he lies, he speaks his native language, for he is a liar and the father of lies.' " (John 8:44)

We don't want to put Satan in the spotlight by bringing any unnecessary attention to him. However, if we are going to be faithful to the teaching of Scripture, we need to recognize that he is a reality. We also have to recognize that our Christian life is not a spiritual playground; rather it's a spiritual battleground.

"Put on the full armor of God so that you can take your stand against the devil's schemes. For our struggle is not against flesh and blood, but against the rulers, against the authorities, against the powers of this dark world and against the spiritual forces of evil in the heavenly realms." (Ephesians 6:11-12)

The good news for us as Christians is that when it comes to this spiritual battle, Satan cannot destroy us. The only thing he can do is shoot his darts of doubt at us. In fact, Jesus makes it very clear that there is absolutely nothing or nobody who can separate us from him.

" 'I give them eternal life, and they shall never perish; no one can snatch them out of my hand.' " (John 10:28)

Satan's strategy is very simple. He tries to get us to doubt God's love, he tries to get us to doubt God's promises, and he tries to get us to doubt God's care for us. It's the same thing that he tried to do to Jesus in the wilderness (see Matthew 4). However, take note of the three things Jesus did to overcome the deceiver and his flaming darts of doubt.

Jesus countered immediately: He didn't let the darts penetrate.
Jesus countered with Scripture: He used truth to overcome the lies.
Jesus countered with authority: He showed Satan who was in control.

As Christians, when the darts of doubt start flying our way today, we can follow the example of Jesus and be victorious. It takes discipline and it takes recognition. But, it's worth it. So, when the darts start coming, don't panic. Instead, counter immediately, counter with Scripture, and counter with the authority you have in Christ. Then, watch those darts wither into nothing

Following the Example of Jesus

(relationship with God, character)

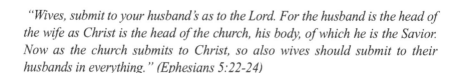

"Wives, submit to your husband's as to the Lord. For the husband is the head of the wife as Christ is the head of the church, his body, of which he is the Savior. Now as the church submits to Christ, so also wives should submit to their husbands in everything." (Ephesians 5:22-24)

It's amazing how many men know these verses, and how many women wish they didn't know these verses! However, these verses are not saying that a wife should be a slave to her husband. Rather, a wife should be a helper and respecter of her husband. She is to honor his leadership and support him by encouraging him (which sometimes includes telling him things he may not want to hear!).

"Husbands love your wives, just as Christ loved the church and gave himself up for her to make her holy, cleansing her by the washing with water through the word." (Ephesians 5:25-26)

It's amazing how many men forget these verses, and how many women wish men would remember them! Husbands are called to a very high standard when it comes to how we treat our wives. How high?

Husbands are to be lovers, not losers: Christ loved, He didn't abuse or disrespect. In like manner, husbands are to be lovers, not self-absorbed dictators.

Husbands are to be givers, not grabbers: Christ demonstrated His love by giving Himself up to save us from our sins. He came to serve, not to be served. In like manner, husbands are to serve their wives in a giving and self-sacrificial way.

Husbands are to be cleansers, not defilers: Christ prayed for and taught truth to His people. He cleansed them by bathing them in prayer and teaching them the Word of truth (His ultimate and perfect cleansing came at the cross). In like manner, husbands are to bathe their wives and families in prayer. Husbands are to bathe their marriage and household in God's truth—learning God's truth, obeying God's truth, and teaching God's truth.

Run to God

(relationship with God, peace, rest)

Life is difficult and crisis circumstances can arise at any time. Perhaps you may be experiencing one of those difficult crisis circumstances right now. How are you handling your crisis circumstance? Are you calling upon the Lord, or are you running from the Lord?

"I call with all my heart; answer me, O Lord, and I will obey your decrees. I call out to you; save me and I will keep your statutes." (Psalm 119:145-146)

The psalmist was experiencing a crisis situation and he was feeling powerless. Yet, he knew where to look for strength and hope. He prayed to God with "all his heart" and trusted that the Lord would hear him and rescue him. Interestingly, many people who experience crisis situations do the exact opposite of the psalmist. They either blame God or they try to run and hide from God. Are you one of those people right now?

"I rise before dawn and cry for help; I have put my hope in your word. My eyes stay open through the watches of the night that I may meditate on your promises." (Psalm 119:147-148)

Notice how the psalmist reacted to his crisis circumstance. He didn't run from God, he ran to God! In fact, he decided that prayer was more important than sleep! A wise person once said: "If a problem is important enough to worry about, then it's important enough to pray about." It seems that the psalmist thought his problems were so big that he needed to use as many hours as he could to pray to God. How about you? Do you think that it's time to stop running from God and start running to God? Make today a day where you spend some time in prayer, meditating on God's promises and looking to Him for your hope. If that means sacrificing some sleep, don't worry. Your time spent with God will be well worth it!

"Hear my voice in accordance with your love; preserve my life, O Lord, according to your laws." (Psalm 119:149)

The Lord's Purpose Prevails

(trust, future, legacy)

"I know that you can do all things; no plan of yours can be thwarted." (Job 42:2)

Do you believe that the Lord can overcome any and all the obstacles in your life right now? Do you believe that no one or nothing can stop God's purpose from being fulfilled in your life? Meditate on the above verse and rejoice in God's power and His perfect plan for you!

"Many are the plans in a man's heart, but it's the Lord's purpose that prevails." (Proverbs 19:21)

Man's plans fail, but God's purposes prevail! Do you believe that God has a wonderful purpose for your life? Do you believe that God's plans for you will absolutely prevail? Meditate on the above verse and rejoice in the fact that the Lord's purpose for you will not fail, rather it will prevail!

"For when David had served God's purpose in his own generation, he fell asleep." (Acts 13:36)

What an incredible legacy! David fulfilled God's purpose, and then he went home to be with the Lord. That is exactly what happened with my father this past February as well. Isn't that what you would like to have happen with your life? Mediate on the above verse and rejoice in the fact that your life down here on earth matters. Thank the Lord that He has a legacy that He wants you to leave. Ask the Lord to guide you to fulfill that legacy. Then go out and live a life that is truly worth living!

Special Creation of God

(identity, words)

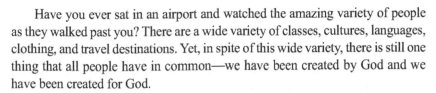

Have you ever sat in an airport and watched the amazing variety of people as they walked past you? There are a wide variety of classes, cultures, languages, clothing, and travel destinations. Yet, in spite of this wide variety, there is still one thing that all people have in common—we have been created by God and we have been created for God.

"You are worthy, our Lord and God, to receive glory and honor and power, for you created all things, and by your will they were created and have their being." (Revelation 4:11)

When was the last time you looked at a person as someone special who has been created by God and for God? If we are honest, many times we focus on the differences found in a person rather than focus on the dignity of that person as a special creation of God. Focusing on the differences often leads to criticism and condemnation. This is wrong and disrespectful, not only to the person, but also to God.

"With the tongue we praise our Lord and Father, and with it we curse men, who have been made in God's likeness. Out of the same mouth come praise and cursing. My brothers, this should not be." (James 3:9-10)

Very sobering words to all of us, aren't they? Perhaps we should all take some time and reflect on how we have been viewing others as of late. In fact, the next time we start to praise God with our mouths (at church or in our private devotions), maybe we should first ask ourselves if the same mouth has been blessing or cursing others.

"So God created man in his own image, in the image of God he created him; male and female he created them." (Genesis 1:27)

Let God Handle Things

(words, trust)

Is there someone in your life who has hurt you? If so, are you trying to figure out ways to get back or get even? Being hurt or betrayed by another person is very difficult to deal with (especially if that person is someone you trusted). However, the Bible gives us the proper perspective when it comes to retaliation and revenge.

"Do not say, 'I'll pay you back for this wrong!' Wait for the Lord, and he will deliver you." (Proverbs 20:22)

The Lord promises that He is the one who can and will straighten out the wrongs that have been inflicted upon us. We can trust this promise because the Lord never lies and the Lord is never late. However, the above verse tells us that there are two conditions that we must fulfill:

Watch our mouths: We are to refrain from making verbal threats towards those who are guilty of causing us pain. Why? Because it will only escalate the problem. In fact, though it may provide a few seconds of relief for us, making verbal threats will inevitably lead towards more anger and frustration. Therefore, get in the habit of taking your anger and frustration to the Lord. He understands and He is the One who will provide the peace to trust that He can and will deliver you.

Wait for the Lord: We are to trust that God's timing is perfect when it comes to handling the wrongs that have been inflicted upon us. However, it can be very difficult to wait upon the Lord. Why? Because we want immediate retribution and immediate results. This can be a huge trap because it may lead us to take matters into our own hands rather than trusting in the Lord's perfect timing and plans. Experience should tell all of us that nothing but more pain and frustration occurs when we attempt to bypass God's plans and try to rush God's timing.

"If it is possible, as far as it depends on you, live at peace with everyone. Do not take revenge, my friends, but leave room for God's wrath, for it is written, 'It is mine to avenge; I will repay,' says the Lord." (Romans 12:18-19)

Are you leaving any room for God to handle things? Or, are you taking up all the room?

God Is Our Deliverer

(trust, faith, stress)

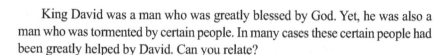

King David was a man who was greatly blessed by God. Yet, he was also a man who was tormented by certain people. In many cases these certain people had been greatly helped by David. Can you relate?

"I am forgotten by them as though I were dead; I have become like broken pottery. For I hear the slander of many; there is terror on every side; they conspire against me and plot to take my life." (Psalm 31:12-13)

Perhaps you don't have people who are actually plotting to take your life. However, you may have people who are slandering you, creating terror and turmoil in your life. How are you handling all of this? Are you listening to them and getting stressed? Or, are you looking up (like King David) and being blessed?

"But I trust in you, O Lord; I say, 'You're my God.' My times are in your hands; deliver me from my enemies and from those who pursue me." (Psalm 31:14-15)

Take a few moments and meditate on what David said. Read it slowly and really think about what he said. Now think about the fact, that we as Christians can say those same exact words! God is our God who has every aspect of our lives in His hands. He is our deliverer. Therefore, we can trust Him with absolutely everything in our lives, including our reputations that are being slandered!

"How great is your goodness, which you have stored up for those who fear you, which you bestow in the sight of men on those who take refuge in you. In the shelter of your presence you hide them from the intrigues of men; in your dwelling you keep them safe from accusing tongues." (Psalm 31:19-20)

God is your God; God is your refuge and shelter; God has every aspect of your life in His hands; and God is your Deliverer from those who are creating terror and turmoil by slandering you! Praise God!

True Source of Your Income

(finances, character, priorities)

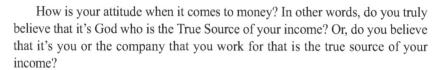

How is your attitude when it comes to money? In other words, do you truly believe that it's God who is the True Source of your income? Or, do you believe that it's you or the company that you work for that is the true source of your income?

"You may say to yourself, 'My power and the strength of my hands have produced this wealth for me.' But remember the Lord your God, for it is he who gives you the ability to produce wealth, and so confirms his covenant, which he swore to your forefathers, as it's today." (Deuteronomy 8:17-18)

God is the One who graciously provides us with the abilities and the opportunities to be able to produce income. Therefore, God not only deserves all the credit and praise, but He also deserves the first fruits of our income as well. Unfortunately, during difficult economic times like these, many seem to forget to honor God with their first fruits, rationalizing that we need it more than God does. But, take a look at what King David had to say about this.

"Wealth and honor come from you; you are the ruler of all things. In your hands are strength and power to exalt and give strength to all. Now, our God, we give you thanks, and praise your glorious name." (1 Chronicles 29:12-13)

David had no doubt that God was the sole reason that he was promoted to his position of king. David also had no doubt that God was the sole reason that he had the wealth and honor that he had. As a result, David clearly understood that everything he had was on loan, not something that he owned. How about you? Do you feel that everything you have is on loan from God? Or, do you feel that you own everything as a result of the work of your hands? The answer to these questions has a direct correlation to your attitude when it comes to money—and to giving.

"Who am I, and who are my people, that we should be able to give as generously as this? Everything comes from you, and we have given you only what comes from your hand." (1 Chronicles 29:14)

Worship the Lord with Gladness

(praise, thankfulness, relationship with God)

"Shout for joy to the Lord, all the earth. Worship the Lord with gladness; come before him with joyful songs." (Psalm 100:1-2)

How are we to respond to the greatness of God? We are to shout for joy, worship Him with gladness, and sing joyful songs. In other words, the Lord doesn't want meaningless lip service. Rather, the Lord wants our hearts and our heads. He wants our all. Why?

"Know that the Lord is God. It is he who made us, and we are his, we are his people, the sheep of his pasture." (Psalm 100:2-3)

Why do we respond to the greatness of God with unbridled joy? Because, He is the Lord. He is the maker and owner of all things. He is the One who chose to create and shape us. He is the One who chose to bring us to Himself through Jesus Christ. As Christians, we are His and He is our ever-faithful shepherd. Why praise God with unbridled joy? Why not!

"Enter his gates with thanksgiving and his courts with praise; give thanks to him and praise his name. For the Lord is good and his love endures forever; his faithfulness continues through all generations." (Psalm 100:4-5)

In a world where love and faithfulness can be fickle, we have a God whose love endures forever and whose faithfulness never stops. Therefore, let the Lord hear you! Shout for joy, worship Him with gladness and sing joyful songs of praise and thanks to Him. Our great God is worthy of our all!

Follow the Example of Christ

(actions, character, evangelism)

The apostle Paul was a man who not only loved Jesus, but he was also a man who lived to represent Jesus before others. Paul also understood that the example of his life could make a huge impact in other lives.

"Follow my example, as I follow the example of Christ." (1 Corinthians 11:1)

Paul was able to confidently invite people to follow the example of His life. He was certain that people would benefit from following his example. How could he be so confident? Paul was certain that people would benefit from his example because He was certain that he was following the example of Christ. How about you? Can people learn what Christ-like living is by following your example? Are people willing to follow you because they trust that you're truly following Christ?

"I praise you for remembering me in everything and for holding to the teachings, just as I passed them on to you." (1 Corinthians 11:2)

As Christians, we have the unspeakable privilege of representing Christ before a watching world. We can represent Him both verbally and visually. In fact, today you have the opportunity to set an incredible example as you follow the example of Christ. Think about it, your family can be blessed by following that example. Your friends and coworkers can be blessed by following that example. Even strangers can be blessed by your Christ-like example today!

"Whatever you have learned or received or heard from me, or seen in me—put into practice. And the God of peace will be with you." (Philippians 4:9)

Seek the Wisdom of God

(wisdom, trust)

Are you looking for wisdom to help you through some challenging times right now? The Bible is very clear that we can either follow the wisdom of the world or we can follow the wisdom of God's Word. Which one are you looking to follow today?

"Counsel and judgment are mine; I have understanding and power." (Proverbs 8:14)

Are you in need of good counsel and discerning judgment? Can you use some keen understanding and confident power to courageously step forward today? Well, wisdom says that she possesses those very things that you're in desperate need of! She invites you right now to come to her and receive the wisdom you need for today (the book of Proverbs often refers to wisdom in the feminine sense).

"I love those who love me, and those who seek me find me." (Proverbs 8:17)

Wisdom tells us she delights in those who seek her. Wisdom also tells us that we will (not might!) find her. However, we need to be proactive and come to her. Far too often we rush into our day without first seeking the wisdom of God. We don't take the time to read God's Book of wisdom, the Bible. We don't take the time in prayer to listen to the wisdom that comes from the Spirit of God. As a result, we end up going out into the world and living our day at the mercy of the wisdom of the world. No wonder we become frustrated and confused!

"My fruit is better than fine gold; what I yield surpasses choice silver. I walk in the way of righteousness, along the paths of justice, bestowing wealth on those who love me and making their treasuries full." (Proverbs 8:19-21)

Focus on Loving God and Others
(trials, character, words)

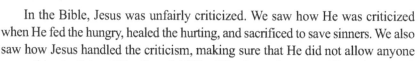

In the Bible, Jesus was unfairly criticized. We saw how He was criticized when He fed the hungry, healed the hurting, and sacrificed to save sinners. We also saw how Jesus handled the criticism, making sure that He did not allow anyone or anything to distract Him from fulfilling His plan and purpose. How about you? How are you handling the criticism that has been coming your way as of late?

Three Practical Points

Don't chase the critics.

"My dear brothers, take note of this: Everyone should be quick to listen, slow to speak and slow to become angry." (James 1:19)

Christian, don't let the critics distract you! The devil would love to see you stop what you're doing and chase down all of your critics. Why? So that you can get distracted and discouraged from fulfilling God's plan for you—a plan that brings glory to God. Yet it's hard to not react and go after the critics, isn't it? That's why Scripture tells us to be quick to listen, slow to speak, and slow to anger. As I write this, I am amazed at how often I am slow to listen, quick to speak, and quick to get angry. Can you relate? We need to understand that not all criticism is bad. A wise person once said; critics can actually be good coaches. How? They can help us recognize things that we need to work on, things that can help us grow into the type of people that bring glory to our great God. That's why we need to be quick to listen, to see if there is any truth to the criticism. If there is, learn from it and grow from it. If there is no truth to it, then brush it off and continue to go forward.

Don't argue with the critics.

"As charcoal to embers and as wood to fire, so is a quarrelsome man for kindling strife." (Proverbs 26:21)

Christian, don't add fuel to the fire! Why argue with a person who is already looking for reasons to criticize you? Why put yourself in a position to hear more and more criticism from that person? A wise person once said: "Criticism often stings like a bee sting." However, far too often we end up turning it into a snake bite. What did this person mean? When we spend our time chasing down and arguing with our critics, we are also spending time reminding ourselves of their criticism against us. We start to dwell on the criticism, we think all kinds of thoughts about the critic, and we end up turning our little bee stings into a snake bite!

Don't become a critic.

"When words are many, sin is not absent, but he who holds his tongue is wise." *(Proverbs 10:19)*

Christian, don't become a critic! That doesn't mean that we condone sin and let people dishonor God. But we do not need to become a carbon-copy of the very critics who have criticized us. In other words, we need to become more like Christ, not like the critic! First, we want our words to be edifying to people and glorifying to God. Second, we have a plan and purpose that God wants us to fulfill. Therefore, we need to spend our time loving God and loving others in a way that makes a difference for eternity. We have been given gifts from God and an expectation by God to take advantage of the opportunities that God provides us. Doesn't it make more sense to focus on that, rather than on our critics?

" 'I have brought you glory on earth by completing the work you gave me to do.'" *(John 17:4)*

The Power Is in God's Word

(the Bible, character)

Jeremiah was a prophet of God who was trying to tell other people about the greatness of God. However, his message was not being enthusiastically accepted. In fact, not only did his message lead to ridicule and rejection, but it also led to intense persecution. This caused Jeremiah to wonder if what he was doing was actually worth it. It also caused him to wonder if he should simply stay silent and not talk about God at all.

"Whenever I speak, I cry out proclaiming violence and destruction. So the word of the Lord has brought me insult and reproach all day long. But if I say, 'I will not mention him or speak any more in His name,' His word is in my heart like a fire, a fire shut up in my bones. I am weary of holding it in; indeed, I cannot." (Jeremiah 20:8-9)

Like Jeremiah, all Christians are called to tell others about the greatness of God. This doesn't mean that all are called to be pastors or preachers. Rather, all are called to share the "Who" and "What" of God. We are called to share who God is and what He has done in our lives. Sounds simple, doesn't it? Yet, so many of us often feel like Jeremiah and would rather remain silent than endure ridicule and rejection from others. Perhaps you're feeling that way right now. Perhaps you're feeling weary of holding back God's Word because you know that you're not doing what you're called to do. How can we overcome our fears and frustrations? By remembering what God says about His powerful Word:

" 'Is not my word like fire,' declares the Lord, 'and like a hammer that breaks a rock into pieces?' " (Jeremiah 23:29)

The power is found in God's Word, not in the person who proclaims it. No matter how hard some hearts may seem when it comes to God's Word; the above verse reminds us, God's Word is like a sledgehammer that can break even the hardest of hearts. Therefore, like Jeremiah, we are called to share God's truth and leave the changing of hearts to the grace of God. This means that silence is not an option for Christians! Instead, we need to pray to the Lord and ask Him to give us the courage and confidence to share the greatness of God that is found in the Word of God.

" 'Ah, Sovereign Lord,' I said, 'I do not know how to speak; I am only a child.' But the Lord said to me, 'Do not say, "I am only a child." You must go to everyone I send you to and say whatever I command you. Do not be afraid of them, for I am with you and will rescue you,' declares the Lord." (Jeremiah 1:6-8)

How Great Is God's Compassion

(compassion, forgiveness)

"Who is a God like you, who pardons sin and forgives the transgression of the remnant of his inheritance? You do not stay angry forever but delight to show mercy." (Micah 7:18)

Are you struggling with guilt right now? Do you feel that your sins are so big that God can't or won't forgive you? Take a look at the above verse and think about this, how great is the mercy of God!

"You will again have compassion on us; you will tread our sins underfoot and hurl our iniquities into the depths of the sea." (Micah 7:19)

Are you in desperate need of some compassion right now? Do you need the comfort of knowing that you're loved by God? Take a look at the above verse and see this, how great is the compassion of God! Do you see what He does with our sins? Take a second and think about what happens to something that sinks to the bottom of the ocean. It's gone forever. That is exactly what God does with our sins through Jesus Christ!

" 'No longer will a man teach his neighbor, or a man his brother, saying, "Know the Lord," because they will all know me, from the least of them to the greatest,' declares the Lord. 'For I will forgive their wickedness and will remember their sins no more.' " (Jeremiah 31:34)

God forgives our sins completely because Jesus was punished for our sins completely. Not only was He punished for our sins as our substitute; He paid for our sins completely. Therefore, if we have trusted in the completely sufficient substitutionary work of Jesus, and we have received His free gift of saving grace, then you need to know God says that you're completely forgiven! Know that completely means completely!

"Then he adds: 'Their sins and lawless acts I will remember no more.' And where these have been forgiven, there is no longer any sacrifice for sin." (Hebrews 10:17-18)

Be Patient and Understanding with Each Other

(relationships, character)

As Christians, we are called to show patience and understanding to our brothers and sisters in Christ. The Bible exhorts us to help, not hurt; to build up, not tear down; to encourage, not discourage.

"We who are strong ought to bear with the failings of the weak and not to please ourselves. Each of us should please his neighbor for his good, to build him up." (Romans 15:1-2)

We must be careful to not read the above verses and think that this is a call to accept or ignore the sins of others. No, these verses tell us that we need to exercise patience and use the failings of others as an opportunity to teach them. The failings of others (especially young Christians) are to be expected. After all, none of us are perfect—including us! Therefore, we need to look for "teachable moments" where we can use the failings of others as a springboard to launch them to maturity in Christ. What should be our primary motivation for doing this?

"For even Christ did not please himself but, as it's written: 'The insults of those who insult you have fallen on me.'" (Romans 15:3)

Why do we need to bear up with the failings of the weak? Because that is exactly what Christ has done for us! Why do we need to be patient and look to bless instead of curse? Because that is exactly what Christ did for us? That is why consistent time in the Bible will give us the correct perspective and motivation when it comes to dealing with others. In fact, if you're struggling when it comes to dealing with the shortcomings of other Christians, maybe you need to look at how much time you have spent in the Scriptures lately.

"For everything that was written in the past was written to teach us, so that through endurance and the encouragement of the Scriptures we might have hope." (Romans 15:4)

A Gift to Be Received

(salvation, sin)

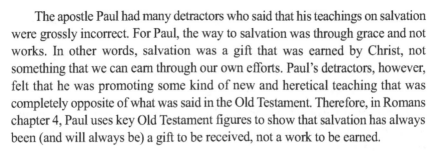

The apostle Paul had many detractors who said that his teachings on salvation were grossly incorrect. For Paul, the way to salvation was through grace and not works. In other words, salvation was a gift that was earned by Christ, not something that we can earn through our own efforts. Paul's detractors, however, felt that he was promoting some kind of new and heretical teaching that was completely opposite of what was said in the Old Testament. Therefore, in Romans chapter 4, Paul uses key Old Testament figures to show that salvation has always been (and will always be) a gift to be received, not a work to be earned.

Paul makes the point that Abraham was saved by grace and not through his own good works:

"What shall we say that Abraham, our forefather, discovered in this matter? If, in fact, Abraham was justified by works, he had something to boast about—but not before God. What does the Scripture say? 'Abraham believed God and it was credited to him as righteousness.'" (Romans 4:1-3)

Paul also uses the example of King David to make the point that salvation is a gift from God:

"Now when a man works, his wages are not credited to him as a gift, but as an obligation. However, to the man who does not work but trusts God who justifies the wicked, his faith is credited as righteousness. David says the same thing when he speaks of the blessedness of the man to whom God credits righteousness apart from works: 'Blessed are they whose transgressions are forgiven, whose sins are covered. Blessed is the man whose sin the Lord will never count against him.'" (Romans 4:4-8)

Abraham and David were both saved by the grace of God. Paul also was saved by the grace of God, and he preached that salvation was through grace alone, by faith alone, in Christ alone, to the glory of God alone. How do you feel that you will be saved? Are you counting on your good works to get you into heaven, or are you counting only on what Christ has done for you through His death and resurrection? Take some time to really think about your answer to those two questions. Why? Because your answer has eternal consequences!

There Is No Such Thing as Luck

(purpose, future)

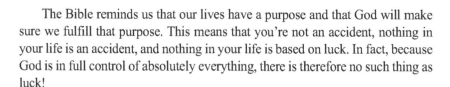

The Bible reminds us that our lives have a purpose and that God will make sure we fulfill that purpose. This means that you're not an accident, nothing in your life is an accident, and nothing in your life is based on luck. In fact, because God is in full control of absolutely everything, there is therefore no such thing as luck!

"All the days ordained for me were written in your book before one of them came to be." (Psalm 139:16)

God tells us that He has planned your days and your steps. God tells us that every one of your days matters (including today!). This means that today is not some purposeless waste of time. No, your day has been specially designed by the great God of this universe. He designed this day before you were ever born! Like an actor in a play, you have been given a script by the divine Director who will make sure that your life becomes a hit!

"My times are in your hands; deliver me from my enemies and from those who pursue me." (Psalm 31:15)

God is saying that He has absolutely everything under control. Do not worry, time won't run out. Why? Because God has your time in His hand! Do not worry; your enemies will never be able to stop you from fulfilling God's purpose for your life. Why? Because God has your time in His hand! Therefore, rejoice in this day God has given you. Make sure to thank God that He has a perfect plan and purpose for you!

Prayer Is Powerful and Effective

(prayer)

One of my seminary professors once told me that as I stand up and preach, I can safely assume that about one third of the people who are listening are right in the middle of some very difficult and challenging circumstances. He also told me that I can safely assume that another third of the people are just starting to come out of what has been very difficult and challenging circumstances. The remaining third of the people—take a guess—they are about to go into some very difficult and challenging circumstances. Well, needless to say, this thing called life can be a very, very tough thing to try to go through—right? So, how do we do it?

"So he said to me, 'This is the word of the Lord to Zerubbabel: Not by might nor by power, but by my Spirit,' says the Lord Almighty." (Zechariah 4:6)

You know, it has been said that Satan trembles when even the weakest Christian is down on his/her knees in prayer. That's because Satan knows that when we are down on our knees, he doesn't stand a chance. Satan clearly recognizes that our Christian life is not a spiritual playground, but rather, it's a spiritual battleground. He knows that the weapon we possess in our spiritual arsenal—the weapon of prayer—is a weapon that he can't possibly overcome.

"Pray in the Spirit on all occasions with all kinds of prayers and requests. With this in mind, be alert and always keep on praying for all the saints." (Ephesians 6:18)

Notice how many "alls" are in that verse? Do you see how important prayer is? In fact, from one end of this Bible to the other, Satan has watched as God's people have dropped down to their knees. They have fervently and earnestly prayed to God. Satan has seen how God has not only answered their prayers, but he has seen how God has answered those prayers in ways that were immeasurably greater than those people could have even hoped for or imagined. It's safe to say that when the Bible tells us in the book of James that the prayers of God's people are powerful and effective that Satan really believes that. But do you believe that?

"The prayer of a righteous man is powerful and effective." (James 5:16)

Freedom from the Fear of Death

(fear, death, salvation)

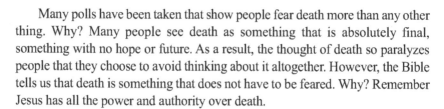

Many polls have been taken that show people fear death more than any other thing. Why? Many people see death as something that is absolutely final, something with no hope or future. As a result, the thought of death so paralyzes people that they choose to avoid thinking about it altogether. However, the Bible tells us that death is something that does not have to be feared. Why? Remember Jesus has all the power and authority over death.

"I am the Living One; I was dead, and behold I am alive forever and ever! And I hold the keys of death and Hades." (Revelation 1:18)

Through His death and resurrection, Jesus decisively defeated our two arch enemies: Sin and death. Jesus didn't just simply defeat sin and death; He victoriously triumphed over them as the conquering King!

"Having disarmed the powers and authorities, he made a public spectacle over them, triumphing over them by the cross." (Colossians 2:15)

What does all of this mean for us? As Christians, we do not have to fear death because Jesus has all power over death. Jesus has all power over death because He triumphed over sin and death by the cross. As the conquering King, Jesus holds the keys to death and says, "I am in control! Those who come to me are free! Death is not the end, it's a continuation of life with me forever!"

"Since the children have flesh and blood, he too shared in their humanity so that by his death He might destroy him who holds the power of death—that is, the devil—and free those who all their lives were held in slavery by their fear of death." (Hebrews 2:14-15)

Freedom from the slavery of death. Freedom from the fear of death. Freedom to live with God forever. How is this all possible? Only through the death and resurrection of our great Lord and Savior, Jesus Christ!

"To him who is able to keep you from falling and to present you before his glorious presence without fault and great joy—to the only God our Savior be glory, majesty, power and authority, through Jesus Christ our Lord, before all ages, now and forever more! Amen." (Jude 24-25)

A Channel of God's Peace

(relationships, actions, character)

Human relationships can be challenging. Why? Because people are different: We have different needs, different habits, and different ways of communicating. As a result, we need to work hard at getting along with each other. In some instances, we have to work very, very hard! Are you dealing with any challenging relationships in your life right now? If your answer is "yes" then perhaps you should take a look at what the Bible has to say about this.

"Love must be sincere. Hate what is evil; cling to what is good. Be devoted to one another in brotherly love. Honor one another above yourselves. Never be lacking in zeal, but keep your spiritual fervor, serving the Lord. Be joyful in hope, patient in affliction, and faithful in prayer. Share with God's people who are in need. Practice hospitality." (Romans 12:9-13)

Love one another, be sincere and devoted to one another, honor each other, keep up your spiritual fervor, and be joyful and patient with each other. How is this all possible? How can we follow the teaching of these verses when we are in the midst of very challenging relationships? The key is found in the last three words of verse 12: Be faithful in prayer. Through prayer we gain the proper perspective. Through prayer we are able to enjoy and appreciate the love of God, which in turn can lead to the love of others. A great example of this is found in the prayer of Mother Teresa , a woman who is famous worldwide for her selfless love, "Lord, help me be a channel of Your peace. That where there is hatred, I may bring love; that where there is wrong, I may bring the spirit of forgiveness; that where there is discord, I may bring harmony; that where there is error, I may bring truth; that where there is doubt, I may bring faith."

"If it is possible, as far as it depends on you, live at peace with everyone." (Romans 12:18)

Perhaps we should all take a few moments and reflect on how we are dealing with the various relationships in our lives right now. Are we doing everything we can to live at peace with those people? In other words, are we being faithful in prayer?

How Are You Sleeping at Night?

(rest, purpose, wisdom)

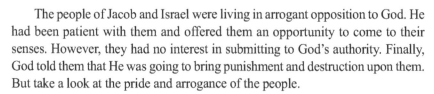

The people of Jacob and Israel were living in arrogant opposition to God. He had been patient with them and offered them an opportunity to come to their senses. However, they had no interest in submitting to God's authority. Finally, God told them that He was going to bring punishment and destruction upon them. But take a look at the pride and arrogance of the people.

"The bricks have fallen down, but we will rebuild with dressed stone; the fig trees have been felled, but we will replace them with cedars." (Isaiah 9:10)

Basically, the people were saying that no matter what God did to them, they would still be able to succeed on their own. They felt they were strong enough and smart enough to accomplish anything. They didn't need God and made it very clear by saying "we will rebuild, we will replace." Unfortunately, their "we will" attitude is still prevalent today. As we are in the midst of some very challenging times, many people refuse to look to God for wisdom and guidance and instead reflect the arrogant attitude of the people during Isaiah's time; "We will rebuild our bank accounts, and we will replace our difficulties with our own success." But take a look at what the Bible says.

"Unless the Lord builds the house, its builders labor in vain. Unless the Lord watches over the city, the watchmen stand guard in vain. In vain you rise early and stay up late, toiling for food to eat—for he grants sleep to those he loves." (Psalm 127:1-2)

As you're looking to build or rebuild things in your life, are you reflecting a "He will" or a "we will" attitude? Are you seeking God's wisdom and guidance, or are you trusting in your own wisdom and guidance? Perhaps a good indicator as to which attitude you're reflecting is to ask yourself the question: "How am I sleeping at night?"

God Judges Our Success

(obedience, success)

From a human standpoint, it's easy to see why Jeremiah complained to God so much. This was a man who served as God's spokesman to Judah for forty years. Yet when he spoke, nobody seemed to listen. Consistently and passionately he urged the people to repent and turn to God, but nobody moved. He was poor and underwent severe difficulties to deliver his prophesies. He was thrown into prison, into a cistern, and he was taken to Egypt against his will. He was rejected by his neighbors, his family and friends, his audience, and the kings. Throughout his life, Jeremiah stood alone, declaring God's message at a huge cost. In the eyes of the world, Jeremiah was not a success.

"O Lord, you deceived me, and I was deceived, you overpowered me and prevailed. I am ridiculed all day long; everyone mocks me. Whenever I speak, I cry out proclaiming the violence and destruction. So the word of the Lord has brought me insult and reproach all day long." (Jeremiah 20:7-8)

Can you relate to Jeremiah's feelings of frustration and fear? Perhaps you have been feeling like your efforts in telling others about the Lord have been a complete waste. Perhaps you have been laughed at and ridiculed, just as Jeremiah was. But in God's eyes, Jeremiah was one of the most successful people in all of history. Success, as measured by God, involves obedience and faithfulness. Regardless of opposition and personal cost, Jeremiah courageously and faithfully proclaimed the Word of God. Jeremiah had to depend on God's love as He developed endurance. It's the same with us. God calls us to be obedient, to trust in Him, and to answer His call—no matter the cost. Although we may feel like our efforts are not producing the fruit we had anticipated, we need to remember that God has the power to reap an abundant harvest if we just don't give up. In fact, God is doing a great work in those very areas where He may seem to be the most absent to you right now!

"Let us not become weary in doing good, for at the proper time we will reap a harvest if we do not give up." (Galatians 6:9)

Trust God to Strengthen You

(trust, fear, trials)

Being in a position of leadership often puts the leader in a position for criticism and unfair accusations. Nehemiah was not an exception to this rule. The wall was almost complete and the opposition's efforts to stop its construction were failing. So, they tried a new approach, centering their attacks on Nehemiah's character. They attacked him personally with rumors, deceit, and false reports. By God's grace, Nehemiah was able to show that these accusations were empty and false. He could prove that these accusations were unfounded, because he lived a life that showed that these accusations were unfounded. Are you dealing with some criticism and unfair accusations right now?

" 'Hear us, O our God, for we are despised. Turn their insults back on their own heads. Give them over as plunder in a land of captivity. Do not cover up their guilt or blot out their sins from your sight, for they have thrown insults in the face of the builders.' " (Nehemiah 4:4-5)

Notice how Nehemiah handled all the attacks on his character. He didn't panic nor pout, he prayed. He continued to keep focused on the task that the Lord gave him to do. Personal attacks hurt, and when the criticism is unjustified, it's easy to despair. We need to understand that we are unable to control these attacks on our character, but we are able to control the validity of these attacks. It's amazing how living a God-centered life of integrity somehow diffuses the worst of these character criticisms. We must learn to follow Nehemiah's example and trust God to strengthen us to overlook unjustified abuse. When opposition builds up against God's people and His work, it's tempting to pray, "God get me out of this situation." But take a look at how Nehemiah prayed:

"But I prayed, 'Now strengthen my hands.' " (Nehemiah 6:9)

Nehemiah showed tremendous determination and character to remain steadfast in his responsibility. This is a great example for all of us today. With the privilege of representing God comes the responsibility of living a life that is worthy of this call—a privilege and responsibility that Nehemiah certainly understood.

"Do not say, 'I'll pay you back for this wrong!' Wait for the Lord, and he will deliver you." (Proverbs 20:22)

Serve the Lord Our God

(priorities, legacy)

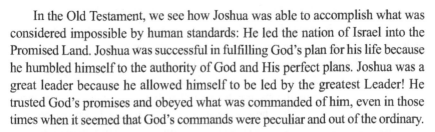

In the Old Testament, we see how Joshua was able to accomplish what was considered impossible by human standards: He led the nation of Israel into the Promised Land. Joshua was successful in fulfilling God's plan for his life because he humbled himself to the authority of God and His perfect plans. Joshua was a great leader because he allowed himself to be led by the greatest Leader! He trusted God's promises and obeyed what was commanded of him, even in those times when it seemed that God's commands were peculiar and out of the ordinary.

" 'But as for me and my household, we will serve the Lord.' " (Joshua 24:15)

Besides fulfilling his call as God's instrument in leading Israel into the Promised Land, Joshua also made sure to prepare the next generation for their responsibility of obeying and following the One True God of Israel. He understood his responsibility of placing the faith firmly in the hands of the next generation. The evidence of Joshua's success is perfectly summarized in the following verse:

"Israel served the Lord all the days of Joshua and all the days of the elders who survived Joshua, and had known all the deeds of the Lord that he had done for Israel." (Joshua 24:31)

Joshua led the people by word and example. His legacy carried on long after he died. What will be your legacy that you leave behind? Will your household still serve the Lord long after you're gone? Will your friends or coworkers be able to say that your words and actions truly impacted them for good? Each day our lives are making a difference, either for good or for bad. May we all think about that as we face our day today.

" 'Now then,' said Joshua, 'throw away the foreign gods that are among you and yield your hearts to the Lord, the God of Israel.' And the people said to Joshua, 'We will serve the Lord our God and obey him.' " (Joshua 24:23-24)

The Lord Is There

(trust, peace)

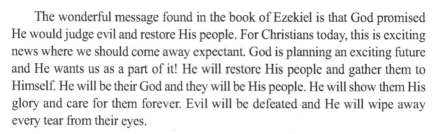

The wonderful message found in the book of Ezekiel is that God promised He would judge evil and restore His people. For Christians today, this is exciting news where we should come away expectant. God is planning an exciting future and He wants us as a part of it! He will restore His people and gather them to Himself. He will be their God and they will be His people. He will show them His glory and care for them forever. Evil will be defeated and He will wipe away every tear from their eyes.

"The name of the city from that time on will be: The Lord is There." (Ezekiel 48:35)

The Lord Is There! Can you only imagine what that will be like? Certainly it will be beyond our wildest imaginations! The triumph of God over evil is a triumph for His people. God's people win because God wins. As God's people turn to Him in large numbers, they will realize that He alone is God, and that He will be their God and they will be His people forever. As Christians, and through the indwelling of the Holy Spirit, we are able to enjoy a foretaste of what is guaranteed to come. What a glorious guarantee that truly is!

"You were also included in Christ when you heard the word of truth, the gospel of your salvation. Having believed, you were marked in him with a seal, the promised Holy Spirit, who is a deposit guaranteeing our inheritance until the redemption of those who are God's possession—to the praise of his glory." (Ephesians 1: 13-14)

Meditate on the above verses for a few minutes. Think about what they mean to your life both now and in the future. Think about the fact that you have been sealed by God, for life with God, and this life is both now and forever more. Now ask yourself this question, "Are the challenges I am facing today truly worth stressing over?" When you really think about it, as Christians, we are too blessed to be stressed!

The Lamb of God

(sin, salvation)

The Day of Atonement was the holiest day in the Old Testament calendar. It was the day when annual atonement was made for the sins of the nation. The rituals and sacrifices proceeded according to the following steps:

The high priest washed and dressed, and then sacrificed a bull as a sin offering for himself.

He entered the Most Holy Place and sprinkled the ark with blood.

He took two goats and by lot chose one to be the scapegoat, the other to be the sin offering.

After sacrificing one goat as the sin offering, he then sprinkled blood on the ark, the outer part of the tabernacle of meeting, and the main alter.

He confessed the sins of the Israelites as he laid hands on the scapegoat's head and then sent the scapegoat into the desert. By doing this, the high priest transferred those sins to the goat and the goat then symbolically carried the people's sins away into the desert.

Christians have long regarded the scapegoat as a type of Christ. The New Testament makes many comparisons between the Day of Atonement and the death of Christ (see Hebrews 9:6-28, 13:11-13). Like the scapegoat of old, Christ was delivered "outside the camp" to be killed outside the walls of Jerusalem.

"So Jesus also suffered outside the city gate to make the people holy through His own blood." (Hebrews 13:12)

As Jesus hung on the cross, God the Father took the sins of His people—past, present and future—and placed them on His Son. Then the Father punished Jesus in our place. Jesus took our sins and then He took the full punishment, condemnation and judgment those sins deserve. He actually became sin in our place. The Father poured out His wrath on His Son bearing our sins and being condemned in our place—Jesus became our substitute. As our sin offering, He is the perfect sacrificial Lamb, who takes away the sins of His people!

"The next day John saw Jesus coming toward him and said, 'Look, the Lamb of God, who takes away the sin of the world!'" (John 1:29)

The Work of the Holy Spirit
(Holy Spirit, spiritual gifts)

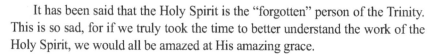

It has been said that the Holy Spirit is the "forgotten" person of the Trinity. This is so sad, for if we truly took the time to better understand the work of the Holy Spirit, we would all be amazed at His amazing grace.

The Holy Spirit is necessary for rebirth. In John 3, Jesus tells Nicodemus, " 'I tell you the truth no one can enter the Kingdom of God unless he is born of water and the Spirit. Flesh gives birth to flesh, but Spirit gives birth to spirit.' " (John 3:5-6)

Regeneration is the gift of God's grace. It's the immediate, supernatural work of the Holy Spirit where He takes an unbeliever from spiritual death to spiritual life.

Before His death, Jesus promised that He and the Father would send to His disciples "another Helper" (John 14:16; 14:26; 15:26; 16:7). The promised Holy Spirit acts as our advocate (1 John 2:1) and Defender before the Father, as well as continually providing encouragement, counsel, and strength for those in whom He dwells.

The Holy Spirit carries on the teaching and testimony that Jesus began (John 14:26). He also testifies and bears witness about Jesus. (John 15:26)

The Holy Spirit convicts the world of sin, righteousness, and of judgment (John 16:8). He guides believers in truth. (John 16:12)

The Holy Spirit grants spiritual gifts so as to enable and empower believers to serve Jesus. (1 Corinthians 12:4-11)

Isn't it amazing to see how much the Holy Spirit has done in our lives? Isn't it amazing to see how much He continues to do in our lives? Take some time right now to thank the Holy Spirit for His amazing work and His amazing grace in your life!

"You did not receive a spirit that makes you a slave again to fear, but you received the Spirit of sonship. And by him we cry, 'Abba, Father.' The Spirit himself testifies with our spirit that we are God's children." (Romans 8:15-16)

The Lord Is Faithful to Forgive Us

(forgiveness, confession)

"No one who is born of God practices sin, because his seed abides in him; and he cannot sin, because he is born of God." (1 John 3:9)

Is perfection possible for born again Christians? There have been those throughout church history who have taken 1 John 3:9, as well as the command of Matthew 5:48 ("Be perfect, therefore, as your heavenly Father is perfect"), and reasoned that since God gives us these commands, He must also give us the ability to obey them perfectly. They claim that God's Word clearly tells us in 1 John 3:9 that it's possible, even necessary, for a real Christian to come to the place where He cannot sin.

Yet this cannot be true, for what the apostle John is saying in 1 John 3:9 is that a Christian cannot persist in habitual, continual sin because he is born of God (the translation from the original Greek language makes this very clear). He cannot sin without a struggle or without a sense of grief so powerful that ultimately, despite his struggles, he will be brought to repentance and a forsaking of sin. What John is declaring to us then, is that sin is no longer natural to the believer. Though for a time he may slip into it, nevertheless, it's now contrary to his nature.

"If we claim to be without sin, we deceive ourselves and the truth is not in us. If we confess our sins, he is faithful and just and will forgive us of our sins and purify us from all unrighteousness." (1 John 1:8-9)

The bad news is that we all make mistakes and transgress the will of God. We can never achieve perfection while on earth. The good news, however, is that the Lord is faithful to forgive us and cleanse us when we come to Him in humble repentance. Perhaps lately you have been feeling that you have been making many mistakes and that the Lord cannot or will not forgive you. Do you truly want to find forgiveness and peace? Are you truly sorry for what has been occurring in your life and do you want to get into a right relationship with the Lord? Well, the Lord is faithful and the Lord is just. He will forgive you and purify you—just come to Him.

" 'Come to me, all you who are weary and burdened, and I will give you rest.' " (Matthew 11:28)

Look Through the Eyes of Grace

(relationships, forgiveness, grace)

"Accept one another, then, just as Christ accepted you, in order to bring praise to God." (Romans 15:7)

Take some time to meditate on what this verse is really saying. Then, ask yourself if you're truly living in a way that is obedient to what this verse teaches.

"Accept one another"—how?

"Just as Christ accepted you"—why?

"In order to bring praise to God"—are we doing this?

One of the secrets to living a God-glorifying life is to develop the mindset of heaven. This means that in order to be able to accept others the way Christ has accepted us, we need to look at them through the blood of Christ. When was the last time you looked at your spouse, friend, or co-worker as someone who is covered by the precious blood of Christ? In other words, when was the last time you looked at them through the eyes of grace, where you see them the same way God the Father sees you in Christ Jesus. How does God the Father look at those who have trusted God the Son, Jesus Christ, as their personal Lord and Savior?

"Therefore, there is now no condemnation for those who are in Christ Jesus." (Romans 8:1)

Please understand, this does not mean that we turn a blind eye to sinful rebellion against God's standard. Rather, it means that we need to look at other Christians with eyes of grace and patience. Why? Because isn't that how God looks at us? Think about it, would any of us want God to treat us the same way we treat others? Accepting others as Christ has accepted us allows us to live a life that literally becomes a "walking billboard" to God's amazing grace. Take some time and ask the Lord to grant you the grace so that your life today can be a "brilliant billboard" that brings all glory and honor to our Great God.

"May the God who gives endurance and encouragement give you a spirit of unity among yourselves as you follow Christ Jesus, so that with one heart and one mouth you may glorify the God and Father of our Lord Jesus Christ." (Romans 15:5-6)

The Power of Prayer

(prayer, trust, stress)

A wise person once said that when God is about to do something great, He starts His people praying. His supernatural strength is available to praying people who are convinced to the core of their beings that He can make a difference. Skeptics may argue that answered prayers are only coincidences, but as an English archbishop once observed: "It's amazing how many coincidences occur when one begins to pray."

"Oh, the depth of the riches of the wisdom and knowledge of God! How unsearchable his judgments, and his paths beyond tracing out! Who has known the mind of the Lord? Or who has been his counselor?" (Romans 11:33-34)

The Bible is very clear about the power of prayer. It's also very clear in showing us God's desire for His people to earnestly pray. For it's only when we have first spent time on our knees before God that we will then be able to go and stand before people. The Bible screams out that we need to focus less on organizing and more on agonizing. Why? Because it's very difficult to stumble when we are on our knees!

"Who has ever given to God, that God should repay him? For from him and through him and to him are all things. To him be the glory forever! Amen." (Romans 11:35-36)

Famous evangelist D. L. Moody was once quoted as saying that he always was looking for opportunities throughout his day to pray and to be filled with the Spirit. When asked by somebody why a godly man such as himself would need to pray so much, he responded: "Because I leak." If a man such as D. L. Moody took prayer as seriously as he did, then perhaps we should as well! Wouldn't you agree? Besides, as the saying goes, you usually end up resembling the one who you most hang out with. Meaning, if we want to become more and more like Jesus, we need to get alone with Him more and more in prayer. How much time are you spending alone with Jesus? Do you have some major problems that you're worried about right now? Well, if your problems are big enough to worry about, then they are big enough to pray about as well. Spend some extra time in prayer today and watch how the Lord will give you the peace and perspective to victoriously move forward in faith.

" 'Don't let your hearts be troubled. Trust in God; trust also in me.' " (John 14:1)

Have You Developed
Spiritual Amnesia?

(thankfulness, praise, trust)

In Numbers, Chapter 11, we find Moses dealing with a group of people who were hungry and who had lost patience. Faced with the task of trying to help them, Moses himself started running out of patience. He lost patience with the people and he started to lose patience with God's timing. Can you relate?

"But Moses said, 'Here I am among six hundred thousand men on foot, and you say, "I will give them meat to eat for a whole month!" Would they have enough if flocks and herds were slaughtered for them? Would they have enough if all the fish in the sea were caught for them?'" (Numbers 11:21-22)

It's amazing how quickly Moses developed "spiritual amnesia" toward God. Moses had witnessed time and again how God could provide for all the various needs. Moses saw firsthand how God was able to accomplish what seemed to be the impossible. Yet, when the pressure came to him from the people, Moses suddenly forgot all that God had done and he developed a case of "spiritual amnesia." Sounds like us, doesn't it? Although Moses had run out of patience, God in His grace remained patient and encouraged Moses to focus on the size of God rather than the size of the problem.

"The Lord answered Moses, 'Is the Lord's arm too short? You will now see whether or not what I say will come true for you.'" (Numbers 11:23)

The Lord graciously reminded Moses of His power and His promises. In other words, the Lord told Moses to stop focusing on the size of the problem and instead focus on the size of God. This is the same message for all of us today. God graciously provided for Moses all that He promised to Moses (even though the consistently rebellious people were disciplined by the Lord). When it comes to the problems you're dealing with today, is the Lord's arm too short to reach down and help you? Is the Lord's arm too weak to straighten out your problems? Will God's promises ever fail? If you have answered "No!" To those three questions (which you should have!), then relax and rejoice—with God on your side, you're on the winning side!

Look to God for Help

(temptation, trials)

It's easy to ask for help when we feel that the person we are asking can relate to our circumstances. It's also easy to ask for help when we feel that the person we are asking can help us overcome our difficulties. In other words, we need someone who understands our pain and someone who has the power to overcome our pain.

"Because he himself suffered when he was tempted, he is able to help those who are being tempted." (Hebrews 2:18)

The above verse assures us that Jesus understands our temptations because He also experienced temptations. Not only does He understand, but Jesus is able to help us overcome our temptations. He can relate and He has the power. Why? Because He is God!

"Therefore, since we have a great high priest who has gone through the heavens, Jesus the Son of God, let us hold firmly to the faith we profess. For we do not have a high priest who is unable to sympathize with our weaknesses, but we have one who has been tempted in every way, just as we are—yet was without sin." (Hebrews 4:14-15)

We can overcome because Jesus overcame! This means that there is absolutely nothing that you're dealing with right now that Jesus can't give you victory over. So, as you face your day today, take some time to get alone with Jesus and look to Him to provide you the help you need. You won't be disappointed! In fact, you may be very surprised at what you receive!

"Let us then approach the throne of grace with confidence, so that we may receive mercy and find grace to help us in our time of need." (Hebrews 4:16)

The Lord Is My Helper

(love, stress)

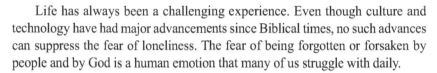

Life has always been a challenging experience. Even though culture and technology have had major advancements since Biblical times, no such advances can suppress the fear of loneliness. The fear of being forgotten or forsaken by people and by God is a human emotion that many of us struggle with daily.

"But Zion said: 'the Lord has forsaken me, the Lord has forgotten me.' " *(Isaiah 49:14)*

Approximately 700 years before the birth of Christ, God's people were fearful that they had been forgotten and forsaken by God. Times were tough and the people were stressed and oppressed. Yet, take a look at how the Lord encouraged His people.

"Can a mother forget the baby at her breast and have no compassion on the child she has borne? Though she may forget, I will not forget you!" (Isaiah 49:15)

What a powerful visual illustration to remind the people back then of God's amazing faithfulness and love. What a powerful illustration to remind all of us today as well! Think about a mother's love and faithfulness for her baby: She cares for her baby, she is always thinking about her baby, she hears the cries of her baby, she knows exactly what her baby needs, and she knows exactly when to give to her baby that which the baby needs. Well, just imagine how much more God cares for His children! Imagine how much more God thinks of His children, hears the cries of His children, knows exactly what His children need, and knows exactly when to provide what His children need.

"Never will I leave you; never will I forsake you. So we say with confidence, 'The Lord is my helper; I will not be afraid. What can man do to me?' " *(Hebrews 13:5-6)*

Friend, if you're currently struggling with loneliness and fear, please try to trust that you're not forgotten and you're not alone. Regardless of all of your challenges and difficulties, God's faithfulness will never fail you! Just think, God's love and care for you is greater and stronger than the greatest love a human mind can conceive—that of a mother towards her child.

God Has a Purpose for Our Trials

(trials, purpose)

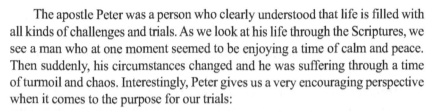

The apostle Peter was a person who clearly understood that life is filled with all kinds of challenges and trials. As we look at his life through the Scriptures, we see a man who at one moment seemed to be enjoying a time of calm and peace. Then suddenly, his circumstances changed and he was suffering through a time of turmoil and chaos. Interestingly, Peter gives us a very encouraging perspective when it comes to the purpose for our trials:

"In this you greatly rejoice, though now for a little while you may have had to suffer grief in all kinds of trials." (1 Peter 1:6)

First, the bad news: 1) We will have trials. 2) We will have a variety of trials. 3) We will have painful trials. There is no getting around it. Life is challenging and it's filled with all kinds of difficult trials. Nobody is exempt. However, praise God that the story doesn't end there!

"These have come so that your faith—of greater worth than gold, which perishes even though refined by fire—may be proved genuine and may result in praise, glory and honor when Jesus Christ is revealed." (1 Peter 1:7)

Now, the good news: God has a purpose for our trials: 1) To test our faith, and 2) to grow our faith, so that 3) our faith can be shown as genuine and bring glory to Jesus Christ. Maintaining this type of "Peter perspective" is the key in being able to survive and even thrive through our trials.

"He knows the way that I take; when he has tested me, I will come forth as gold." (Job 23:10)

Your trials are not meant to beat you down; they are meant to build you up. God's purpose is to bring you forth as gold! So as you're facing your trials and challenges today, rather than asking, "God, what are You doing?" Perhaps you can say, "God, thank You that You know what You're doing!"

"Praise be to the God and Father of our Lord Jesus Christ! In his great mercy he has given us new birth into a living hope through the resurrection of Jesus Christ from the dead." (1 Peter 1:3)

Have You Checked Your Heart Temperature Lately?

(thankfulness, priorities)

Have you checked your "heart temperature" lately? What do we mean? Generally, grateful people are joyful people. Grateful people are joyful people because they maintain a healthy focus on all that they have. They are grateful and joyful because they realize that all they have is from God. Ungrateful people, however, usually have an unhealthy focus on all that they don't have. They fail to remember all of their blessings from God, focusing instead on getting more and more. Therefore, ungrateful people in general are dissatisfied and unhappy. Please understand, there's nothing wrong with wanting to improve your life. It's safe to say, we all would like to see certain improvements in our lives . . . regardless of how blessed we currently are. However, the problem occurs when we forget all that God has graciously given us; developing instead an unhealthy desire to get more and—no matter what it takes and who it hurts.

"After these events, King Xerxes honored Haman, son of Hammedatha, the Agagite, elevating him and giving a seat of honor higher than that of all the other nobles. All the royal officials at the king's gate knelt down and paid honor to Haman, for the king had commanded this concerning him. But Mordecai would not kneel down or pay him honor." (Esther 3:1-2)

Haman seemed to have it all. He was honored by the king, he was respected by all the officials, and the people even bowed down to him—all except one man, Mordecai. You would think that Haman would have been satisfied and grateful with all that he had. You would think that Haman would have been joyful for the great honor he had been given. But he wasn't. Why? Because he didn't focus on all that he had, instead he focused on the one thing that he didn't have—the respect of Mordecai.

"When Haman saw that Mordecai would not kneel down or pay him honor, he was enraged. Yet having learned who Mordecai's people were, he scorned the idea of killing only Mordecai. Instead Haman looked for a way to destroy all Mordecai's people, the Jews, throughout the kingdom of Xerxes." (Esther 3:5-6)

183

As I stated earlier, ungrateful people in general are not joyful people. Why? They have an unhealthy desire for more and more, focusing exclusively on what they don't have, and failing to remember all that they've been graciously given. Haman is a perfect example of this. Mordecai became his obsession—he wanted respect from this Jewish man, and if he couldn't get it he would kill Mordecai and all the Jewish people. How did Haman get to this point? He didn't check his heart temperature. He didn't ask two very important questions:

1) Why am I so upset?

2) Where have I been focusing?

Although none of us will get to the point that Haman did (hopefully not!), nevertheless we can all fall into the same type of trap that he did. An insatiable desire for more and more leads to dissatisfaction and ungratefulness for all that we have been graciously given. That is why it's important to consistently check the temperatures of our hearts by asking two very important questions: 1) Why am I so upset? and 2) Where have I been focusing as of late?

The Purpose of God's Law
(the Bible, sin)

Some people say that a true believer is one who follows the law in order to try to please God: "God gave us His laws and we are required to keep them." Others say that because we are saved by grace through faith in Jesus, the law is no longer important to us: "Jesus wiped out the law and we are free to live how we want." Who do you believe is correct? What do you believe is the purpose of God's law?

"Now we know that whatever the law says, it says to those who are under the law, so that every mouth may be silenced and the whole world held accountable to God. Therefore, no one will be declared righteous in his sight by observing the law; rather, through the law we become conscious of sin." (Romans 3:19-20)

The purpose of God's law is to make us conscious that we are unable to keep the law. Consequently, we realize that we fall short of God's standard (that's called sin), and are therefore in need of a Savior to save us (that's called grace). In other words, the purpose of the law is to point us to the cross. However, once we enter into a saving relationship with Jesus through grace, we do not simply dismiss God's law as though it's not important for our lives.

" 'Why do you call me, 'Lord, Lord,' and do not do what I say? I will show you what he is like who comes to me and hears my words and puts them into practice.' " (Luke 6:46-47)

Just as the purpose of the law is to point us to the cross, the purpose of the cross is to point us back to the law. In other words, as people saved by grace, we now desire to live a life that is pleasing to God. Why? Not to earn our salvation, but out of gratitude for the gift of our salvation. Therefore, we desire to learn God's standards and put God's standards into practice in our lives. We desire to submit to God's perfect wisdom and plan for our lives. This desire is consistently fueled by immense gratitude for the gracious gift of eternal life.

"Blessed is he whose transgressions are forgiven, whose sins are covered. Blessed is the man whose sin the Lord does not count against him and in whose spirit there is no deceit." (Psalm 32:1-2)

As Christians, do we realize how truly blessed we are? In fact, we are too blessed to be stressed! Take some time right now and ask the Lord to give you the strength and desire to follow and obey Him. Ask the Lord to give you the ability to live a life that is pleasing to Him. In other words, ask the Lord to give you an attitude of gratitude.

Being Under the Lordship of Jesus

(trust, submission)

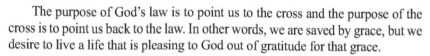

The purpose of God's law is to point us to the cross and the purpose of the cross is to point us back to the law. In other words, we are saved by grace, but we desire to live a life that is pleasing to God out of gratitude for that grace.

"What then? Shall we sin because we are not under the law but under grace? By no means!" (Romans 6:15)

The apostle Paul utterly rejected the idea that believers are free to ignore the laws of God. Grace was not an excuse to disobey God. Rather, grace was a reason to want to obey God. As Christians, we recognize and rejoice that we have been set free from the slavery of sin. We also recognize and rejoice that we now live a life of freedom through Jesus Christ.

"Thanks be to God that, though you used to be slaves to sin, you wholeheartedly obeyed the form of teaching to which you were entrusted. You have been set free from sin and have become slaves to righteousness." (Romans 6:17-18)

These are very interesting verses because they describe our lives of slavery. At one time we were enslaved under the deadly master of sin. But now, as Christians, we have been set free to become slaves to a new master: Jesus Christ. What? We are still slaves and under the authority of a master? But as Christians aren't we free? Yes, when Jesus sets you free, you're free indeed. You're free from the slavery of sin, self and Satan. You're free from the curse of the law by no longer trying to earn your salvation through the law. However, you now are living your life under the Lordship of the true Master, Jesus Christ.

"Now that you have been set free from sin and have become slaves to God, the benefit you reap is holiness, and the result is eternal life. For the wages of sin is death, but the gift of God is eternal life in Christ Jesus our Lord." (Romans 6:22-23)

Look at the benefits that come from your new Master. Look at the result of being under the Lordship of Jesus. Look at the gift you have received from your new Master. If you understand all that you have because of all that has been done for you, doesn't it make sense to try your best to please Him?

Serve One Another in Love

(love, grace)

We have seen that the purpose of the law is to point us to grace (the cross), and the purpose of the cross is to point us back to the law (God's Word). But some people may ask: "Since we are saved and have the free gift of eternal life, then why do we need to listen to what the Bible tells us? After all, God loves us and He doesn't want to burden us with a bunch of rules."

"You my brothers were called to be free. But do not use your freedom to indulge the sinful nature; rather, serve one another in love." (Galatians 5:13)

A story is told about Abraham Lincoln and how one day he entered a village where a young black girl was being auctioned to the highest bidder. After listening for several minutes as many people frantically made bids to purchase this young girl, Abraham Lincoln calmly and compassionately called out the highest bid. He bid a price that was significantly higher than the other people. Taking the girl from the auction stand, Lincoln then led her to a place outside the village. Suddenly, and much to the girl's surprise, Lincoln pulled out a key and started unlocking the shackles that bound the scared young girl. He then looked her in the eyes and compassionately said, "You're free." The girl, in obvious shock, then asked Lincoln, "You paid that huge price for me and you're saying that I am free to go wherever I want to go and do wherever I want to do? You mean that I am not required to stay with you and obey you even though you bought me at a huge price?" Lincoln simply responded, "My precious child, you're free." Thinking about it for a few seconds, the young girl looked at Lincoln and joyfully said, "I'm staying with you!"

"For you know that it was not with perishable things such as silver or gold that you were redeemed from the empty way of life handed down to you from your forefathers, but with the precious blood of Christ, a lamb without blemish or defect." (1 Peter 1:18-19)

Do you truly understand the price that was paid for your freedom? Do you truly understand the compassion and mercy that has been granted to you through Jesus Christ? At one time we all were enslaved in the shackles of our sin nature. But, we were bought at a huge price. Our great Redeemer has set us free, free indeed! Therefore, doesn't it make sense to honor, obey, and live for the One who bought us from the auction block of sin and death?

The Crown of God's Creation

(identity, thankfulness)

How appreciative are you for the blessings that God has graciously provided you? Read Psalm 8 and see the example of King David. David looked back and looked up to gain a greater appreciation of how blessed he truly was. Let's see how David also took the time to look around and rejoice at all the blessings God crowned him with.

"Yet you have made him a little lower than the heavenly beings and crowned him with glory and honor. You have given him dominion over the works of your hands; you have put all things under his feet, all sheep and oxen, and also the beasts of the field, the birds of the heavens, and the fish of the sea, whatever passes along the paths of the seas." (Psalm 8:5-8)

I can imagine King David looking around in wonder at all the various animals God had created. Suddenly, he started to rejoice in the fact that God had actually crowned him with authority over all that God had made. Realizing that humans are the crown of God's creation, David was amazed at the honor he had been given. How about you? When was the last time that you looked around at God's amazing creation and rejoiced in the authority and honor God has given you? When was the last time that you broke out in praise for the fact that you're the crown of God's creation? In fact, when was the last time that we as Christians broke out in praise for the fact that we are the crown of God's new creation?

Perhaps today, we all should take some time to look around and see the honor and dignity we truly have as new creations in Christ. Not only do we have authority and honor over God's creation, we also have dignity and honor as a child of the Creator! How should we respond to that amazing truth? In the same joyful way that King David did:

"O Lord, our Lord, how majestic is your name in all the earth!" (Psalm 8:9)

How appreciative are you for the blessings that God has graciously provided you? It depends on where you're looking. May we follow the example of King David in Psalm 8. May we all slow down and take the time to:

Look back and rejoice in the victories God has provided us.

Look up and recognize who we are, compared to who God is.

Look around and rejoice in all the blessings God has crowned us with.

The Lord's Prayer as a Guide

(prayer)

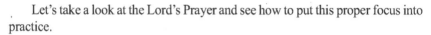

Let's take a look at the Lord's Prayer and see how to put this proper focus into practice.

" 'This, then, is how you should pray: Our Father in heaven, hallowed be your name, your kingdom come, your will be done on earth as it is in heaven.' " *(Matthew 6:9-10)*

Jesus gave us the Lord's Prayer as a guide to help us maintain the proper focus that is pleasing to God. However, we have to be careful to not let this prayer degenerate into heartless and mindless babble. Did you notice the pronouns in the verses above? Your name, Your kingdom, Your will. In other words, Jesus is directing our focus first to God, not to our requests. Why? To make sure that our motives are proper, that they are God-centered, not self-centered. Take a few moments now and ask God to purify your motives in such a way that today you will be seeking to glorify His name, impact His kingdom, and live according to His will.

" 'Give us today our daily bread. Forgive us our debts, as we also have forgiven our debtors. And lead us not into temptation, but deliver us from the evil one.' " *(Matthew 6:11-13)*

Did you notice the change of pronouns in the above verses? Give us, forgive us, and lead us. Jesus makes it clear that it's perfectly proper to come to God with our needs. He is our loving Father who cares for His children. However, we first need to focus our prayers on God: His name, kingdom and will. Then, we can focus on our needs and requests: Our daily bread (physical needs), our forgiveness (spiritual needs), and our temptations (moral needs). Why does Jesus guide us in this way? Because when we first focus on God, then when it comes time to making our requests, we will be filled with peace rather than panic. We will have the proper motives that in turn will give us the proper perspective: "God, I am trusting You to take care of my physical, spiritual and moral needs today in such a way that Your name is honored, Your kingdom is advanced, and Your perfect will is done?" Take a few moments now and present your requests to the Lord. Maintain focus and experience peace in knowing that you're praying in a way that is pleasing to our God!

189

Honor God by Forgiving Others

(forgiveness, relationships)

Today, we will look at the idea of forgiveness in the Lord's Prayer—learning from Jesus how to maintain a God honoring focus in our forgiveness.

" 'Forgive us our debts, as we also have forgiven our debtors.' " (Matthew 6:12)

Famous evangelist John Stott states, "Forgiveness is as dispensable to the life and health of the soul as food is for the body." Maybe we should all take a few moments and really think about what we are asking of God in this prayer. Basically, we are asking God to forgive us in the same way we forgive others. I can't tell you how many times I prayed that prayer in my younger days and had absolutely no clue what I was saying. I was babbling with an unfocused mind and heart. How about you? Do you really want God to forgive you the same way you have forgiven others?

" 'If you forgive men when they sin against you, your heavenly Father will also forgive you. But if you do not forgive men their sins, your Father will not forgive your sins.' " (Matthew 6:14-15)

We need to understand that forgiveness of others does not earn us the right to be forgiven. God's gracious and merciful act of forgiveness is based solely on unmerited and undeserved grace and mercy. However, God forgives those who understand they need to be forgiven. In other words, God forgives those who have a humble and penitent heart. One of the best ways to see a humble and penitent heart is through our forgiveness of others. Why? Because we realize that the offenses that others have committed against us are so small in comparison to our offenses against a holy and righteous God.

" 'Shouldn't you have had mercy on your fellow servant just as I had on you?' " (Matthew 18:33)

Are you struggling with forgiving someone right now? Are you dealing with so much emotional pain that you simply can't find the desire to forgive the person(s) who hurt you? Meditate on the verses above and ask the Lord to slowly soften your heart. In fact, a good passage to read is Matthew 18:21-35. It's there that we can see how Jesus perfectly handled Peter's question about forgiveness. Forgiveness is difficult, but it's not impossible with God. Ask Him to grant you the grace and mercy you need to be able to show the grace and mercy that others need—even those who have hurt you.

What Does the Bible Say About Gossip?

(character, gossip)

A wise person once said that gossip is a universal language that cuts through all barriers. In other words, gossip can be a very popular form of communication throughout the world. Yet, though it may be popular, it's very unproductive and extremely destructive. What does the Bible say about gossip?

"A perverse man stirs up dissension, and a gossip separates close friends." *(Proverbs 16:28)*

Although gossip may be able to cut through all cultural barriers, it also has the ability to cut through and destroy relationships. Gossip stirs up anger and dissension among people. It has the power to separate even the closest of friends. Can you relate? It's painful to have others gossip about us. However, it's even more painful when it's a close friend or family member who is doing the gossiping.

"With the tongue we praise our Lord and Father, and with it we curse men, who have been made in God's likeness. Out of the same mouth come praise and cursing. My brother, this should not be." (James 3:9-10)

When we criticize others, we actually are criticizing God. We are dishonoring the God of creation by gossiping about His creation. This can be a very sobering thought. Hopefully, it can also be a thought that comes to our mind before we open our mouths to gossip. It's not wrong to make judgments about people when they are acting in a way that is contrary to God. The Bible is clear that we are our brother's keeper; that we should not accept that which dishonors God and His creation. However, we have to be very careful not to allow ourselves to fall into the gossip trap.

"Without wood a fire goes out; without gossip a quarrel dies down." (Proverbs 26:20)

Isn't that verse amazingly accurate and relevant? No wood, no fire; no gossip, no quarrelling. Where are you when it comes to this idea of gossip? Have you been recently hurt by others who have gossiped about you? Or, have you been the one doing the hurting (and dishonoring of God) by gossiping about others? Stay tuned, for there is much more to learn about this deceptive and destructive thing called gossip.

How Do We Stop Gossiping?

(character, gossip)

Previously we looked at the topic of gossip. We have seen what the Bible has to say about gossip. Today we will look at how we can better control ourselves when it comes to gossip. In doing so, we will see that it's very important to think before we speak. The best way to think is to ask ourselves five key questions. How do we stop gossiping?

T-H-I-N-K!

T—Is what I am about to say true?

If not, then don't even think about saying it.

H—Is what I am about to say hurtful?

If it is, then perhaps you need to think twice before saying it.

I—Would I like the same thing to be said about me?

If not, then think about how the other person may feel.

N—Do I have negative motives?

"All a man's ways seem innocent to him, but motives are weighed by the Lord." (Proverbs 16:2)

K—What kind of feeling am I giving the Holy Spirit?

"Do not let any unwholesome talk come out of your mouths, but only what is helpful for building others up according to their needs, that it may benefit those who listen. And do not grieve the Holy Spirit of God, with whom you were sealed for the day of redemption." (Ephesians 4:29-30)

Gossip hurts others and dishonors God. As Christians, we are called to a higher standard. That is why we need to T-H-I-N-K before we speak. We won't always be successful in our battle against gossip, but hopefully we can become more disciplined and dedicated. Who knows, maybe your example can be one that God uses to positively impact others as well.

" 'A new command I give you: Love one another. As I have loved you, so you must love one another. By this all men will know that you're my disciples, if you love one another.' " (John 13:34-35)

The Principle: God Cannot Be Mocked

(character, relationships, love)

"Do not be deceived: God cannot be mocked. A man reaps what he sows. The one who sows to please his sinful nature, from that nature will reap destruction; the one who sows to please the Spirit, from the Spirit will reap eternal life." *(Galatians 6:7-8)*

You will reap what you sow.

You must consider what and where you sow.

The Question: Where are you sowing?

Are you sowing in the field of the Spirit?

"The fruit of the Spirit is love, joy, peace, patience, kindness, goodness, faithfulness, gentleness and self-control. Against such things there is no law." *(Galatians 5:22-23)*

Are you sowing in the field of the Spirit?

"The acts of the sinful nature are obvious: sexual immorality, impurity and debauchery; idolatry and witchcraft; hatred, discord, jealousy, fits of rage, selfish ambition, dissensions, factions and envy; drunkenness, orgies, and the like. I warn you, as I did before, that those who live like this will not inherit the kingdom of God." *(Galatians 5:19-21)*

The Harvest: What are you reaping?

Are you reaping fruit from the field of the Spirit?

Fruit when it comes to God: love, joy, peace.

Fruit when it comes to others: patience, kindness, goodness.

Fruit when it comes to ourselves: faithfulness, gentleness, self-control.

Are you reaping fruit from the field of the flesh?

Fruit when it comes to God: idolatry, witchcraft.

Fruit when it comes to others: hatred, discord, jealousy, factions, envy.

Fruit when it comes to ourselves: sexual immorality, impurity, debauchery, drunkenness, orgies, fits of rage, selfish ambition.

The Reminder: God cannot be mocked!

"Do not be deceived: God cannot be mocked. A man reaps what he sows. The one who sows to please his sinful nature, from that nature will reap destruction; the one who sows to please the Spirit, from the Spirit will reap eternal life." *(Galatians 6:7-8)*

The Bad News

(sin, salvation)

"I am not ashamed of the gospel, because it is the power of God for the salvation of everyone who believes; first for the Jew, then for the Gentile." (Romans 1:16)

The Gospel means good news. However, before we can understand the good news, we first need to understand the bad news.

The bad news is that we all have come into this world physically alive, but spiritually dead—spiritually disconnected—to God. Why? This is because of what happened with Adam and Eve back in the Garden of Eden. Because Adam and Eve disobeyed God by eating the forbidden fruit; God punished them with the punishment of death—not physical but spiritual death. The Bible tells us that what Adam and Eve did contaminated the entire human race. So, we are all born into this world as sinners in God's sight, sinners who are facing God's eternal judgment.

"As for you, you were dead in your transgressions and sins, in which you used to live when you followed the ways of this world and of the ruler of the kingdom of the air, the spirit who is now at work in those who are disobedient. All of us also lived among them at one time, gratifying the cravings of our sinful nature and following its desires and thoughts. Like the rest, we were by nature objects of wrath." (Ephesians 2:1-4)

The Bible also tells us that there is absolutely nothing that we can do through our own efforts to change this situation. We cannot walk our way into heaven. We cannot talk our way into heaven. We cannot do enough good works to earn our way into heaven. There is nothing that we can do through our own efforts to make ourselves right in God's sight. That is bad news.

"As it is written, 'There is no one righteous, not even one; there is no one who understands, no one who seeks God. All have turned away, they have together become worthless; there is no one who does good, not even one.' " (Romans 3:10-12)

These are some very sobering verses, aren't they? Yet, so many people laugh at the thought that we are sinners who need a Savior. They scoff at the idea that they do not have the intellect or ability to save themselves. Who are you counting on to save you from your sins? Are you counting on yourself, or are you counting on a Savior? Your answers to these questions carry the weight of your eternal destiny. Make sure you know that you know the correct answer. Why? Because, if you're wrong, the news is bad—very, very bad.

Lip Service or Love Service?

(serving, love)

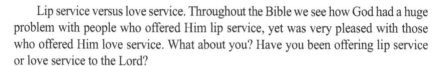

Lip service versus love service. Throughout the Bible we see how God had a huge problem with people who offered Him lip service, yet was very pleased with those who offered Him love service. What about you? Have you been offering lip service or love service to the Lord?

"He replied, 'Isaiah was right when he prophesied about you hypocrites; as it is written: These people honor me with their lips, but their hearts are far from me. They worship me in vain; their teachings are but rules taught by men.'" (Mark 7:6-7)

Why were these people considered hypocrites and liars? After all, the verses above show us that they were trying to honor the name of God; they were trying to worship Him. The problem is that these were people who professed the name of the Lord with their lips, but did not show it with their lives. They were playing a game by using the Lord's name—even though their lives showed that they had no true clue as to who the Lord really was.

Jesus replied: "'Love the Lord your God with all your heart and with all your soul and with all your mind.' This is the first and greatest commandment.'" (Matthew 22:37-38)

The Lord deserves our attention and our adoration; He deserves to be our love from both our lips and our lives. We love the Lord because of who He is and what He has done for us—and continues to graciously do for us on a daily basis. Although we can never love Him perfectly on this side of heaven in a way that He truly deserves; nevertheless we are to strive to give Him our hearts, heads and hands in a way that shows we truly do love Him.

" 'Greater love has no one than this, that he lay down his life for his friends. You are my friends if you do what I command. I no longer call you servants, because a servant does not know his master's business. Instead, I have called you friends, for everything that I learned from my Father I have made known to you. You did not choose me, but I chose you and appointed you to go and bear fruit—fruit that will last.'" (John 15:13-16)

Christian, one of the greatest ways to protect ourselves from lip service is to truly understand the Scripture above. Why do we love Jesus? Not only did Jesus love us first, not only did He show the magnitude of that love on the cross, but He also calls us His friend! Wow—let that one sink in for a while! Then watch how your love service towards the Lord explodes!

Practicing Thankfulness

(thankfulness, praise)

Why is it that we, the people of God, so often grumble against our God? Maybe it's the hurry in our lives that leads to worry—and whining. Perhaps it's our busyness in our lives that causes us to develop a mild case of "spiritual amnesia." Whatever the reason, we very often resemble the grumbling attitude of the early Israelites.

"Celebrate the Feast of Unleavened Bread, because it was on this very day that I brought your divisions out of Egypt. Celebrate this day as a lasting ordinance for the generations to come." (Exodus 12:17)

God commanded His people to celebrate their miraculous deliverance from oppression and bondage in Egypt. They did . . . briefly. However, once they realized the Egyptians were coming after them, the Israelites stood at the edge of the Red Sea and complained bitterly. Their praise turned to panic and their worship turned to whining.

"As Pharaoh approached, the Israelites looked up, and there were the Egyptians, marching after them. They were terrified and cried to the Lord. They said to Moses, 'Was it because there were no graves in Egypt that you brought us to the desert to die? What have you done to us by bringing us out of Egypt? Didn't we say to you in Egypt, "Leave us alone; let us serve the Egyptians? It would have been better for us to serve the Egyptians than to die in the desert." ' " (Exodus 14:10-12)

Isn't it amazing to see how quickly the Israelites forgot all that God had done for them? Isn't it amazing how quickly we do the same? The Bible tells us that through Jesus we have been set free. We have been set free from the evil bondage of sin and Satan. When Jesus set us free, He set us free indeed! We are now in the family of God. We serve a new Master who is caring and compassionate. He promises us life in abundance; one that begins here on earth and lasts throughout eternity. Yet when faced with some difficult circumstances, we often end up forgetting and complaining in a way that often resembles the verses above. Christian, think of your last few days: Would you say that your attitude has been one of praise or panic? Have your days been filled with worship and gratitude? Or have they been filled with worry and grumbling?

"Be joyful always; pray continually; give thanks in all circumstances, for this is God's will for you in Christ Jesus." (1 Thessalonians 5:16-18)

The Charcoal of Criticism

(character, trials, words)

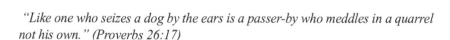

"Like one who seizes a dog by the ears is a passer-by who meddles in a quarrel not his own." (Proverbs 26:17)

Have you ever tried to aggressively grab a dog by its ears? Not a pretty sight, right? The Scriptures tell us that the same type of result can occur when we get ourselves involved in things that aren't our business. Yes, we are our brother's keeper. Yes, we do have an obligation to point out error and sin. However, we need to make sure that our motives are not meddling, and our actions are not attacks.

"As charcoal to embers and as wood to fire, so is a quarrelsome man for kindling strife." (Proverbs 26:21)

Constant criticism of others can be a type of charcoal that ignites a fire among people. Gossip and backbiting can also do the same. A quarrelsome attitude often inflames such bitter strife, that the best of relationships can suddenly be destroyed. Are you currently involved in creating some "forest fires" in your home, school, or work place? Are you carrying the "charcoal of criticism" in your pocket right now? In other words, is your life leaving a trail of strife?

"You my brothers, were called to be free. But do not use your freedom to indulge the sinful nature; rather, serve one another in love. The entire law is summed up in a single command: 'Love your neighbor as yourself.' If you keep on biting and devouring each other, watch out or you will be destroyed by each other." (Galatians 5:13-15)

Love builds up, back biting devours and destroys. As Christians, we are called to be free and to use our freedom to bless our God by being a blessing to others. Each day we are faced with the opportunity to build up and bless, or to back bite and destroy. Take some time right now and think about your attitude over the past few days. Meditate on the Scriptures we have looked at today and ask the Lord to set your heart right in His sight. Ask Him to guide you and strengthen you so that your life does not leave a trail of strife today.

"Get rid of all bitterness, rage and anger, brawling and slander, along with every form malice. Be kind and compassionate to one another, forgiving each other, just as in Christ God forgave you." (Ephesians 4:31-32)

Commit Your Plans to the Lord

(future, trust, purpose)

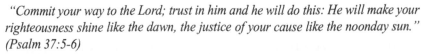

"Commit your way to the Lord; trust in him and he will do this: He will make your righteousness shine like the dawn, the justice of your cause like the noonday sun." *(Psalm 37:5-6)*

Commit: Have you taken the time to commit your career, calling, or even your current concerns to the Lord?

Trust: Are you committed to trust the Lord when it comes to your career, calling, or current concerns?

Wait: Are you willing to wait for the Lord, trusting that He is faithful to lift the darkness and to shine His light on your career, calling or current concerns?

"Commit to the Lord whatever you do, and your plans will succeed." *(Proverbs 16:3)*

Your plans will succeed because you have committed yourself to the plans of the Lord. The key is to make a commitment. Commitment then leads to trust. Your plans will succeed because you trust the Lord to work out His perfect plans in and through your life. Commitment and trust allow us to have the patience to wait. Your plans will succeed because you're waiting on the Lord's perfect timing to be revealed in and through your life.

"As the eyes of slaves look to the hand of their master, as the eyes of a maid look to the hand of her mistress, so our eyes look to the Lord our God, till he shows us his mercy." *(Psalm 123:2)*

What a wonderful picture of faith! What a wonderful example of commitment, trust and patience to wait on the Lord. How about you? Can you set that same example in your life right now? It's not always easy to do so. We want to, but we often take back that commitment—which causes us to trust in ourselves or others more than in the Lord . . . which then causes us to be impatient and not wait on the Lord. The result: frustration and failure. Can you relate? Yet, in spite of our faulty faithfulness, the Lord is always faithful. He is faithful to bring about His perfect plan for our lives, and He is faithful to bring it about in His perfect timing. Thanks be to God!

"Unless the Lord had given me help, I would have soon dwelt in the silence of death. When I said, "My foot is slipping," your love, O Lord, supported me. When anxiety was great within me, your consolation brought joy to my soul." *(Psalm 94:17-19)*

Let Your Light Shine Before Men

(evangelism, relationships, character)

Recently my wife and I missed our connecting flight to Croatia and were forced to stay in Paris for ten hours. I know you're thinking, "What a blessing!" Well, when I heard the news that we were going to be delayed for ten hours, I must admit that I didn't act as if it were a blessing. Instead, I became rather impatient with the poor man who gave us the news, even though he had absolutely nothing to do with our minor inconvenience.

"Live such good lives among pagans that, though they accuse you of doing wrong, they may see your good deed and glorify God on the day he visits us." (1 Peter 2:12)

I do not know if the man who worked at the airport was a follower of Christ or not. I'm sure that, if asked, he might wonder if I was a follower of Christ after my little outburst! However, I do know that I am to represent my Lord in a way that brings honor and glory to Him—no matter how many times my schedule and plans get inconvenienced. Having our schedules interrupted is a part of life. Minor inconveniences due to events outside of our control are all part of being human. It's not if we are going to be inconvenienced, it's how will we react when we are inconvenienced. I know I didn't do so well at the Paris airport. It was a good lesson for me, and hopefully one that may speak to you as well. As Christians, every day is an opportunity to bring glory to our great God. Very often, God will provide what we perceive to be inconveniences that can actually be opportunities—if we are prepared for them.

"But in your hearts set Christ apart as Lord. Always be prepared to give an answer to everyone who asks you to give a reason for the hope that you have. But do this with gentleness and respect." (1 Peter 3:15)

Obviously, I wasn't prepared in that Paris airport. It's obvious from my confession that I wasn't very gentle or respectful. Although my opportunity for witness was wasted, nevertheless I praise God for His gentle mercy and grace in forgiving me! My hope in sharing this story is that you will not make the same mistake that I did. Remember, God will often provide what we often perceive to be inconveniences that actually are opportunities in disguise—opportunities to give a reason for our hope and faith in Christ. My prayer is that you (and me!) will be prepared the next time the opportunity comes.

"In the same way, let your light shine before men, that they may see your good deeds and praise your Father in heaven." (Matthew 5:16)

The Step of Faith

(faith, trust)

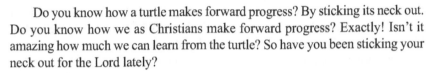

Do you know how a turtle makes forward progress? By sticking its neck out. Do you know how we as Christians make forward progress? Exactly! Isn't it amazing how much we can learn from the turtle? So have you been sticking your neck out for the Lord lately?

"Without faith it is impossible to please God, because anyone who comes to him must believe that he exists and that he rewards those who earnestly seek him." (Hebrews 11:6)

Too often, we say to God, "Show me first and then I will step forward." However, God says, "Step first and then I will show you." In other words, we need to first stick out our necks like a turtle in order to move forward. This takes faith—a faith that believes that God is who He says He is and that He can do what He says He can do . . . even if we can't see every step of the way.

"By faith Abraham, when called to go to a place he would later receive as an inheritance, obeyed and went, even though he did not know where he was going." (Hebrews 11:8)

That is the type of faith that honors God. That is the type of faith we need to exercise in our daily lives. Is God calling you to trust Him right now on a particular issue? Is this call of trust stretching your faith like never before? Well, take a lesson from Abraham (and the turtle!) and take the step of faith. It can be scary, but God is with you every step of the way.

"Because he loves me," says the Lord, "I will rescue him; I will protect him, for he acknowledges my name. He will call upon me, and I will answer him; I will be with him in trouble, I will deliver him and honor him." (Psalm 91:14-15)

Think about the journey of a turtle. Although the pace is slow, the turtle keeps sticking its neck out and moving forward, eventually getting to its desired destination. Maybe today you're feeling like you have been moving at a turtle's pace, wondering if you will ever get to where God wants you to be. Take heart; faithfully keep going forward. Although you may feel like you're going slow, remember that God knows the way and that He is never late!

"Now faith is being sure of what we hope for and certain of what we do not see. This is what the ancients were commended for." (Hebrews 11:1-2)

The Call to Persevere

(faith, trust)

Previously we took a look at the example of Abraham, as well as a turtle, to see that God is honored by our step of faith. We must realize, however, that God is not asking us to take a blind step of faith. Rather, the Spirit of God encourages us through the Word of God that we can trust in the faithfulness of God every step of the way.

"See, I am sending an angel ahead of you to guard you along the way and to bring you to the place I have prepared. Pay attention to him and listen to what he says. Do not rebel against him; he will not forgive your rebellion, since my Name is in him." (Exodus 23:20-21)

Many scholars agree that this Angel of the Lord is none other than a manifestation of Jesus Christ in the Old Testament. The good news is that God is saying the same thing to us today as He was saying to His people back then. He has sent the Spirit of Christ ahead of us to prepare a place for us. Maybe He is preparing a place for your future employment or education. Or, perhaps He has gone ahead to prepare your future mate or ministry. Regardless of what it is , the Lord is faithful to do His part. He is faithful to guard us, guide us, and bring us to the place He has for us. Yet, He requires that we step forward in faith, paying attention to His promptings and listening to His Word of truth.

"So do not throw away your confidence; it will be richly rewarded. You need to persevere so that when you have done the will of God, you will receive what he has promised." (Hebrews 10:35-36)

This call to persevere is a call to persevere to the end. It's a call to persevere in our journey toward our heavenly home secured for us through Jesus Christ. It's through the Spirit of Christ that we are being guarded, guided and brought to the place that is prepared for us—here on earth as well as in heaven. The Scriptures are clear, we need to pay attention and persevere as we are led to the place prepared for us. This takes faith—a faith that believes the Lord is perfectly faithful to do His part. Do you believe that the Spirit of the Lord is ahead of you preparing a place for your employment or education? Do you have the faith to step forward trusting that the Spirit of the Lord will guard you and bring you to your future mate or ministry?

"Let us hold unswervingly to the hope we profess, for he who promised is faithful. And let us consider how we may spur one another on toward love and good deeds." (Hebrews 10:23-24)

Walk in Fear of the Lord

(character, integrity)

"The Lord abhors dishonest scales, but accurate weights are his delight."
(Proverbs 11:1)

The Lord delights in honesty and integrity; however He is disgusted by duplicity and falsehood. As you prepare to go to work or school today, are you preparing to bring delight to the Lord? How about when it comes to your family or other relationships today? Will the Lord see honesty and integrity, or will He see the exact opposite? Take some time and pray that the Lord will be pleased with the work and integrity of your hands today.

"The Lord detests men of perverse heart but he delights in those whose ways are blameless." (Proverbs 11:20)

Once again, we see that the Lord delights in a certain lifestyle, while He detests the other. Although none of us can be perfect and blameless in the Lord's sight; we would all like to have hearts that are a delight to the Lord, not hearts that are detestable to Him. Take some time right now and ask the Lord to set your heart right in His sight. Ask Him to give you a heart that is devoted to fulfilling His desires today.

"Blessed is the man who always fears the Lord, but he who hardens his heart falls into trouble." (Proverbs 28:14)

Do you want to be blessed? Do you want the favor of the Lord on your work, school and family? Then walk in fear of the Lord. Fear means awe and reverence for the Lord. Fear means submission and respect to the Lord. Fear means recognizing that the Lord's ways are better than our ways. In other words, fear of the Lord relies on wisdom from the Lord, which leads to blessings from the Lord. However, lack of fear leads to a fall—a fall into trouble. The contrast is clear, fear of the Lord leads to favor from the Lord; lack of fear leads to a frightful fall. Favor or a fall, which one do you want to characterize your day with today? Take some time right now and ask the Lord to give you a heart and hands that show awe and reverence for His holy name. Ask Him to lead you today in His path of righteousness for the sake of His holy name.

"He whose walk is blameless is kept safe, but he whose ways are perverse will suddenly fall." (Proverbs 28:18)

Are You Having a "Tea Bag" Moment?

(trials, stress)

It has been said; people are like tea bags, you find out how strong they are once they are put in hot water. Are you feeling a bit like a "tea bag" right now? Is there some heat that you're feeling right now?

"If you falter in times of trouble, how small is your strength." (Proverbs 24:10)

This was the verse that God used in my life eight months ago when my father went home to be with the Lord. On one hand, I was extremely grateful for the privilege of having had my father for forty four years, and I was also full of peace in knowing that my father was with Jesus. On the other hand, however, I was feeling so weak and confused that I didn't have the strength to take the next step. Can any of you relate? Yet, as I look back on that "very hot tea bag" moment in my life, I can see how God used it to show me my faith and to strengthen my faith. To be more precise, God used that time to show me His faithfulness and His sufficient strength in my life. Without Him, I have no idea how I would have survived that time. However, with Him, I can see how He carried me through it and brought me to another level in my relationship with Him—and others.

"Consider it pure joy, my brothers, whenever you face trials of many kinds, because you know that the testing of your faith develops perseverance." (James 1:2-3)

God has a purpose for all of our "tea bag" moments. He wants to grow us and develop us into the type of people who can live the type of life He has for us. Being dipped into "hot water" is not easy or comfortable, but God is not going to burn you or let you drown. He loves you and has a purpose for everything that comes your way—including those "tea bag" trials you're facing right now.

"Perseverance must finish its work so that you may be mature and complete, not lacking in anything." (James 1:4)

Christian, there will come a time when you will look back on these "tea bag" moments that you're currently facing and be amazed at how God worked in and through your life. I say this, not as a pastor, but as a person just like you. I say this as a person who recently experienced an extremely hot "tea bag" moment. I say this as a person who, now by God's grace, is a different person. Praise God!

How Do We Respond When Our Plans Are Suddenly Changed?

(trust, perspective, trials)

Do we start to get nervous? "What happened?" "How could that have happened?"

Do we start to pout? "Poor me." "Why did that have to happen to me?"

Do we then start to shout? "You're at fault." "I want what I want, and I want it now!"

"What causes fights and quarrels among you? Don't they come from your desires that battle within you? You want something but don't get it. You kill and covet, but you cannot have what you want. You quarrel and fight. You do not have, because you do not ask God." (James 4:1-2)

How should we respond when our plans are suddenly changed?

Maybe this is an opportunity to share the love of God.

"Be wise in the way you act toward outsiders; making the most of every opportunity. Let your conversation be always full of grace, seasoned with salt, so that you may know how to answer everyone." (Colossians 4:5-6)

Maybe this is an opportunity to fulfill the will of God.

"Many are the plans in a man's heart, but it's the Lord's purpose that prevails." (Proverbs 19:21)

Maybe this is an opportunity to bring glory to God.

"In the same way, let your light shine before men, that they may see your good deeds and praise your Father in heaven." (Matthew 5:16)

Rather than getting nervous, then beginning to pout and shout, perhaps we should look at our inconveniences as potential opportunities. It won't be easy. But wouldn't you love to be able to share the love of God with somebody today? Maybe an inconvenience today will actually provide that opportunity for you today. Wouldn't you love to fulfill the will of God in your life today? Maybe an inconvenience today will be the opportunity to set you on the path of God's perfect plan and purpose for you. Wouldn't you love to bring glory to God today? Perhaps all those inconveniences that you face today will actually provide opportunities for you to bring glory to God—all day!

Praise Be to My Rock!

(trials, relationship with God)

Moses was a man who was called by God to lead the people of God into the Promised Land. Yet, it seemed he always had to deal with challenging circumstances and challenging people. Can you relate?

"Then Moses said to him, 'If your Presence does not go with us, do not send us up from here. How will anyone know that you are pleased with me and with your people unless you go with us? What else will distinguish me and your people from all the other people on the face of the earth?'" (Exodus 33:15-16)

Moses knew that his only hope for success was that God would be with him every step of the way. Moses was willing to deal with the all the challenges of leadership. He was willing to lead through all the challenging circumstances, and he was willing to put up with all the challenging people. However, Moses knew his only hope for success (and sanity!) was the Presence of God. In other words, if God wasn't leading the way, Moses knew there was no way.

"And the Lord said to Moses, 'I will do the very thing you have asked, because I am pleased with you and I know you by name.'" (Exodus 33:17)

Think about your prayers over the past week or so. What have you been asking for? Have you been asking God to make your challenging circumstances go away, or have you been asking God to be with you in the midst of those circumstances? Have you been asking God to be with you as you deal with those challenging people, or have you been asking God to do something else with those people?!?

"For who is God besides the Lord? And who is the Rock except our God? It's God who arms me with strength and makes my way perfect. He makes my feet like the feet of a deer; he enables me to stand on the heights." (Psalm 18:31-33)

The key to success and sanity is to know that God is with us. The key to peace and perspective is to know that God is leading us. Perhaps we should all take some time and reflect on what Moses was saying to the Lord. Then, we should take the time to pray in a way similar to Moses; "Lord, please pour out Your presence upon my family today, upon my place of employment, upon my school, upon my ministry. Do not let me try to do this on my own. Lord, I need You leading me every step of the way."

"The Lord lives! Praise be to my Rock! Exalted be God my Savior!" (Psalm 18:46)

Build Up and Bless Others

(character, relationships)

Are you adding value to the lives of others? In other words, are the people in your family getting better because of your influence on them? Or, are they getting bitter? How about in your place of employment? Are you adding value to the people you work with? What about those you go to school with? Are people growing because of your impact, or are they groaning?

"A generous man will prosper; he who refreshes others will himself be refreshed." (Proverbs 11:25)

This verse tells us we are to be in the business of building up and blessing others. The benefit of doing this is that people are refreshed because of your influence on them. They feel better and are becoming better because of the impact you're having on them. However, the benefits do not stop there. As you refresh others, you also will be refreshed. You will experience the refreshing joy and contentment of knowing that your life matters, that you're actually making a difference in the lives of others—bringing glory to our great God. Think about it, you have the privilege and opportunity to influence lives, making both a temporal difference on earth and an eternal difference for heaven!

"Let us not become weary in doing good, for at the proper time we will reap a harvest if we do not give up." (Galatians 6:9)

There may be some of you who feel you have blown it when it comes to being a refreshing blessing in the lives of others. Perhaps you're feeling you have not been a refreshing blessing in your marriage or with your children. Maybe you're feeling your attitude has not been so refreshing at work, in school, or even in your ministry. Today is a new day! By God's grace you can start to focus on being a refreshing influence in those very lives where you feel you have blown it—it's not too late! Do not become weary and don't throw in the towel, for the Lord tells us that there will be a harvest of blessing—if we do not give up!

"May the God who gives endurance and encouragement give you a spirit of unity among yourselves as you follow Christ Jesus, so that with one heart and mouth you may glorify the God and Father of our Lord Jesus Christ." (Romans 15:5-6)

How Do You Respond to Bad News?

(trials, character)

How do you respond when you're surprised by bad news? King David was devastated by the sudden onslaught of bad news. One day he came upon the city of Ziklag, his headquarters, and saw that it was destroyed by his enemies. Not only that, but his family and the families of his soldiers were kidnapped by the enemy as well. To top it all off, the soldiers blamed David for these problems and were considering stoning him to death. Talk about a bad day!

How did David respond?

He lost all his strength.

"When David and his men came to Ziklag, they found it destroyed by fire and their wives and sons and daughters taken captive. So David and his men wept aloud until they had no strength left to weep." (1 Samuel 30:3-4)

David was real when it came to dealing with his emotions. He didn't suppress his emotions, nor did he try to bury his emotions in an unhealthy or ungodly way. David poured out his heart to the Lord. What about you? How are you dealing with your emotions right now?

He found his strength in the Lord.

"But David found strength in the Lord his God." (1 Samuel 30:6)

God in His grace provided the strength David needed to heal and deal with the onslaught of bad news. It's as if David emptied himself of himself, leaving room for God's sufficient grace and perfect power to fill him up. The result? David was strengthened in the Lord. How about you? Where are you finding your strength right now?

He sought wisdom from the Lord.

"And David inquired of the Lord, 'Shall I pursue this raiding party? Will I overtake them?' 'Pursue them,' he answered. 'You will certainly overtake them and succeed in the rescue.'" (1 Samuel 30:8)

Show Your Love by Obeying His Commands

(obedience, character)

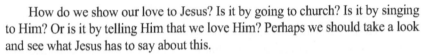

How do we show our love to Jesus? Is it by going to church? Is it by singing to Him? Or is it by telling Him that we love Him? Perhaps we should take a look and see what Jesus has to say about this.

" 'Whoever has my commands and obeys them, he is the one who loves me.' " (John 14:21)

Jesus is very clear that obedience to Him is a clear sign of our love for Him. Our obedience is not out of obligation, thinking that we must obey in order to earn our salvation. Rather, our obedience comes from an attitude of gratitude for the free gift of our salvation. We want to obey Jesus because of who He is and what He has done for us—and continues to do for us on a daily basis. Although it's good that we go to church, this is not the main way to prove our love to Jesus. Likewise, although it's good to sing to Jesus and tell Him that we love Him, this also is not the main way to prove our love to Jesus. Those who have His commands and obey His commands are those who show their love to Jesus. Look at the promise Jesus makes to those who show their love to Him:

" 'He who loves me will be loved by my Father, and I too will love him and show myself to him.' " (John 14:21)

Do you want to see more of Jesus? Then show your love to Him by trying to live in obedience to Him. Do you want to see more of Jesus working in and through your life? Then show your love to Him by obeying Him. None of us will be perfect in our obedience to Jesus. We all fall short. However, as Christians, we should all have a desire to continue to try to obey Him—even after we fail. In other words, we should have the desire to obey Jesus when it comes to our marriages—even if we have fallen short as of late. We should have a desire to obey Jesus when it comes to our work or school—even if we have fallen short as of late. We should have a desire to obey Jesus when it comes to our ministries—even if we have fallen short as of late. The question is: Do you have that desire?

"Jesus replied, 'If anyone loves me, he will obey my teaching. My Father will love him, and we will come to him and make our home with him. He who does not love me will not obey my teaching. These words you hear are not my own; they belong to the Father who sent me.' " (John 14:23-24)

Pray with A Focused Heart and Mind

(prayer)

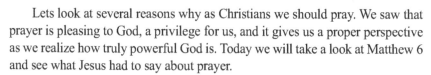

Lets look at several reasons why as Christians we should pray. We saw that prayer is pleasing to God, a privilege for us, and it gives us a proper perspective as we realize how truly powerful God is. Today we will take a look at Matthew 6 and see what Jesus had to say about prayer.

Pray with a focused heart.

" 'When you pray, do not be like the hypocrites, for they love to pray standing in the synagogues and on the street corners to be seen by men. I tell you the truth, they have received their reward in full. But when you pray, go into your room, close the door and pray to your Father, who is unseen. Then your Father, who sees what is done in secret, will reward you.' " (Matthew 6:5-6)

Notice that Jesus didn't say "if" you pray. He said "when" you pray. In these verses, Jesus criticized many of the religious leaders who used prayer as a means of showing off. These leaders liked to parade their prayers out in the open where all could see how holy and righteous they were. Yet, Jesus didn't view them as holy or righteous. He called them hypocrites. Interestingly, the word for hypocrite comes from a Greek word describing an actor who performs on a stage. This actor wore many different masks to portray many different characters in the performance. Wearing different masks for a stage performance is acceptable because the audience knows that they are coming for a show. However, prayer is not a performance or show that is to be paraded in front of an audience. This does not mean that we cannot or should not pray publicly in church or in small groups with others. Rather, the point that Jesus is making is that the only "audience" we should be concerned with is our heavenly Father. Our hearts need to be focused on God alone, for He is the One to whom we are praying to. Therefore, whether praying publicly in church, in a small group, or praying alone in the privacy of our homes, we need to make sure that our hearts are focused on our loving God who hears us and can answer us.

Pray with a focused mind.

" 'When you pray, do not keep on babbling like pagans, for they think they will

be heard because of their many words. Do not be like them, for your Father knows what you need before you ask Him.'" (Matthew 6: 7-8)

Once again, notice that Jesus didn't say "if" you pray. He said "when" you pray. In these verses, Jesus criticized those who felt that they could impress and influence God with their many words. These people were simply babbling with their mouths without even using their minds. Interestingly, this can easily happen with those of us who regularly attend church as well. We can lapse into mindless prayers and meaningless songs of praise. The point that Jesus was making was that our heavenly Father is not impressed with the number of words in our prayers. He is impressed with heartfelt and mind focused interaction.

Pray with a focused perspective.

"This, then, is how you should pray: 'Our Father in heaven, hallowed be your name.'" (Matthew 6:9)

Notice that Jesus instructs us to focus first on the One to whom we are praying. Why? It gives us the proper perspective. God is our loving Father. This should give us confidence that He cares for us. He is also our Great God who reigns from heaven. This should give us confidence that He has the power to answer our prayers. It's the holy name of our compassionate and all-powerful God that we desire to see honored and revered. This should give us confidence that we desire that which God Himself desires. Isn't it amazing to think about what we are actually saying when we pray the first verse of the Lord's Prayer?

Perfectly United in Mind and Thought

(relationships, forgiveness)

It's extremely sad and devastating when there is jealousy and arguing within the body of Christ. Unhealthy discord not only causes pain within the body of Christ, it also promotes laughter and ridicule outside the body of Christ: "Look at those people who call themselves Christians. They can't even get along with each other, why would we ever want to join their little fight club?"

"I appeal to you, brothers, in the name of our Lord Jesus Christ, that all of you agree with one another so that there may be no divisions among you and that you may be perfectly united in mind and thought." (1 Corinthians 1:10)

The apostle Paul was making this appeal to the Christian church in Corinth. Why? They were getting involved in all kinds of petty arguments that caused all kinds of problems within the church. Paul made his appeal in the name of Christ, and he did it for the unity and health of the body of Christ. He was not telling them to be united in mind and thought when it came to sinful living or false teaching. Both of his letters to the Corinthians are very clear on this, and both letters emphasize that Christians are not expected to compromise God's standards for the sake of unity. Rather, Paul was telling them to grow up and stop acting like little babies.

"Brothers, I could not address you as spiritual but as worldly—mere infants in Christ. I gave you milk, not solid food, for you were not ready for it. Indeed, you are still not ready. You are still worldly. For since there is jealously and quarreling among you, are you not acting like mere men? For one says, 'I follow Paul,' and another, 'I follow Apollos,' are you not mere men?" (1 Corinthians 3:1-4)

Not a very pretty picture of the Christians in the Church of Corinth, is it? They were acting like mere babies, arguing and creating petty rivalries as to whom they felt was a better leader and teacher within the church. Unfortunately, this type of childish behavior still happens today. For the sake of Christ, shouldn't we all attempt to honor the body of Christ? Out of gratitude to Christ, shouldn't we all attempt to build up and bless the body of Christ? After all, we are a part of His body because of what He allowed to have happen to His body on that cross.

"Don't you know that you yourselves are God's temple and that God's Spirit lives in you? If anyone destroys God's temple, God will destroy him; for God's temple is sacred, and you're that temple." (1 Corinthians 3:16-17)

His Amazing Grace and Love

(God's character, love)

"For God so loved the world that he gave his one and only Son, that whoever believes in him shall not perish but have eternal life." (John 3:16)

God the Lover.

The Bible tells us that we all have come into this world as sinners with a basic nature that is in rebellion to God. The sad truth is that we want nothing to do with God, we do not want to obey God, and we do not want to bring glory to God. In other words, we are not in love with God. Yet, God in His grace decided to show His love towards us in the most amazing way.

God the Giver.

God the Father gave His beloved Son (God the Son) as a sacrifice and substitute for sinners. Can you imagine the love that God has for us that He would give His Son to be punished for us? In other words, God didn't simply say that He loves us. He showed His love for us by giving His one and only Son to be the way to forgiveness, peace and eternal life.

God the Savior.

Why did God decide to show His love for us by giving His Son? To save us! As sinners, we have no hope for salvation through our own efforts. The Bible is very clear on this. However, God did for us that which we could never do on our own—He saved us. How? He punished His perfect, beloved Son in our place as our substitute. God is holy, righteous and just. He cannot simply accept or ignore sin. He must punish anything or anyone who falls short of His perfect standard. If He punished us, we would all be eternally damned. Instead, in His amazing love for us, as Jesus was on the cross, God the Father placed our sins on Jesus and punished Him in our place as our substitute. Jesus then died the death we deserve. However, three days later He rose in victory—Jesus overcame sin and death for us! God in His grace offers forgiveness and eternal life as a free gift, based solely on what Jesus did for us. That's why it's called grace—amazing grace!

"God demonstrates his own love for us in this: While we were still sinners, Christ died for us. Since we have now been justified by his blood, how much more shall we be saved from God's wrath through him!" (Romans 5:8-9)

God Can Calm Your Stormy Seas

(trials, stress)

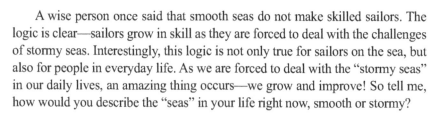

A wise person once said that smooth seas do not make skilled sailors. The logic is clear—sailors grow in skill as they are forced to deal with the challenges of stormy seas. Interestingly, this logic is not only true for sailors on the sea, but also for people in everyday life. As we are forced to deal with the "stormy seas" in our daily lives, an amazing thing occurs—we grow and improve! So tell me, how would you describe the "seas" in your life right now, smooth or stormy?

"He got up, rebuked the wind and said to the waves, 'Quiet! Be still!' Then the wind died down and it was completely calm. He said to his disciples, 'Why are you so afraid? Do you still have no faith?' They were terrified and asked each other, 'Who is this? Even the wind and the waves obey him!' " (Mark 4:39-41)

As Christians, we serve and trust in the One who has all authority over all circumstances. Yet, it's so easy to forget that when the seas start to get stormy, isn't it? Are your circumstances overwhelming you to the point that you're feeling afraid and fragile in your faith right now? The disciples felt the same way, yet look what Jesus graciously did for them. The good news is that the same Jesus who calmed the stormy seas for His disciples back then is the same exact Jesus who can calm the stormy seas that you're facing today. How can we be so certain?

"Jesus Christ is the same yesterday and today and forever." (Hebrews 13:8)

Do you believe that God has a purpose for your life? Do you also believe that God may be allowing the seas to get a bit stormy in your life right now because He wants to grow you in such a way so that you can fulfill the purpose He has for you? It's not easy to go through the stormy seas. But God is with us through these stormy circumstances. And God has all authority and power over every stormy circumstance that you're facing—or will ever face.

"Fear not, for I have redeemed you; I have summoned you by name, you are mine. When you pass through the waters, I will be with you; and when you pass through the rivers, they will not sweep over you. When you walk through the fire, you will not be burned; the flames will not set you ablaze." (Isaiah 43:1-2)

A Step of Faith

(sin, perspective)

A wise person once said that you do not need to be great to start, but you need to start to be great. In other words, we cannot wait for the perfect time and the perfect scenario in order to start something. Why? Because there is never the perfect time and perfect scenario! Of course, God has His perfect time and scenario for everything, but we are not God. Therefore, we need to take a step of faith, trusting in Him and His call for our lives. Greatness comes by starting, making mistakes, and learning from those mistakes.

"Not that I have already obtained all this, or have already been made perfect, but I press on to take hold of that for which Christ took hold of me." (Philippians 3:12)

The apostle Paul was saying that he wasn't going to sit around and come up with reasons to procrastinate. He knew that he wasn't perfect, and he also knew that he wasn't going to wait for the perfect time or scenario to fulfill God's call on his life. Instead, he said that he was going to press on, he was going to seize the opportunity and take hold of the life that God had graciously granted him. How about you? Are you willing to press on, or do you simply want to wait?

"Brothers, I do not consider myself yet to have taken hold of it. But one thing I do: forgetting what is behind and straining toward what is ahead, I press on toward the goal to win the prize for which God has called me heavenward in Christ Jesus." (Philippians 3:13-14)

The apostle Paul was saying that he wasn't going to let himself get distracted from fulfilling God's plan for his life. Did he have failures in his life? Of course he did. But, he said that he was going to forget what was behind and strain toward what was ahead. He learned from his mistakes, he certainly did not want to repeat them, but he was not going to let the fear of making more mistakes slow him down. How about you? Do you feel that you're meant to do more in your life than you're doing now? It's not that what you're doing now isn't important, but do you feel that God has something bigger for you to do? If so, are you moving in that direction? Are you praying about it with a sense of fervor and excitement? Are you diligently seeking the Scripture for God's guidance and wisdom? Are you seeking counsel and wisdom from godly people? In other words, are you starting to forget what is behind and straining toward what is ahead?

"We live by faith, not by sight. We are confident, I say, and would prefer to be away from the body and at home with the Lord. So we make our goal to please him, whether we are at home in the body or away from it." (2 Corinthians 5:7-9)

Chosen by God to Belong to Him

(character, sin)

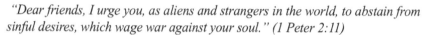

"Dear friends, I urge you, as aliens and strangers in the world, to abstain from sinful desires, which wage war against your soul." (1 Peter 2:11)

The Scripture above tells us that we as Christians are involved in a constant war. Interestingly, this war is waged within, where we are actually at war with ourselves! This is a war where our enemy sin nature is constantly trying to attack passions that lead us down the wrong path. Can you relate?

"Live such good lives among the pagans that, though they accuse you of doing wrong, they may see your good deeds and glorify God on the day he visits." (1 Peter 2:12)

As Christians, our primary purpose is to bring glory to God. One of the ways we do this is to live our lives in such a way that others will bring glory to God. The stakes are high. Eternity hangs in the balance. Yet how do we do this when we are constantly being bombarded by our enemy sin nature that is waging war against us?

"You are a chosen people, a royal priesthood, a holy nation, a people belonging to God, that you may declare the praises of him who called you out of darkness into his wonderful light." (1 Peter 2:9)

One of the best ways to win this war is to remember who we are because of whose we are. As Christians, we have been chosen by God to belong to God. But that is not all. We have been chosen by God to belong to God, and to also bring praises to God—remembering that He rescued us out of darkness and death, bringing us into His light and life. In other words, our motivation to win this internal war comes from an attitude of gratitude. We are grateful that God has saved us through His beloved Son, Jesus Christ. We also want to live a God-honoring and God-glorifying life because we are His! Therefore, Christian, stand up and fight back when it comes to the internal desires that are waging war against you. Be prepared and don't give up. Bring glory to the One who has given His all for you!

"Once you were not a people, but now you are the people of God; once you had not received mercy, but now you have received mercy." (1 Peter 2:10)

Trust in the Truth of God

(spiritual warfare, identity)

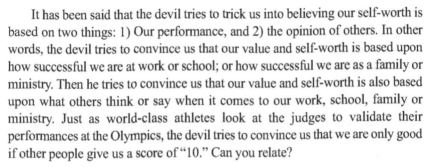

It has been said that the devil tries to trick us into believing our self-worth is based on two things: 1) Our performance, and 2) the opinion of others. In other words, the devil tries to convince us that our value and self-worth is based upon how successful we are at work or school; or how successful we are as a family or ministry. Then he tries to convince us that our value and self-worth is also based upon what others think or say when it comes to our work, school, family or ministry. Just as world-class athletes look at the judges to validate their performances at the Olympics, the devil tries to convince us that we are only good if other people give us a score of "10." Can you relate?

"You created my inmost being; you knit me together in my mother's womb. I praise you because I am fearfully and wonderfully made; your works are wonderful, I know that full well." (Psalm 139:13-14)

It's funny, but God's truth says something completely opposite to that of the lies from the devil. This shouldn't surprise us, should it? The Bible tells us we are special and unique people who have been divinely designed by our great God. Therefore, we have value and dignity because we have been created with value and dignity! In other words, your performance, as well as the opinion of others, does not give you value and dignity—you already have it!

"My frame was not hidden from you when I was made in the secret place. When I was woven together in the depths of the earth, your eyes saw my unformed body. All the days ordained for me were written in our book before one of them came to be." (Psalm 139: 15-16)

As you live your life today, you have a choice: You can listen to the lies of the devil, or you can trust in the truth of God. Are you going to let the devil tell you that you're only as good as your latest performance? Are you going to base your self-worth on the opinion of others? Or are you going to relax and rejoice in the fact that you're a wonderful creation of God and that you're a person of value and dignity?

"How precious to me are your thoughts, O God! How vast is the sum of them! Were I to count them, they would outnumber the grains of sand. When I awake, I am still with you." (Psalm 139:17-18)

A Spirit of Power

(success, grace, fear)

Rule # 1: We all make mistakes.

Rule # 2: Mistakes can be a good thing.

If we are trying new things and looking to improve, chances are we will make mistakes. Yet our path to improvement is often through the very mistakes that we make. How? Mistakes can be good if we learn from them, because this new knowledge allows us to move forward with a greater sense of clarity and confidence. Isn't this what usually happens with scientific discoveries? The greatest advances have come only after a series of many mistakes. Scientists were able to learn what didn't work; which then allowed them to discover what actually worked. It's the same with our lives. If we are making mistakes, this means we are trying to do something with our lives. We are standing up and stepping out into the unknown. The key is to learn and grow from our mistakes, not to repeat them, and to keep stepping forward in faith. In fact, the only way to be certain we will not make mistakes is to play it safe and not try to do anything with our lives—which actually is the greatest mistake we can make!

"For this reason I remind you to fan into flame the gift of God, which is in you through the laying on of my hands." (2 Timothy 1:6)

The apostle Paul wrote these words to a young man named Timothy. Paul was in prison and he was trying to encourage Timothy to do something with his life. With Paul gone, Timothy was suddenly given the responsibility to oversee a large ministry—something he felt very inadequate to do. Timothy was a rather timid person, afraid to make mistakes—that's why Paul had to remind him to step up and use the gifts that God had given him. Maybe right now you're feeling a bit like Timothy. You feel inadequate and afraid to take on a certain responsibility. You know that you need to step up and step forward in faith, yet you're afraid to make a mistake, thinking that you will blow it—for yourself and others. Friend, don't let fear paralyze your faith. Remember rule #1: We all make mistakes. Also, remember rule #2: Mistakes can be a good thing. Therefore, step forward and don't be afraid of mistakes. Expect to makes some mistakes, look to learn and grow from your mistakes, and always remember rule #3: God never makes mistakes!

"For God did not give us a spirit of timidity, but a spirit of power, of love and of self-discipline." (2 Timothy 1:7)

Build Up and Encourage

(relationships, encouragement)

Are you a people builder? Do you encourage and build up people, or do you discourage and tear down people? Businesswoman Mary Kay Ash has stated, "Everyone has an invisible sign hanging from their neck that says, 'Make me feel important.' " How important are you making people feel?

"We who are strong ought to bear with the failings of the weak and not to please ourselves. Each of us should please his neighbor for his good, to build him up." (Romans 15:1-2)

Please understand, the Scripture above is not telling us to condone sin. As Christians, we are not in the business of encouraging disobedience to God. However, we are in the business of building up people and encouraging them to become all that God has called them to be. We all need to be encouraged from time to time, and we all need to become more consistent encouragers. Why? Because courage is something that often leaks. As the old English proverbs states, "old praise dies, unless you feed it."

"Let us therefore make every effort to do what leads to peace and to mutual edification." (Romans 14:19)

Today is a day where you can build up and encourage someone. Perhaps it's a friend or family member. Maybe it's a person at work, at school, or in your ministry. Whoever it may be, and wherever it may be, try to picture that invisible sign and let that person know that he or she is important. You will be amazed at how you can brighten someone's day—including your own!

"A generous man will prosper; he who refreshes others will himself be refreshed." (Proverbs 11:25)

The greatest exercise for your heart is to reach down and lift someone up. Take the time to make the time to be a blessing to someone else today. It won't take much effort, but the reward will be phenomenal. Set a goal to make a positive difference in the life of someone today. Look for reasons to encourage that person, and let them know that they are important.

"May the God who gives endurance and encouragement give you a spirit of unity among yourselves as you follow Christ Jesus, so that with one heart and mouth you may glorify the God and Father of our Lord Jesus Christ." (Romans 15:5-6)

Be a "Bright" Christian

(character, evangelism)

" 'You are the light of the world. A city on a hill cannot be hidden. Neither do people light a lamp and put it under a bowl. Instead they put it on its stand, and it gives light to everyone in the house.' " (Matthew 5:14-15)

Jesus tells us that we are to be "bright" Christians. What exactly does that mean? The main function of light is to dispel darkness. During the days of Jesus there was no electricity. Therefore, lamps were used to light a house. This is a practice that is still used in many parts of the world today. By telling us to be "bright" Christians, Jesus is saying that we need to live our lives in such a way that we bring light to this dark world. Why is this world in darkness? People are living in darkness as a result of sin and the devil.

"The god of this age has blinded minds of unbelievers, so that they cannot see the light of the gospel of the glory of Christ, who is the image of God." (2 Corinthians 4:4)

As Christians, our light can shine both verbally and visually. In other words, what we say and what we do can be a source of light that dispels darkness. However, we must be careful that our light does not come across so strong that it shines like high beams of a car—causing people to turn away. Remember, we are called to be ambassadors for Christ, not jerks for Jesus!

"We are therefore Christ's ambassadors, as though God were making his appeal through us. We implore you on Christ's behalf: Be reconciled to God. God made him who knew no sin be sin for us, so that in him we might become the righteousness of God." (2 Corinthians 5:20-21)

That is good news that will bring light into any dark life! By the way, do you see the focus? It's all on what God has done for us through Jesus. It's all about God's love, God's mercy, and God's grace. Christian, those are some "powerful lamps" that can brighten up this dark world! Think about it, as we verbally and visually live our lives in joyful gratitude of God's love, mercy and grace, other people will start to see the light of God's love, mercy and grace in and through us. What will be the result?

" 'In the same way, let your light shine before men, that they may see your good deeds and praise your Father in heaven.' " (Matthew 5:16)

May all of us endeavor to be "bright" Christians this upcoming Christmas season. And may we never forget—it's all about God's grace, therefore God gets all the glory!

His Promise Preserves Our Lives

(trials, stress, trust)

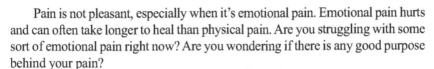

Pain is not pleasant, especially when it's emotional pain. Emotional pain hurts and can often take longer to heal than physical pain. Are you struggling with some sort of emotional pain right now? Are you wondering if there is any good purpose behind your pain?

"It was good for me to be afflicted so that I might learn your decrees. The law from your mouth is more precious to me than thousands of pieces of silver and gold." (Psalm 119:71-72)

The writer of this Psalm looked at his afflictions as something that drew him closer to God's Word, thus drawing him closer to God. It's safe to say that he wasn't happy while going through his afflictions. Can you relate? Rather, he was happy as he looked back and saw the result of his going through his afflictions. What was that result? He had a closer and more intimate relationship with God through His Word. Do you see yourself drawing closer to God and His Word as a result of the pain you're now experiencing?

"Before I was afflicted I went astray, but now I obey your word. You are good, and what you do is good; teach me your decrees." (Psalm 119:67-68)

A wise person once said that we do not recognize the worth of the anchor until we first feel the stress of a storm. That often happens with our relationship with God. When things are smooth and easy, it's very tempting to think that we can handle things without God. However, it's amazing how quickly we turn to God when we start to feel the storm of afflictions in our lives. Can you relate? Isn't it amazing how patient and gracious God is? Rather than forgetting us, God instead allows us to come to Him, anchoring our lives through the security of His amazing love and strength.

"May your unfailing love be my comfort, according to your promise to your servant. Let your compassion come to me that I may live, for your law is my delight." (Psalm 119:76-77)

Going through pain and affliction is never easy. However, it's a reality of life. The good news is that you're not alone—you have a God who cares for you and who can help you in your time of need. Not only can He help you, He actually wants to help you!

"Remember your word to your servant, for you have given me hope. My comfort in my suffering is this: Your promise preserves my life." (Psalm 119:49-50)

Through Christ Our Comfort Overflows

(trials, stress, trust)

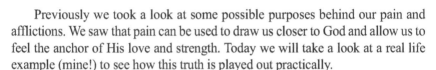

Previously we took a look at some possible purposes behind our pain and afflictions. We saw that pain can be used to draw us closer to God and allow us to feel the anchor of His love and strength. Today we will take a look at a real life example (mine!) to see how this truth is played out practically.

"Praise be to the God and Father of our Lord Jesus Christ, the Father of compassion and the God of all comfort." (2 Corinthians 1:3)

A while back my father-in-law had surgery in America for a very serious illness. At the same time, my wife was getting the test results in Croatia on something that we were told was "abnormal." Needless to say, that was a very challenging time in our lives. However, we can praise God for His compassion and we can look to him for His comfort. As I think about how much I love my wife and father-in-law, I can't help but find comfort in the fact that our God of all compassion loves them even more than me! This means He is watching over them and that He is already working things for our good and His glory! What is my response to all of this? Praise be to the God and Father of our Lord Jesus Christ! But wait, there is more.

"Who comforts us in all our troubles, so that we can comfort those in any trouble with the comfort we ourselves have received from God." (2 Corinthians 1:4)

Do you see another purpose behind our problems? As we receive comfort from the God of all comfort and compassion, we then are able to comfort others who may be going through similar pain and afflictions. Therefore, as I received tremendous comfort from God's Word, my hope is that maybe you can be comforted as well. Perhaps you can relate to something that you are going through, and hopefully you can find comfort in the verses that have blessed us. I know that my wife and I have drawn closer to God and each other through our difficulties. For that, we are grateful. I also know that we have learned to appreciate the gift of health and a new day through all of this. For that, we are grateful. I also know that God has shown forth His comfort and compassion in the most amazing ways through all of this. We praise Him for the strength and faith to keep going on!

"For just as the sufferings of Christ flow into our lives, so also through Christ our comfort overflows." (2 Corinthians 1:5)

God is Your Refuge

(trials, stress, hope)

King David was having one of those really bad days. He was hiding from his enemies in a cave, and his life seemed to be spinning out of control. Can you relate with David's cave experience? Better yet, are you having one of those "cave" experiences right now?

"I cry to the Lord; I lift up my voice to the Lord for mercy. I pour out my complaint before him; before him I tell my trouble." (Psalm 142:1-2)

One of the blessings of the "cave" is that there is no one else there to distract you. It's just you and the Lord. You can pour out your heart to Him because you can give complete attention to Him—something that is very difficult for us when we are in the fast lane of our normal everyday lives.

"When my spirit grows faint within me, it is you who know my way. In the path where I walk men have hidden a snare for me. Look to the right and see; no one is concerned for me. I have no refuge; no one cares for my life." (Psalm 142:3-4)

Can any of you relate to what David was feeling? Are you struggling with a weak spirit, fearing that you may step into a snare at any moment? Do you feel like you're all alone and that no one seems to care for you and your struggles? If so, look at how David found his strength to carry on.

"I cry to you, O Lord; I say, "You are my refuge, my portion in the land of the living." Listen to my cry, for I am in desperate need; rescue me from those who pursue me, for they are too strong for me." (Psalm 142:5-6)

Despite his cave experience, David found hope. How? Because he remembered where his help came from—he remembered the goodness of God, and he recognized the grace of God. David understood the sad truth that his enemies were too strong for him, but he also rejoiced in the unchangeable truth that his enemies were no match for God. How did He come to this conclusion? It was there in that cave David realized that God was all that he had. It was also there in that cave that he realized that God was all that he needed. You see, like David, your "cave" that you are burdened in right now may actually turn out to be your "cave" that produces all kinds of blessings from God. Trust in the goodness of God, and look to Him as your refuge—He won't fail you!

"Set me free from my prison, that I may praise your name. Then the righteous will gather about me because of your goodness to me." (Psalm 142:7)

The Lord Is My Strength and My Song

(stress, thankfulness)

"Give thanks to the Lord, for He is good; His love endures forever." (Psalm 118:1)

What are you thankful for right now? Has the Lord shown His goodness and love to you over this past week? If so, have you taken the time to give Him thanks? Or, have you been so busy moving to the next project in your life that you have simply given a nod to God?

"I was pushed back and about to fall, but the Lord helped me. The Lord is my strength and my song; he has become my salvation. Shouts of joy and victory resound in the tents of the righteous: The Lord's hand has done mighty things!" (Psalm 118:13-15)

The writer of this psalm understood how great of a victory he had experienced. He also clearly understood that is was the Lord's hand that was the sole reason for this victory. Therefore, the psalmist broke out in shouts of joy and gratitude to the Lord. As you look back over the past week, can you see how the Lord's hand has graciously blessed you? If so, are you shouting for joy to the Lord, or are you stressed and forgetful of the Lord?

"You are my God, and I will give you thanks; you are my God, and I will exalt you. Give thanks to the Lord, for he is good; his love endures forever." (Psalm 118:28-29)

The psalmist concluded this psalm in the same way that he began—he was full of thanks and praise to the God whose love endures forever. Perhaps you're feeling alone right now, wondering how you're going to make it through this season in your life. Or, perhaps you're feeling the financial stress these days, worrying how you're going to pay all the bills. Meditate on the verses that we looked at today. Be reminded that our God is an awesome God—He is your joy and salvation. God is your refuge and strength, an ever-present help in our time of trouble. In other words, no matter the size of your challenges that you're facing right now, God's love for you is much bigger and better! Give your burdens to the Lord!

"It is better to take refuge in the Lord than to trust in man. It is better to take refuge in the Lord than to trust in princes." (Psalm 118:8-9)

Digging Deeper into Your Relationship with the Lord

(relationship with God, prayer)

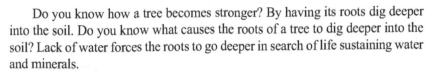

Do you know how a tree becomes stronger? By having its roots dig deeper into the soil. Do you know what causes the roots of a tree to dig deeper into the soil? Lack of water forces the roots to go deeper in search of life sustaining water and minerals.

"To you I call, O Lord my Rock; do not turn a deaf ear to me. For if you remain silent, I will be like those who have gone down into the pit. Hear my cry for mercy as I call to you for help, as I lift up my hands toward your Most Holy Place." (Psalm 28:1-2)

Do you know how a Christian becomes stronger? By having to dig deeper in prayer. Do you know what very often causes a Christian to dig deeper in prayer? Lack of what we feel is a clear answer from God forces us to go deeper in our prayers, as we search for God's life sustaining guidance and grace. Perhaps you have been feeling that God has not heard your prayers as of late. Maybe you're wondering if you are wasting your time as you continually search for the Lord's guidance and grace in prayer. Friend, you're not wasting your time—you're doing exactly what you should be doing! You're digging deeper in your relationship with the Lord. The result will be that the Lord will not only give you the guidance and grace you're searching for, but you will also grow into a stronger and more mature follower of Christ.

"Praise be to the Lord, for he has heard my cry for mercy. The Lord is my strength and my shield; my heart will trust in him, and I am helped. My heart leaps for joy and I will give thanks to him in song." (Psalm 28:6-7)

A wise person once said that Christians are wisest and safest when they are on their knees in prayer. Why? Because it's pretty hard to stumble when you're on your knees. Christian, don't get discouraged into thinking that God doesn't hear your prayers. Don't get depressed when you feel that you're not getting a clear answer to your prayers. Like the roots of a tree, keep digging—because you will be amazed with the blessing you will find!

"The Lord is the strength of his people, a fortress of salvation for his anointed one. Save your people and bless your inheritance; be their shepherd and carry them forever." (Psalm 28:8-9)

Patiently Persevering in Prayer

(prayer)

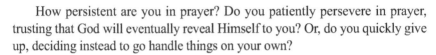

How persistent are you in prayer? Do you patiently persevere in prayer, trusting that God will eventually reveal Himself to you? Or, do you quickly give up, deciding instead to go handle things on your own?

Then Jesus told his disciples a parable to show them that they should always pray and not give up. He said: "In a certain town there was a judge who neither feared God nor cared about men. And there was a widow in that town who kept coming to him with the plea, 'Grant me justice against my adversary.' "For some time he refused. But finally he said to himself, 'Even though I don't fear God or care about men, yet because this widow keeps bothering me, I will see that she gets justice, so that she won't eventually wear me out with her coming!' " (Luke 18:1-5)

Jesus was telling this parable to people who must have been wondering if it's worth it to keep persistently praying to God. In other words, He was telling this parable to people just like us! Do you ever wonder if your prayers are passing the ceiling? Have you been waiting and waiting for an answer from heaven, yet it seems like nothing is happening? Well, this parable is perfect you. Christian, God hears your prayers and God will answer your prayers. We don't know when or how long. But there is one thing that we do know: God cares for His children and God will take care of His children.

"And the Lord said, 'Listen to what the unjust judge says. And will not God bring about justice for his chosen ones, who cry out to him day and night? Will he keep putting them off? I tell you, he will see that they get justice, and quickly. However, when the Son of Man comes, will he find faith on the earth?' " (Luke 18:6-8)

A wise person once said: "If your problems are big enough to worry about, then your problems are big enough to pray about." Therefore, present your requests to the Lord and keep presenting them to Him. Don't come to Him with rehearsed formulas or stagnant statements. Use your mind and your heart, and cry out to your heavenly Father—cry out to Him day and night. Trust in His love and faithfulness. Trust that He hears your prayers and that He will not keep putting you off. Christian, you're not wasting your time when you pray to God. You're investing your time in the wisest of ways!

Come to Christ and Be Blessed

(wisdom, salvation, stress)

How are you feeling this season? Are you feeling blessed, or are you feeling stressed? Are you excited to spend time with family and friends, or are you dreading the thought of seeing anybody?

"It is for freedom that Christ has set us free. Stand firm, then, and do not let yourselves be burdened again by a yoke of slavery." (Galatians 5:1)

There are many ways we can allow ourselves to become burdened and enslaved. Fear due to finances can burden and enslave us. Stress due to relationships can burden and enslave us. Worry due to work or school can burden and enslave us. The verse above reminds us that Christ has set us free—free indeed! The verse also encourages us to stand up and stand firm—and keep standing firm! Christian, do not let yourself be robbed of the joy of this season. Stand up and stand firm, you have been set free by the Lord your Savior!

"For to us a child is born, to us a son is given, and the government will be on His shoulders. And He will be called Wonderful Counselor, Mighty God, Everlasting Father, Prince of Peace." (Isaiah 9:6)

Do you need insight and wisdom right now? Don't stress—come to Christ and be blessed. He is the Wonderful Counselor and He can guide you in the perfect way. Do you feel burdened about some challenges you have been facing this past year? Don't stress—come to Christ and be blessed. He is Mighty God and He can carry all of your burdens on His shoulders. Are you concerned about how you're going to provide for you and your family? Don't stress—come to Christ and be blessed. He is the Possessor of all eternity and He can provide for all of your needs. Are you experiencing panic as you think about the future? Don't stress—come to Christ and be blessed. He is the Prince of Peace and He can turn your worry into worship.

"Of the increase of his government and peace there will be no end. He will reign on David's throne and over his kingdom, establishing and upholding it with justice and righteousness from that time on and forever. The zeal of the Lord Almighty will accomplish this." (Isaiah 9:7)

The Gift of Our Lord and Savior

(salvation)

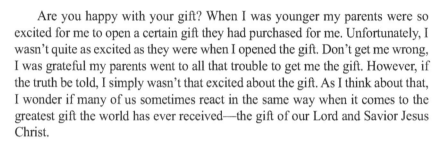

Are you happy with your gift? When I was younger my parents were so excited for me to open a certain gift they had purchased for me. Unfortunately, I wasn't quite as excited as they were when I opened the gift. Don't get me wrong, I was grateful my parents went to all that trouble to get me the gift. However, if the truth be told, I simply wasn't that excited about the gift. As I think about that, I wonder if many of us sometimes react in the same way when it comes to the greatest gift the world has ever received—the gift of our Lord and Savior Jesus Christ.

" 'Today in the town of David a Savior has been born to you; he is Christ the Lord. This will be a sign to you: You will find a baby wrapped in cloths and lying in a manger.' Suddenly a great company of the heavenly host appeared with the angel, praising God and saying, 'Glory to God in the highest, and on earth peace to men on whom His favor rests.' " (Luke 2:11-13)

It's not that we Christians do not appreciate the gift of Jesus and the gift of eternal life He graciously grants to us. But are we are as excited about the birth of Jesus as the great company of heavenly hosts were? It's hard to continue to be excited about a birth that occurred 2,000 years ago, isn't it?

"Praise be to the God and Father of our Lord Jesus Christ! In his great mercy he has given us new birth into a living hope through the resurrection of Jesus Christ from the dead, and into an inheritance that can never perish, spoil or fade—kept in heaven for you." (1 Peter 1:3-4)

Think about it, the birth of Jesus led to our birth—a new birth—where we are now alive to God and members of His family. The birth of Jesus has also led to an inheritance for us, an inheritance in heaven that far exceeds any and all of our favorite gifts combined! With this in mind, take some time today to really think about how blessed you are that Jesus came to this earth 2,000 years ago. Perhaps you can find a quiet place to praise God for the gift of His beloved Son. Maybe you can also share your joy with your family and friends. Remember Christian, He came for you. May we all be forever grateful for the greatest gift there is—the gift of our Lord and Savior Jesus Christ.

Be a People of the Highest Integrity

(character, relationships, integrity)

The New Year brings in all kinds of New Year's resolutions. Some people resolve to lose a certain amount of weight. Others resolve to achieve a certain business or educational goal. Still others resolve to break a certain habit. However, I wonder how many of us resolve to be people of the highest integrity when it comes to our finances.

"The Lord abhors dishonest scales, but accurate weights are his delight." (Proverbs 11:1)

Are you resolved to be honest and ethical in your business dealings? Are you willing to make a commitment to seek to bring delight to the Lord when it comes to the handling of your money?

"The wages of the righteous bring them life, but the income of the wicked brings them punishment." (Proverbs 10:16)

God has graciously entrusted a certain amount of money to us. In fact, He has also blessed us with certain gifts that allow us to make money. The question is: will we be a people who resolve to make money God's way? Will we be a people who resolve to manage God's money God's way? Will we be a people of the highest integrity?

"The Lord does not let the righteous go hungry but he thwarts the craving of the wicked." (Proverbs 10:3)

We all need to understand that the Lord takes care of His people—He takes care of those who are resolved to obey and honor Him. This doesn't mean that the Lord must bless us if we are obedient. The truth is that He doesn't owe us anything. Rather, we owe Him everything. This also doesn't mean that our main motive for obedience should be that we are expecting the Lord to bless us. Yes, the Lord does bless obedience. However, that shouldn't be our main motive. Rather, we should desire to obey and honor God because of our love for and gratitude to God. In other words, we want to honor Him with our finances because of who He is and because of how He is. With this in mind, are you willing to make that kind of resolution when it comes to your finances?

"The man of integrity walks securely, but he who takes crooked paths will be found out." (Proverbs 10:9)

Faithful to God, Not to the Crowd

(peer pressure)

Each day is filled with new hopes and new dreams. It also is an opportunity to take a stand in your commitment to the Lord. In other words, this new day is a time to make a devoted commitment to walk in the ways of the Lord.

"The Lord was with Jehoshaphat because in his early years he walked in the ways his father David had followed. He did not consult the Baals but sought the God of his father and followed his commands rather than the practices of Israel." (2 Chronicles 17:3-4)

King Jehoshaphat began his reign as a man who walked in obedience to God. He was not interested in fitting in with the crowd. Rather, he was willing to stand up and stand out from the crowd. He was a man of character and integrity, one who was devoted to the Lord his God. Is that your goal for this new day? Are you willing to be faithful to God, seeking His approval, and looking to please Him—even if it means saying "no" to the crowd?

"The fear of God came upon all the kingdoms of the countries when they heard how the Lord had fought against the enemies of Israel. And the kingdom of Jehoshaphat was at peace, for his God had given him rest on every side." (2 Chronicles 20:29-30)

The Lord blessed the faithfulness of Jehoshaphat. He had said "yes" to God and "no" to the crowd—and God granted amazing grace and blessings to Jehoshaphat. Jehoshaphat did have his moments of weakness. He made some mistakes by making the wrong alliances. Although he did fall into the trap of following the crowd a few times, nevertheless he kept his heart devoted and faithful to the Lord.

" 'There is, however, some good in you, for you have rid the land of the Asherah poles and have set your heart on seeking God. " (2 Chronicles 19:3)

None of us will be perfectly faithful to our Lord. Jehoshaphat made his mistakes, and so will we. This sad, but true reality is one that is a constant challenge for all of us as Christians. However, God is not expecting us to be perfect. He is pleased with a heart that seeks to please Him, one that is devoted to trying to be faithful. Are you willing to make that commitment for this new day? In other words, are you willing to be faithful to God, seek His approval, and look to please Him—even if it means saying "no" to the crowd?

Bring Pleasure to God

(humility, obedience)

"Has not my hand made all these things, and so they came into being?" declares the Lord. 'This is the one I esteem: He who is humble and contrite in spirit, and trembles at my word.' " (Isaiah 66:2-3)

God tells us that He is pleased with the person who is humble and contrite. How can we be people who are humble and contrite? We can do this by being people who honor and submit to God's holy Word. Do you see the logic? As we honor and obey God's perfect Word, we become people who understand who God is and who we are. In other words, we start to understand that God is God, and that we are not! This causes us to be humble and contrite, seeing ourselves as sinners who are so unbelievably blessed to be able to have a relationship with our great God. This proper perspective is one that brings pleasure to God and blessings to us.

"You do not delight in sacrifice, or I would bring it; you do not take pleasure in burnt offerings. The sacrifices of God are a broken spirit; a broken and contrite heart, O God, you will not despise." (Psalm 51:16-17)

Do you want to bring pleasure and joy to God? Do you want God's favor and blessings on your life? Scripture is clear: God's hand is on the humble, and His care is on the contrite. Obviously, this is completely opposite to what the world tells us. Therefore, as Christians, we have a choice to make. Are we going to listen to God's Word, or are we going to listen to the world's ways? Are we going to try to please God by obeying His standards, or are we going to try to be popular in the world by following its standards?

"In God, whose word I praise, in the Lord, whose word I praise—in God I trust; I will not be afraid. What can man do to me? I am under vows to you, O God; I will present my thank offerings to you." (Psalm 56:10-12)

May this day be one where you bring pleasure to God. Remember, He is pleased with a humble and contrite heart. May this day also be one where God pours out His gracious blessings upon you. Remember, God loves to bless those who obey and trust in Him!

God's Wonderful Masterpiece

(identity, love)

The Bible tells us that we are unique and wonderful creations of God. Yes, we have been tainted by sin, and we do have a depraved sin nature that we daily have to deal with. However, the Bible is clear, we are people with dignity who have been specially created by our special God. This means that you are a very special and unique person. You have been specifically created for a special purpose that has been specially planned and designed for you.

"For you created my inmost being; you knit me together in my mother's womb. I praise you because I am fearfully and wonderfully made; your works are wonderful, I know that full well. My frame was not hidden from you when I was made in the secret place. When I was woven together in the depths of the earth, your eyes saw my unformed body. All the days ordained for me were written in your book before one of them came to be." (Psalm 139:13-16)

As you enter into this day, step forward with a sense of excitement and anticipation. God has a wonderful plan for the wonderful and special you He has created! The fun really starts as you begin to slowly discover that plan, and then go out and start to fulfill that plan for the glory of God. Christian, you are a person with dignity because you have been designed by the divine Designer—and He does not make mistakes! Be joyful about today. Get excited about this new day. But, stay humble. Remember, you are who you are because of Him. God specially designed you for His glory, so make sure to give Him that glory!

"For we are God's workmanship, created in Christ Jesus to do good works, which God prepared in advance for us to do." (Ephesians 2:10)

In the original language, the word "workmanship" means "masterpiece." This means that you are God's wonderful masterpiece, and He has planned certain works for you to do that will paint a wonderful masterpiece of a life for you. May you have a most wonderful and special day!

"Oh, the depth of the riches of the wisdom and knowledge of God! How unsearchable his judgments, and his paths beyond tracing out! Who has known the mind of the Lord? Or who has been his counselor? Who has ever given to God, that God should repay him? For from him and through him and to him are all things. To him be the glory forever! Amen." (Romans 11:33-36)

The Discipline of God

(discipline, trials, stress)

The Bible tells us, discipline from God is actually a blessing from God. That may be difficult for some to accept, especially for those who are experiencing God's discipline right now! However, the Bible is clear that one of the ways to know we are loved by God is to experience the discipline of God.

"You have forgotten that word of encouragement that addresses you as sons: 'My son, do not make light of the Lord's discipline, and do not lose heart when he rebukes you, because the Lord disciplines those he loves, and he punishes everyone he accepts as a son.'" (Hebrews 12:5-6)

Are you feeling the Lord's discipline right now? Rejoice that you are a child of God who is loved by God! Have you been wondering why the Lord has been disciplining you as of late? Because you are a child of God who needs to be changed by God—a change that is meant to make you better, not bitter! Perhaps you have been stuck in some sin that you have not been able to overcome. Or maybe you have been stuck in the safety and comfort of living your life in cruise control. Whatever it may be, we all need to understand that one of the ways God grows us and shows us His love is by disciplining us.

"Endure hardship as discipline; God is treating you as sons. For what son is not disciplined by his father? If you are not disciplined [and everyone undergoes discipline], then you're illegitimate children and not true sons." (Hebrews 12:7-8)

The Bible tells us to persevere and hang in there when we are experiencing discipline from the Lord. One of the ways to do this is to recognize that He disciplines His true children. In other words, the discipline you're experiencing right now is actually a way for you to know with certainly that you're a child of God. What a blessing! Another way to endure discipline is to remember that God is perfect in His discipline. His discipline is never too much or too little. He knows exactly what you need, and He knows exactly how much you need—so that you can become the person He created and saved you to be. What a blessing!

"No discipline seems pleasant at the time, but painful. Later on, however, it produces a harvest of righteousness and peace for those who have been trained by it." (Hebrews 12:11)

The Lord Is Our Helper

(stress, finances)

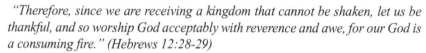

"Therefore, since we are receiving a kingdom that cannot be shaken, let us be thankful, and so worship God acceptably with reverence and awe, for our God is a consuming fire." (Hebrews 12:28-29)

Over the past few years, we have seen that the stock market and real estate market can be shaken. We have also seen that seemingly strong businesses can be shaken. In fact, we have even seen that the strongest countries can be shaken. However, the Bible encourages us that there is one kingdom that can never be shaken—the kingdom of God. The good news is, through Jesus Christ, we as Christians are members of that very kingdom! The question is, do we realize how blessed we truly are?

"Keep your lives free from the love of money and be content with what you have, because God has said, 'Never will I leave you; never will I forsake you.' So we say with confidence, 'The Lord is my helper; I will not be afraid. What can man do to me?'" (Hebrews 13:5-6)

Not only are we part of an eternal and unshakable kingdom, we also have an eternal and unshakable King who says that He is with us and will never leave us. This should give us incredible confidence, especially when daily we have to face the "shakiness" of various markets and businesses. God tells us that He is our Helper and protector, He promises to guide and guard us, and He reminds us that He is much mightier than even the mightiest of human enterprises. Think about it, as a Christian you're part of a kingdom that can never be shaken. You also have the great God of this universe on your side, and He can never be shaken or defeated. What should our response to all of this be?

"What, then, shall we say in response to this? If God is for us, who can be against us? He who did not spare his own Son, but gave him up for us all—how will he not also, along with him, graciously give us all things?" (Romans 8:31-32)

Take some time and meditate on the verses from today. Think about how they apply to your life. More specifically, think about how they apply to some of the "shakable" circumstances you have been facing as of late. Then take some time to rejoice that you are part of an amazing kingdom, and that your King is more than able to give you everything you need to keep you from being shaken!

Peace Should Reign in Our Hearts

(peace, relationships)

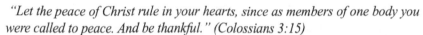

"Let the peace of Christ rule in your hearts, since as members of one body you were called to peace. And be thankful." (Colossians 3:15)

Christians are called to be peace lovers, peace livers, and peace makers. In other words, peace should reign in our hearts as we live our life to honor Jesus, the Prince of Peace. Think about it, we have been brought into a peace relationship with God through Jesus. We have also been brought into a peace relationship with other Christians who are now part of God's family through Jesus. Therefore, peace should be an attribute that permeates our actions and attitudes. Is this true of you? Are you a peace lover, peace liver, and peace maker?

"Therefore, as God's chosen people, holy and dearly loved, clothe yourselves with compassion, kindness, humility, gentleness and patience. Bear with each other and forgive whatever grievances you may have against one another. Forgive as the Lord forgave you." (Colossians 3:12-13)

Peace will only permeate our actions and attitudes when we have the proper perspective. What is that perspective? Forgive as the Lord has forgiven us. The peace we have with God is a result of God pursuing peace with us. God the Father chose to punish God the Son in our place so that our sins could be forgiven. God the Son chose to hang on that cross and be punished as our substitute so that we could be brought into a peace relationship with the Father. God the Holy Spirit chose to come live within those of us who have trusted Jesus, sealing our salvation forever. Christian, we must never forget that God is the One who made the choice to pursue peace with us. Pursuing peace with others is much easier when we have this perspective. However, without this perspective, the pursuit of peace is painful. Can you relate?

"Over all these virtues put on love, which binds them all together in perfect unity." (Colossians 3:14)

Is there somebody you need to pursue peace with? Better yet, is there somebody in the family of God who you're really struggling to forgive? Remember, we are called to be peace lovers, peace livers, and peace makers. May God give you the peace and perspective to pursue peace for the glory of His name and unity in His family.

Feeling the Heat of God's Iron

(discipline, stress)

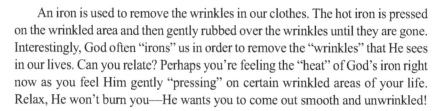

An iron is used to remove the wrinkles in our clothes. The hot iron is pressed on the wrinkled area and then gently rubbed over the wrinkles until they are gone. Interestingly, God often "irons" us in order to remove the "wrinkles" that He sees in our lives. Can you relate? Perhaps you're feeling the "heat" of God's iron right now as you feel Him gently "pressing" on certain wrinkled areas of your life. Relax, He won't burn you—He wants you to come out smooth and unwrinkled!

"Consider it pure joy, my brothers, whenever you face trials of many kinds, because you know the testing of your faith develops perseverance. Perseverance must finish its work so that you may be mature and complete, not lacking anything." (James 1:2-4)

It seems that God is constantly seeing wrinkles in my life. Some are very large wrinkles and others are less noticeable, however, they are wrinkles that need to be smoothed out. You see, God wants His people to "look good" so that we can properly represent Him. As Christians, our lives are to be lived in such a way that others praise God. However, if our lives are full of all kinds of "wrinkles" (unholy actions and attitudes), people will be distracted and therefore not give praise to our God. Therefore, God in His grace will gently apply "heat" on the actions and attitudes of our lives. He will gently press down where needed, and then He will gently smooth over those large and small wrinkles. The result is that our actions and attitudes start to look so good that others begin to give praise and glory to God.

"In the same way, let your light shine before men, that they may see your good deeds and praise your Father in heaven." (Matthew 5:16)

Are you interested in seeing God glorified in and through your life? Be prepared for God to "iron" you. Do you want to see your actions and attitudes cause others to praise God? Be prepared to feel the "heat" of God's iron gently press on you. Don't worry, God is not only perfect in seeing the wrinkles, He is also perfect when it comes to gently smoothing out the wrinkles. Therefore, don't panic, but rejoice—God's "iron" is doing a wonderful work in and through you!

"May the God of hope fill you with all joy and peace as you trust in him, so that you may overflow with hope by the power of the Holy Spirit." (Romans 15:13)

God on Our Side

(hope)

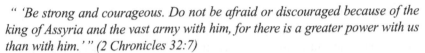

" 'Be strong and courageous. Do not be afraid or discouraged because of the king of Assyria and the vast army with him, for there is a greater power with us than with him.' " (2 Chronicles 32:7)

King Hezekiah and the people of Judah were being threatened by the evil Assyrians. Assyria was a powerful empire that was led by King Sennacherib. He was an arrogant man who believed that he was unstoppable. He and his army had destroyed nation after nation, and Sennacherib now had his sights set on capturing the people of God. It was a seemingly hopeless situation for King Hezekiah and the people of Judah. From a human standpoint, they were outnumbered and powerless. However, they were not fighting simply from a human standpoint— they had God on their side.

" 'With him is only the arm of flesh, but with us is the Lord our God to help us and fight our battles.' And the people gained confidence from what Hezekiah the king of Judah said." (2 Chronicles 32:8)

Yes, Sennacherib was a powerful man. However, he was only a man. Consequently, he was no match for the all-powerful and Almighty God of this universe. This perspective gave Hezekiah and the people the peace and patience they needed to trust in the Lord. How about you? Are you dealing with some powerful opposition in your life right now? Maybe it's a powerful person that is opposing you. Or perhaps it's a powerful circumstance that is opposing you. Christian, look at those words from Hezekiah again—and now apply them to your particular situation. Think about it: If God is on your side, who or what can defeat you? It does not matter how strong the opposition may seem—the opposition is not bigger and more powerful than our great God. This perspective can be difficult for us to remember all the time—especially when the "Sennacherib's" in our life start to come against us. Yet, it's the perspective that we need to maintain. Why? Because it's true! What is against us is only the arm of flesh, but with us is the Lord to help us and fight our battles!

"So the Lord saved Hezekiah and the people of Jerusalem from the hand of Sennacherib king of Assyria and from the hand of all others. He took care of them on every side. Many brought offerings to Jerusalem for the Lord and valuable gifts for Hezekiah king of Judah. From then on he was highly regarded by all the nations." (2 Chronicles 32:22-23)

What Does Your Personal "Stamp" Say About You?

(actions, identity)

My wife and I started a non-profit organization in the United States in 2007. The name of the organization is "Gospel on the Go Ministries" and we have a stamp with the name of the organization on it. We use this stamp on our documents, stamping the name of the organization on all papers where it's required. We are also in the process of starting a non-profit organization in Croatia as well. We have requested the name to be "Lighthouse of Life," and once we are officially registered with the government we will then receive a stamp with the name of the new organization on it. Interestingly, the stamps for both organizations are limited, for they can only state the name of each organization. However, the stamps cannot truly describe who we are and what we do. The stamps cannot describe if we are people of character and integrity. The stamps cannot describe if we are people of love and humility. Only our actions over time will let people know who we truly are. In other words, our actions and attitudes will be the "real stamps" of our organizations.

"We want to avoid any criticism of the way we administer this liberal gift. For we are taking pains to do what is right, not only in the eyes of the Lord but also in the eyes of men." (2 Corinthians 8:20-21)

As I think about it, every one of us has a "stamp" that describes who we truly are. For example, every family has a "stamp" that not only describes the name of the family, but it also describes the values and character of that family. Parents, what will that "stamp" of your family really say? Every employer and employee has a "stamp" that describes who they truly are. What will your personal "stamp" say about you? Will you be proud of what your "stamp" says about your character and values at work? As we enter into this New Year, may we all think about what the "stamps" of our lives will truly say. May we strive to be a people of Christlike character and integrity. May we strive to be a people who are consistent in our actions and attitudes. May we also be a people who are proud of what the "stamps" of our lives say about us.

"As water reflects a face, so a man's heart reflects the man." (Proverbs 27:19)

Your Shield of Protection and Peace

(peace, stress)

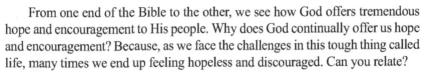

From one end of the Bible to the other, we see how God offers tremendous hope and encouragement to His people. Why does God continually offer us hope and encouragement? Because, as we face the challenges in this tough thing called life, many times we end up feeling hopeless and discouraged. Can you relate?

"The Lord is a refuge for the oppressed, a stronghold in times of trouble. Those who know your name will trust in you, for you, Lord, have never forsaken those who seek you." (Psalm 9:9-10)

Are you feeling oppressed and overwhelmed? The Lord is your Rock and Refuge. Are you feeling stress and worry because of some troubling circumstances? The Lord is your Stronghold and Security. He promises to be with those who trust in Him and will never forget or forsake those who call upon Him.

"Many are saying of me, 'God will not deliver him.' But you are a shield around me, O Lord; you bestow glory on me and lift up my head. To the Lord I cry aloud, and he answers me from his holy hill. I lie down and sleep; I wake again, because the Lord sustains me. I will not fear the tens of thousands drawn up against me on every side." (Psalm 3:2-6)

Are you feeling surrounded by all kinds of difficult people or difficult circumstances? The Lord is your Shield of protection and peace. He is the One who will lift you up, He is the One who will give you the peace to sleep, and He is the One who will give you the strength to get up and get going. In other words, the Lord is the One who will cover you and sustain you through your times of trouble.

"I love you, O Lord, my strength. The Lord is my rock, my fortress and my deliverer; my God is my rock, in whom I take refuge. He is my shield and the horn of my salvation, my stronghold. I call to the Lord, who is worthy of praise, and I am saved from my enemies." (Psalm 18:1-3)

Take some time and meditate on the verses we looked at today. Pick out certain words of hope and encouragement that are meaningful to you. Then, think about how these words of hope and encouragement can be applied to the particular circumstances that you're facing today. Finally, take some time and rejoice—for with God on your side, you're on the winning side!

Seek and Work
Wholeheartedly for the Lord

(work, actions)

"This is what Hezekiah did throughout Judah, doing what was good and right and faithful before the Lord his God. In everything that he undertook in the service of God's temple and in obedience to the law and the commands, he sought his God and worked wholeheartedly. And so he prospered." (2 Chronicles 31:20-21)

King Hezekiah trusted in the Lord, but he also worked hard for the Lord. He sought the Lord, trusting in God's grace and wisdom. He also worked wholeheartedly for the Lord, fulfilling his human responsibility. This is a great example of how God's sovereignty does not cancel out our human responsibility. Yes, God is in full control and has a perfect foreordained plan that cannot be changed. Therefore, we need to seek the Lord and trust in the Lord. However, we don't just sit back and wait for His plan to unfold. We have a role and responsibility to do our part, to work wholeheartedly for the Lord. In doing so, God's sovereignty and our human responsibility come together in such a way that we end up fulfilling God's perfect purpose and plan for our lives—a purpose and plan that often exceeds even our wildest dreams! This same principal of God's sovereignty and human responsibility can be seen in the life and ministry of the apostle Paul as well.

"But by the grace of God I am what I am, and his grace to me was not without effect. No, I worked harder than all of them—yet not I, but the grace of God that was with me." (1 Corinthians 15:10)

Like Hezekiah, Paul trusted in the grace of God. However, he also worked wholeheartedly for God. In fact, he worked harder than most others. Why? He clearly understood that God's sovereignty and human responsibility worked hand in hand. How about you? First, how much time do you spend seeking the Lord's purpose and plan for your life? In other words, are you looking to the Lord and trusting in His sovereignty? Second, how hard are you working for the Lord? In other words, are you fulfilling your human responsibility by working wholeheartedly for the Lord? Remember, God has a perfect plan for our lives, but He expects us to do our part to discover and fulfill this plan. May we all be a people who seek the Lord and work wholeheartedly for the Lord . . .trusting that His perfect plan will exceed even our wildest expectations!

Bring Honor to Christ through Your Words and Lives

(words, actions)

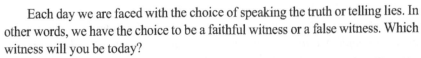

Each day we are faced with the choice of speaking the truth or telling lies. In other words, we have the choice to be a faithful witness or a false witness. Which witness will you be today?

"A truthful witness does not deceive, but a false witness pours out lies." (Proverbs 14:5)

As Christians, our lips and our lives can be a powerful witness for the glory of Christ. People are looking for someone they can trust, someone who will not deceive them. This means that today you will have the opportunity to bless someone and bring honor to your Lord and Savior.

"A truthful witness saves lives, but a false witness is deceitful." (Proverbs 14:25)

As Christians, our lips and our lives can also bring dishonor to Christ. Today will also be a day where you will be faced with the temptation of being a false witness—bringing hurt to others and dishonor to your Lord and Savior. As you embark on this new day, what kind of witness do you want to be—a faithful or false witness—in your family, workplace, school, or ministry? Do you want to bring blessings to others and honor to Christ? Or, do you want to bring pain to others and dishonor to Christ?

"But when he, the Spirit of truth, comes, he will guide you into all truth. He will not speak on his own; he will speak only what he hears, and he will tell you what is yet to come. He will bring glory to me by taking from what is mine and making it known to you. All that belongs to the Father is mine. That is why I said the Spirit will take from what is mine and make it known to you." (John 16:13-15)

As Christians, we have the Spirit of truth with us and living in us. God the Holy Spirit is our Guide and our Teacher. He wants our lives to be lives that are defined by truth, not by deception. He wants our lives to bring glory to God the Father and God the Son. Think about it: God the Holy Spirit lives in you, right? This means that He is with you everywhere you go. This also means that He will be right there with you today when you're faced with the choice of being a faithful or a false witness. What choice will you make?

God's Word of Truth Refreshes and Sustains Us

(God's Word, stress)

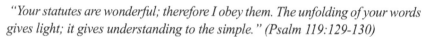

"Your statutes are wonderful; therefore I obey them. The unfolding of your words gives light; it gives understanding to the simple." (Psalm 119:129-130)

The psalmist was so excited about God's wonderful word of truth. He was so excited to learn God's Word; for he knew God's Word would provide light and understanding for his journey in life. He was also excited to obey God's Word, because he knew obedience would lead to joy and blessings. How about you? How excited are you to read and obey God's Word of truth? Do you open the Bible with a sense of excitement and anticipation, trusting that God will graciously provide light and wisdom for your daily journey?

"I open my mouth and pant, longing for your commands." (Psalm 119:131)

What a beautiful picture of a person who was committed to learning and living according to God's Word. Yet I wonder how many of us say the same thing about God's Word. Perhaps the psalmist was tired and exhausted from the pressures of life. Can you relate? Yet he knew exactly where to go to find refreshment—God's wonderful Word. He was so thirsty and he knew exactly what could satisfy that thirst. This picture reminds me of the new kitten we recently purchased for my mother. She is only seven weeks old, yet she already rules the house! When she woke up this morning she was so excited to explore her new surroundings that she ended up running and jumping to the point of exhaustion. Do you know what the poor thing did? She looked straight at her water dish, went over to it, and started drinking up the cool water—for about five minutes! As I sat there watching her, I couldn't help but think how much smarter she is than I am. She knew what to do when she was exhausted. She knew where to go for refreshment—and she stayed there until she was satisfied. All this from a seven-week-old animal!

"Your word is a lamp to my feet and a light for my path. I have taken an oath and confirmed it, that I will follow your righteous laws." (Psalm 119:105-106)

May we all learn from the example of the psalmist—and my Mom's kitten! May we all grow in our desire for the Lord and His refreshing Word of truth, and may our lives be filled with light and wisdom that only comes from the wonderful Word of the Lord.

A Good and Faithful Servant

(laziness, actions)

"I went past the field of the sluggard, past the vineyard of the man who lacks judgment; thorns had come up everywhere, the ground was covered with weeds, and the stone wall was in ruins." (Proverbs 24:30-31)

The Bible does not pull any punches when it comes to describing a lazy person. Someone who is lazy is called a sluggard and a fool. Doesn't sound very "politically correct," does it? Yet, the Bible is very clear in warning us of the dangers of being lazy and irresponsible.

"I applied my heart to what I observed and learned a lesson from what I saw: A little sleep, a little slumber, a little folding of the hands to rest—and poverty will come on you like a bandit and scarcity like an armed man." (Proverbs 24:32-34)

Please understand, not all poverty is a consequence of laziness and irresponsibility. Likewise, not all financial difficulties are a direct result of laziness and irresponsibility. However, it's safe to say that laziness and irresponsibility can lull us into a false sense of security only to wake us up with the loud alarm of major financial hardship. Can you relate? When financial challenges arise, it's very easy to blame other people or other circumstances. However, it may be better to first look at ourselves and ask if laziness or irresponsibility had anything to do with our problems. An honest personal assessment may be the first step on the road of financial recovery. We do not need to beat ourselves up about the mistakes we have made. However, we do need to learn from them and make sure that we do not repeat them.

"We hear that some among you are idle. They are not busy; they are busybodies. Such people we command and urge in the Lord Jesus Christ to settle down and earn the bread they eat. And as for you, brothers, never tire of doing what is right." (2 Thessalonians 3:11-13)

As Christians, we have been entrusted with certain gifts and responsibilities from God. God wants a return on His investment. This doesn't mean that our lives should become immersed in work to the point that we sacrifice our health, family and relationship with the Lord. Rather, we should work in such a way that we rely on the grace of God with the goal of bringing glory to God. After all, it's much better to be called a good and faithful servant by the Lord, rather than a lazy, foolish sluggard. Wouldn't you agree?

A Heart of Integrity

(character, legacy)

"Neither before nor after Josiah was there a king like him who turned to the Lord as he did—with all his heart and with all his soul and with all his strength, in accordance with all the Law of Moses." (2 Kings 23:25)

Look at the legacy King Josiah left. He was a godly man who made a positive difference in a very ungodly environment. Josiah wasn't perfect (neither are we!), yet he left a God-centered and God-glorifying legacy for all to follow. Wouldn't you like to leave that type of legacy for your family to follow? Look closely at the epitaph that was written about him. He was a man who followed the Lord with all his heart, soul and strength. Wouldn't you like to have that same type of epitaph written about you? Think about how proud your family would be to have those wonderful words written about you.

"He chose David his servant and took him from the sheep pens; from tending the sheep he brought him to be the shepherd of his people Jacob, of Israel his inheritance. And David shepherded them with integrity of heart; with skillful hands he led them." (Psalm 78:70-72)

King David also left an incredible legacy for all to follow. He was a godly man who made a positive and God-glorifying legacy in spite of all kinds of obstacles and opposition. Although he made mistakes (we all do!), nevertheless, he was a man who had a heart for God (that is the key!). He led with integrity of heart and skillful hands. Wouldn't you like the same to be said about you? Wouldn't it be great to be remembered as a person with a heart of integrity and hands that were skillful?

"However, I consider my life worth nothing to me, if only I may finish the race and complete the task the Lord Jesus has given me—the task of testifying to the gospel of God's grace." (Acts 20:24)

Look at those Words of the apostle Paul. He was determined to fulfill his calling, he was dedicated to leaving a God-centered and God-glorifying legacy, and he was not going to let anything or anyone distract him from getting the job done. Once again, we see a man who left a legacy for all to follow. We also see a wonderful epitaph of a man who was driven to please the Lord. Remember, Paul wasn't perfect (neither are we!), yet he was determined and dedicated to not get distracted from finishing the race. May God grant us the grace, so the same may be said about us.

The Prayer Rut

(prayer)

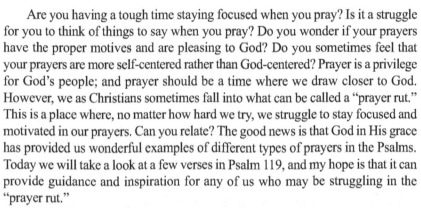

Are you having a tough time staying focused when you pray? Is it a struggle for you to think of things to say when you pray? Do you wonder if your prayers have the proper motives and are pleasing to God? Do you sometimes feel that your prayers are more self-centered rather than God-centered? Prayer is a privilege for God's people; and prayer should be a time where we draw closer to God. However, we as Christians sometimes fall into what can be called a "prayer rut." This is a place where, no matter how hard we try, we struggle to stay focused and motivated in our prayers. Can you relate? The good news is that God in His grace has provided us wonderful examples of different types of prayers in the Psalms. Today we will take a look at a few verses in Psalm 119, and my hope is that it can provide guidance and inspiration for any of us who may be struggling in the "prayer rut."

Teach me.

"Teach me, O Lord, to follow your decrees; then I will keep them to the end. Give me understanding, and I will keep your law and obey it with all my heart." (Psalm 119:33-34)

Direct me.

"Direct me in the path of your commands, for there I find delight." (Psalm 119:35)

Turn me.

"Turn my heart toward your statutes and not toward selfish gain. Turn my eyes away from worthless things; preserve my life according to your word." (Psalm 119:36-37)

Fulfill for me.

"Fulfill your promise to your servant, so that you may be feared. Take away the disgrace I dread, for your laws are good." (Psalm 119:38-39)

Preserve me.

"How I long for your precepts! Preserve my life in your righteousness." (Psalm 119:40)

If you're having a tough time staying focused when you pray, or if it's a struggle for you to think of things to say when you pray, try praying through the Psalms. You will not have to wonder if your prayers have the proper motives, and you can rest in the fact that your prayers are following God's Word of truth. In other words, you will find yourself joyfully climbing out of that "prayer rut!"

What Does Church Mean to You? (Part 1)

(church, the body of Christ)

What does church mean to you? What are some things that you really enjoy about church? What are some other things that you wish would be different about church? Although there may be varying opinions as to what the church is and should look like, the Bible gives us very clear answers as to what God wants His church to be.

1) The church is people.

"You are a chosen people, a royal priesthood, a holy nation, a people belonging to God, that you may declare the praises of him who called you out of darkness into his wonderful light. Once you were not a people, but now you are the people of God; once you had not received mercy, but now you have received mercy." (1 Peter 2:9-10)

Notice that the church is people, not buildings. In other words, God has called people out of darkness and brought people to Himself. He has not called bricks and buildings out of darkness into His wonderful light. This is not to say that church buildings are wrong or evil, rather it is to say that God's church is comprised of God's people—people who once were not a people of God, but by God's grace and mercy are the people of God forever. May the people of God give praise to God! By the way, bricks and buildings can't do that!

2) The church is a body.

"God has combined the members of the body and has given greater honor to the parts that lacked it, so that there should be no division in the body, but that its parts should have equal concern for each other. If one part suffers, every part suffers with it; if one part is honored, every part rejoices with it. Now you are the body of Christ, and each one of you is a part of it." (1 Corinthians 12:24-27)

Notice that the church is a living body, not a stagnate organization. This isn't to say that an organization is evil or wrong. Rather, it is to say that the church is a living and active organism. It's comprised of the people of Christ, living members of the body of Christ—called to build and bless the body of Christ, all for the glory of Christ. Christian, you are part of the body of Christ, and you are a vital part of the body of Christ. May the body of Christ give praise to Christ! By the way, an inanimate organization or institution can't do that!

3) The church is a family.

"How great is the love the Father has lavished on us, that we should be called children of God! And that is what we are! The reason the world does not know us is that it did not know him." (1 John 3:1)

Notice that the church is the family of God, not a long list of names on a membership roster. This is not to say that church membership rosters are wrong. Rather, it is to say that the church is the living, active, blessed family of God. Christian, you are part of the greatest family there is! We are the children of God who have been chosen by God—before the foundation of the world. We are the people of God who have been purchased by the Son of God—at the cross 2000 years ago. We have been adopted into the family of God—marked and sealed by the Holy Spirit—guaranteeing our inheritance and inclusion in God's family forever! May God's family praise our Great God!

What Does Church Mean to You? (Part 2)

(church, the body of Christ)

What does church mean to you? Previously we saw that the Bible describes the church as being the people of Christ, the body of Christ, and the family of Christ. This means that the church is living and active . . . coming into existence because of the grace of Christ and looking to bring glory to Christ. Today we are going to look at some of the roles that Christ has for His people in the church.

1) The role of the pastor.

"It was he who gave some to be apostles, some to be prophets, some to be evangelists, and some to be pastors and teachers, to prepare God's people for works of service, so that the body of Christ may be built up until we all reach unity in the faith and in the knowledge of the Son of God and become mature, attaining to the whole measure of the fullness of Christ." (Ephesians 4:11-13)

What is the role of the pastor? The pastor's role is to build up and encourage God's people in the work of the ministry. Notice that the pastor is not to be a star, where he is adored and worshiped by the people. Rather, he is to be a servant, where he serves the people and equips them to use their gifts to build up the body of Christ. Also, notice that the pastor is not the one who does all the work. He should not selfishly hold onto all the responsibilities, nor should the people sit back and expect him to assume all the responsibilities. Rather, the pastor serves the people by helping prepare the people to serve the body of Christ.

2) The role of the people.

"Each one should use whatever gift he has received to serve others, faithfully administering God's grace in its various forms. If anyone speaks, he should do it as one speaking the very words of God. If anyone serves, he should do it with the strength God provides, so that in all things God may be praised through Jesus Christ. To him be the glory and the power for ever and ever. Amen." (1 Peter 4:10-11)

The people of Christ are called to serve the body of Christ. As Christians, we all have been given spiritual gifts. Though our gifts may vary, our purpose is the same ... to serve the body of Christ for the glory of Christ. This means that a non-serving Christian is an anomaly. Why? As Rick Warren of Saddleback Church loves to say, we are saved to serve. This also means that every Christian has an important contribution to make to the body of Christ. There is no gift that is more important than the other. Every Christian matters and every gift matters. Remember, pastors prepare the people, the people serve the body, and God is glorified.

3) The role of the church.

"His intent was that now, through the church, the manifold wisdom of God should be made known to the rulers and authorities in the heavenly realms, according to his eternal purpose which he accomplished in Christ Jesus our Lord." (Ephesians 3:10-11)

In Part Three, we will take a look at the role of the church. In the meantime, ask yourself this important question, "As a Christian who is part of the body and family of Christ, am I fulfilling my role in such a way that I am bringing glory to Christ?"

What Does Church Mean to You? (Part 3)

(church, the body of Christ)

What does church mean to you? In part one, we saw that the Bible describes the church as being the people of Christ, the body of Christ, and the family of Christ. In part two, we took a look at the role that Christ has for the pastor and the people in the church. Today we are going to take a look at the role Christ has for the church.

1) The role of the church.

"His intent was that now, through the church, the manifold wisdom of God should be made known to the rulers and authorities in the heavenly realms, according to his eternal purpose which he accomplished in Christ Jesus our Lord." (Ephesians 3:10-11)

The primary purpose of the people/church of Christ is to bring glory and honor to its Lord and Savior, Jesus Christ. Jesus paid a huge price for His church, and as Christians we are members of His body because He chose to bring us into His body. Therefore, He deserves our adoration and affection. Interestingly, the verses above tell us that there is an additional purpose for the church. God is using sinful, yet saved, people like you and me to show the heavenly beings the wisdom and power of God. In other words, God is using us to display the manifold wisdom of God. That is absolutely incredible! Think about it, the angels are watching in awe as they see how God's grace and mercy saves His people through the gospel; they stand in amazement as they see the transformed people of Christ joyfully and selflessly serving the body of Christ; they are stunned as they see the church impacting communities, countries and continents for Christ . . . causing them to break out in constant praise and worship to the King, Jesus Christ. This is happening because God has chosen to reveal His wisdom and power through sinners like us—absolutely amazing!

"It was revealed to them that they were not serving themselves but you, when they spoke of the things that have now been told you by those who have preached the gospel to you by the Holy Spirit sent from heaven. Even angels long to look into these things." (1 Peter 1:12)

As Christians, we are the people of Christ, and we are members of the body and family of Christ forever. We are called to serve the body of Christ for the praise and glory of Christ . . . praises that not only happen from people down here on earth, but praises that also happen from the angels in heaven. Amazing, absolutely amazing— what an indescribable privilege to be in the family of God!

Keeping the Main Thing the Main Thing

(simplicity, God's will)

A wise person once said that if you want to reduce complexity and increase productivity, strive for simplicity. In other words, we need to keep the main thing the main thing. However, in this age of ever increasing opportunities and options, how can we learn to keep the main thing the main thing?

"Do not conform any longer to the pattern of this world, but be transformed by the renewing of your mind. Then you will be able to test and approve what God's will is—his good, pleasing and perfect will." (Romans 12:2)

Parents, are you trying to reduce complexity and increase productivity when it comes to the raising of your children? Employers and employees, are you trying to reduce complexity and increase productivity at your work place? How about those of you involved in ministry? Are you working at keeping the main thing the main thing? The Bible tells us that God is a God of order; He is not a God of confusion. Thus, He is a God who is more than able to reduce confusion and complexity in your life. He is a God who is more than able to increase productivity in your life. He is a God who is more than able to give you the wisdom you need to keep the main thing the main thing. However, we have to make the disciplined choice to daily seek the wisdom of His Word rather than the wisdom of the world. We need to daily look for God's perfect Word to reduce the complexity and confusion in our lives, trusting that He will guide us in simplicity and increased productivity. In other words, we need to daily look at God's perfect Word to reveal His good, pleasing and perfect will for our lives.

"Your statutes are wonderful; therefore I obey them. The unfolding of your words gives light; it gives understanding to the simple." (Psalm 119:129-130)

Every day we're faced with a choice: follow the wisdom of the world and fall into the trap of complexity and confusion. Or, follow the wisdom of God's Word and avoid the trap of complexity and confusion. Christian, do you want to keep the main thing the main thing? Do you want to reduce complexity and increase productivity? Then strive for simplicity.

Keeping things in Godly Perspective
(comparison, identity)

"We do not dare to classify or compare ourselves with some who commend themselves. When they measure themselves by themselves and compare themselves with themselves, they are not wise." (2 Corinthians 10:12)

Comparison is not wise. Why? When we compare ourselves to others, we will either become prideful or disappointed. In some cases, we will become prideful because we feel that we are doing better than someone else. In other cases, we will become disappointed because we feel that we are not doing as well as someone else. In either case, comparison is not wise or healthy.

"We, however, will not boast beyond proper limits, but will confine our boasting to the field God has assigned to us, a field that reaches even to you." (2 Corinthians 10:13)

The apostle Paul understood that comparison was unwise and unhealthy. He also understood that any success he was experiencing was all as a result of the Lord. It was the Lord who placed him in the field of service he was in. It was also the Lord who produced the fruit in the field that Paul was in. Therefore, he kept his comparison and boasting in perspective. If he was bearing more fruit than someone else, it was all because of the Lord. Therefore, he didn't get prideful. If someone else was bearing more fruit than Paul, it was all because of the Lord. Therefore, he didn't get discouraged. However, this perspective didn't cause Paul to get lazy and indifferent. No, he understood that he had a responsibility to give his best in all that he did, trusting that the Lord would graciously grant the results.

"But by the grace of God I am what I am, and his grace to me was not without effect. No, I worked harder than all of them—yet not I, but the grace of God that was with me." (1 Corinthians 15:10)

Once again, the apostle Paul kept things in perspective. He gave his best, working harder than others. Yet, he also understood that it was God's grace that gave him the ability and energy to outwork others. Therefore, he didn't boast in anything other than God's grace. By the way, did you notice how many times he used the word "grace" in that verse? How about you? How are you dealing with the ever-present temptation of comparison? Perhaps we should all start comparing ourselves to the Lord Jesus, the perfect One from heaven. In doing so, we will see that we all fall woefully short in comparison to Him. Yet, at the same time we will also see that we are who we are by His grace—and that any success we experience is all because of His amazing grace. Therefore, He gets all the glory!

Receive the Peace of God

(worry, peace, trust)

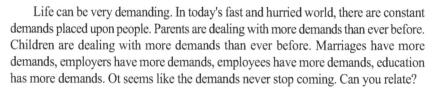

Life can be very demanding. In today's fast and hurried world, there are constant demands placed upon people. Parents are dealing with more demands than ever before. Children are dealing with more demands than ever before. Marriages have more demands, employers have more demands, employees have more demands, education has more demands. Ot seems like the demands never stop coming. Can you relate?

"I sought the LORD, and he answered me; he delivered me from all my fears. Those who look to him are radiant; their faces are never covered with shame. This poor man called, and the LORD heard him; he saved him out of all his troubles. The angel of the LORD encamps around those who fear him, and he delivers them." (Psalm 34:4-7)

This is a great passage because it tells the truth about life—it will not always be easy! The sobering reality is that there will be pressures, there will be demands, and there will be troubles. However, the good news is that the Lord hears and helps those who call upon Him. He lifts them and delivers them from their pressures, demands and troubles. He protects and provides for those who look to Him for help and healing. In other words, Christian, you're not alone when it comes to all of those difficult demands that life is throwing at you right now!

"So do not fear, for I am with you; do not be dismayed, for I am your God. I will stregnthen you and help you; I will uphold you with my righteous right hand." (Isaiah 41:10)

Chrisitan, with the mighty Lord on your side, you are on the winning side! Or, as the Bible reminds us—if God is with us, who or what can be against us! The pressure and demands of this world are exactly that—they are pressures and demands from the world. However, the peace and promises from the Lord are exactly that—peace and promises from our great God who never lies or changes His mind!

"God is not a man, that he should lie, nor a son of man, that he should change his mind. Does he speak and then not act? Does he promise and not fulfill?" (Numbers 23:19)

Today is the day that you can trade the demands of the world and receive the peace of God. Today is the day when you can release the pressures of the world and relax in the promises of God. Today is the day that the Lord has made—go out and live it all for His glory!

God Grants You Victory

(praising God, trust)

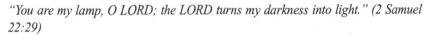

"You are my lamp, O LORD; the LORD turns my darkness into light." (2 Samuel 22:29)

These words come from King David, and these words are his song of praise to the Lord. He was nearing the end of his life, and as he thought about all that God had graciously done for him, he couldn't help but break out in joyous praise. How about you? Can you think of some examples where the Lord has been your lamp? In other words, can you think of some examples where the Lord suddenly turned a dark circumstance into a wonderful blessing of light?

"With your help I can advance against a troop; with my God I can scale a wall." (2 Samuel 22:30)

In spite of what seemed to be overwhelming odds, David was able to experience amazing victories because of God's amazing grace. As he thought back on some of those victories, he couldn't help but break out in joyous praise. How about you? Have you recently experienced any amazing victories because of God's amazing grace? In other words, can you think of a circumstance where God granted you victory in spite of what seemed to be overwhelming odds?

"As for God, his way is perfect; the word of the LORD is flawless. He is a shield for all who take refuge in him. For who is God besides the LORD? And who is the Rock except our God?" (2 Samuel 22:31-32)

David was able to offer joyous praise, because David had the proper perspective. He understood that with God on his side, he was on the winning side! He trusted that God was perfect and that all of his ways were perfect. Therefore, David knew that God would lead and guide, as well as protect and provide, like no one else. David had this perspective because he knew that the Lord was the true living God of the universe . . . the sovereign Creator and Sustainer of the universe! How about you? Can you say those same words of praise that David said? Do you believe that God can perfectly lead and guide your life? Do you believe that God can perfectly protect and provide like no one else when it comes your life? In other words, can you offer joyous praise like David because you have the same perspective as David?

"It is God who arms me with strength and makes my way perfect. He makes my feet like the feet of a deer, he enables me to stand on the heights." (2 Samuel 22:33-34)

Share God's Word with Humility
(love, evangelism)

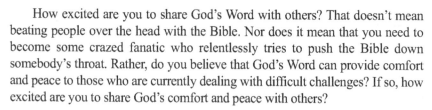

How excited are you to share God's Word with others? That doesn't mean beating people over the head with the Bible. Nor does it mean that you need to become some crazed fanatic who relentlessly tries to push the Bible down somebody's throat. Rather, do you believe that God's Word can provide comfort and peace to those who are currently dealing with difficult challenges? If so, how excited are you to share God's comfort and peace with others?

"Whenever I speak, I cry out proclaiming violence and destruction. So the word of the LORD has brought me insult and reproach all day long." (Jeremiah 20:8)

The prophet Jeremiah met with all kinds of opposition as he shared the Word of the Lord. In fact, he got to the point where he didn't want to share God's Word anymore. He was tired of being mocked and ridiculed—he was tired of feeling like he was wasting his time. Yet, look at what he said:

"But if I say, 'I will not mention him or speak any more in his name,' his word is in my heart like a fire, a fire shut up in my bones. I am weary of holding it in; indeed I cannot." (Jeremiah 20:9)

Jeremiah couldn't help but obediently share God's truth. He knew that it was the only hope for comfort and correction to a people who so desperately needed it. How about you? Do you know of some people who desperately need the comfort and correction of God's Word? Perhaps you're saying to yourself; "Yes, I know someone I could share God's word with; but I know they're going to look at me like I'm weird. They definitely will not be open to me sharing the Bible with them."

"Then the word of the LORD came to Jeremiah: 'I am the LORD, the God of all mankind. Is anything too hard for me?'" (Jeremiah 32:26-27)

A wise person once said that before we go to people about God, we need to first go to God about the people. In other words, we need to pray before we proclaim. In doing so, we're reminded that God can prepare even the hardest of hearts to receive the word He wants us to share with them. We also are reminded that we need to show respect and humility as we share God's Word with others. Therefore, obediently take the step of faith and trust in the power and wisdom of God—you may be very surprised by the results!

Live a Life that Honors God (Part 1)

(discipleship, Christlike)

"How great is the love the Father has lavished on us, that we should be called children of God! And that is what we are! The reason the world does not know us is that it did not know Him." (1 John 3:1)

Christian, it's amazing to think that we are children of God . . . and that is what we are! It's amazing to think that we are members of God's family forever . . . and that is what we are! However, with the privilege of being children of God comes the responsibility to live in a way that honors our great God. So, how is it that we as children of God are to live in the family of God?

1)   We need to put off falsehood and put on truth.

"Therefore each of you must put off falsehood and speak truthfully to his neighbor, for we are all members of one body." (Ephesians 4:25)

Jesus tells us that He is the way, the truth and the life (see John 14:6). He also tells us that the devil is the father of lies (see John 8:44). Therefore, members of God's family need to remember who they are representing. We need to be a people who speak truth in love, and we need to be a people who do not fall into the trap of falsehood.

2)   We need to put off anger and put on peace.

" 'In your anger do not sin': Do not let the sun go down while you are still angry, and do not give the devil a foothold." (Ephesians 4:26-27)

Jesus is the Prince of Peace (see Isaiah 9:6-7). Therefore, as members of His family we need to strive for peace. This doesn't mean that we won't get angry; everybody gets angry from time to time. However, we need to make sure that we pursue peace, and that we make every effort to maintain peace in the family. Why? We do not want to give the devil an opportunity to take unresolved anger and turn it into a full-blown forest fire of chaos.

3)   We need to put off laziness and put on God-honoring work.

"He who has been stealing must steal no longer, but must work, doing something

useful with his own hands, that he may have something to share with those in need." (Ephesians 4:28)

As Christians, we need to remember that we work for our Lord and we work for the glory of our Lord (see Colossians 3:23). Therefore, we need to be the hardest and best workers we can be. Think about it, we have the Spirit of God living in us and we have the word of God guiding us. We have every advantage there is—and no excuses for laziness!

"You were taught, with regard to your former way of life, to put off your old self, which is being corrupted by its deceitful desires; to be made new in the attitude of your minds; and to put on the new self, created to be like God in true righteousness and holiness." (Ephesians 4:22-24)

Live a Life that Honors God (Part 2)
(discipleship, Christlike)

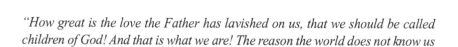

"How great is the love the Father has lavished on us, that we should be called children of God! And that is what we are! The reason the world does not know us is that it did not know him." (1 John 3:1)

As Christians, we have the amazing privilege of being called children of God. However, with that privilege comes the responsibility to live in a way that honors our great God. In Part One, we saw that we need to put off our old ways and put on Christ's new ways. Today we will continue to look at a few more things we need to put off and put on.

1)   We need to put off destructive talk and put on constructive talk.

"Do not let any unwholesome talk come out of your mouths, but only what is helpful for building others up according to their needs, that it may benefit those who listen." (Ephesians 4:29)

As members of God's family, we are called to be positive encouragers, not negative discouragers. This doesn't mean that we approve of or encourage sin.

Rather, it means that we try to build people up in a way that benefits them in their relationship with the Lord. This also means that gossip, back-biting and back-stabbing are things that don't belong in the family of God. Wouldn't you agree?

2) We need to put off bitterness and put on forgiveness.

"Do not grieve the Holy Spirit of God, with whom you were sealed for the day of redemption. Get rid of all bitterness, rage and anger, brawling and slander, along with every form of malice. Be kind and compassionate to one another, forgiving each other, just as in Christ God forgave you." (Ephesians 4:30-32)

God's people are called to be compassionate and forgiving. This means that there is no room for bitterness and brawling in God's family. What is our motivation for forgiving others? We have been forgiven by God in Christ. However, we need to understand the difference between trust and forgiveness. We are called to forgive immediately, but we are not called to trust automatically. Trust is something that has to be earned . . . and it may take time for someone to re-earn trust. Christian, we have the amazing privilege of being called children of God. Yet, with that privilege comes the responsibility to live in a way that honors our great God. May we all live in such a way that blesses others and brings glory to the One whose family name we bear.

"You were taught, with regard to your former way of life, to put off your old self, which is being corrupted by its deceitful desires; to be made new in the attitude of your minds; and to put on the new self, created to be like God in true righteousness and holiness." (Ephesians 4:22-24)

Look to God and Lean on God for Help

(fear, trust)

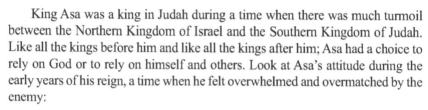

King Asa was a king in Judah during a time when there was much turmoil between the Northern Kingdom of Israel and the Southern Kingdom of Judah. Like all the kings before him and like all the kings after him; Asa had a choice to rely on God or to rely on himself and others. Look at Asa's attitude during the early years of his reign, a time when he felt overwhelmed and overmatched by the enemy:

"Then Asa called to the LORD his God and said, 'LORD, there is no one like you to help the powerless against the mighty. Help us, O LORD our God, for we rely on you, and in your name we have come against this vast army. O LORD, you are our God; do not let man prevail against you.' " (2 Chronicles 14:11)

Asa trusted in the Lord and he completely relied on the Lord for protection and victory. He didn't rely on his own power nor did he rely on the power of other human alliances. Rather, he understood that there was no God but the true living God; and he trusted in His power and fought for His name. How about you? How have your prayers looked as of late? Have you been praying like Asa, looking to God and leaning on God for help? Or, have you been looking to man and leaning on man for help? Look at the result of Asa's faithful trust in the Lord:

"The LORD struck down the Cushites before Asa and Judah. The Cushites fled, and Asa and his army pursued them as far as Gerar. Such a great number of Cushites fell that they could not recover; they were crushed before the LORD and his forces. The men of Judah carried off a large amount of plunder." (2 Chronicles 14:12-13)

Asa looked to God for victory against seemingly impossible circumstances, and Asa received victory from God in spite of those seemingly impossible circumstances. God graciously rewarded Asa's faith, showing that it's absolutely impossible for man to prevail against the Lord. Christian, God is more than able to do the same for you—regardless of the seemingly impossible circumstances you may now be facing. May we all follow the example of Asa, looking to the Lord and leaning on His power to prevail!

"But as for you, be strong and do not give up, for your work will be rewarded." (2 Chronicles 15:7)

Are You Involved in the Game of Blame? (Part 1)

(blame, repentance, confession)

Are you involved in the game of blame? Are you finding it easier to pass the blame on to others rather than admitting that you should take responsibility? It's very easy to fall into the blame game; where our fingers automatically point outward toward others rather than pointing inward toward ourselves.

"He said, 'Who told you that you were naked? Have you eaten from the tree that I commanded you not to eat from?' The man said, 'The woman you put here with me—she gave me some fruit from the tree, and I ate it.'" (Genesis 3:11-12)

Where does blame come from? It all started back in the Garden of Eden. Once Adam and Eve disobeyed God by eating the forbidden fruit, contamination came into the world. Their sin introduced death into the world. Their sin also introduced shame and blame into the world. Thus, upon being confronted by God, Adam failed to take responsibility and repent. Instead he pointed his finger outward and immediately started playing the blame game—he blamed the woman and he blamed God for giving him the woman! Can you think of some recent examples from your life where you have done the same thing?

"Then the LORD God said to the woman, 'What is this you have done?' The woman said, 'The serpent deceived me, and I ate.'" (Genesis 3:13-14)

Notice how easily and how quickly the woman learned to play the blame game from her husband. When God confronted her, she also failed to take responsibility and repent. Instead, she pointed her finger outward and basically said, "The devil made me do it!" Can you think of some recent examples from your life where you have done the same thing?

"The sacrifices of God are a broken spirit; a broken and contrite heart, O God, you will not despise." (Psalm 51:17)

Since we have a sin nature that we inherited from Adam and Eve; we also have a propensity to follow the example of Adam and Eve when it comes to the blame game. However, as Christians we also have the Holy Spirit living inside of us. Therefore, we have the opportunity to do what is right in the Lord's sight.

What is that which is pleasing to the Lord? Pleasing to the Lord is a humble and repentant heart; a heart that is willing to admit our mistakes to the Lord and seek forgiveness from the Lord; and a heart that understands that our fingers should first point inward rather than outward.

Are You Involved in the Game of Blame (Part 2)
(repentance, confession)

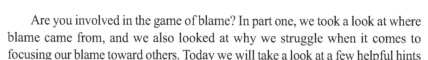

Are you involved in the game of blame? In part one, we took a look at where blame came from, and we also looked at why we struggle when it comes to focusing our blame toward others. Today we will take a look at a few helpful hints from Jesus that can help us when it comes to the blame game.

" 'Why do you look at the speck of sawdust in your brother's eye and pay no attention to the plank in your own eye? How can you say to your brother, "Let me take the speck out of your eye," when all the time there is a plank in your own eye?' " (Matthew 7:3-4)

Jesus tells us to forget the speck and recognize our log. It is very easy to find reasons to criticize and shift blame to others. If you look hard enough you can always find some sort of "speck" to criticize and blame. However, Jesus tells us that we first need to recognize that we have a "big log" sticking out of our own eye that makes it very difficult to properly judge, criticize or blame others.

" 'You hypocrite, first take the plank out of your own eye, and then you will see clearly to remove the speck from your brother's eye.' " (Matthew 7:5)

Jesus tells us to forget the speck and first remove the log. Notice that Jesus doesn't say it's completely wrong to judge, criticize or pass blame. At certain times we may have to do these very things. As Christians, we're called to maintain the integrity of God's truth and to uphold the holiness of God's name. This means that we can't be passive and watch other Christians habitually disobey God's Word and bring dishonor to God's name. However, before we decide to be "our brother's keeper," we need to forget their speck for a moment and focus first on our log. We need to make sure that our motives are pure and our desire is to help and protect the other person, not to hurt and pulverize the other person. In other words, we need to make sure that when we remove the speck, we do it with respect.

" 'For in the same way you judge others, you will be judged, and with the measure you use, it will be measured to you.' " (Matthew 7:2)

May we be committed to not falling into the trap of the blame game. May we all be careful when it comes to being the critic and judge of someone else. In addition, may we remember the steps we learned today:

1) Forget the speck and recognize your log.

2) Forget the speck and first remove the log.

3) Remove the speck, but do it with respect.

Replace Your Fear with Faith

(fear, worry)

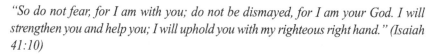

"So do not fear, for I am with you; do not be dismayed, for I am your God. I will strengthen you and help you; I will uphold you with my righteous right hand." (Isaiah 41:10)

Fear is something that can immobilize our faith. Fear is something that can cause us immense worry and doubt. Fear is something that can lead to frustration and confusion. Can you relate? Are you dealing with some kind of fear right now that is immobilizing your faith? Are you feeling confused and worried, frustrated and doubtful? Re-read the verse above and really concentrate on what God is saying:

1) Do not fear. Why? I am with you.
2) Do not be dismayed. Why? I am your God.
3) Do not fear. Why? I will strengthen you.
4) Do not be dismayed. Why? I will help you.
5) Do not fear or be dismayed. Why? I will uphold you with my righteous right hand.

"For I am the LORD, your God, who takes hold of your right hand and says to you, Do not fear; I will help you." (Isaiah 41:13)

Are you still feeling confused and worried, frustrated and doubtful? Re-read the verse above and really concentrate on what God is saying:

1) I am the Lord who is your God.
2) I am the Lord who takes your right hand.
3) I am the Lord who says to you, "Do not be afraid."
4) I am the Lord who says to you, "I will help you."

As Christians, we all experience fear and frustration. We still deal with worry and doubt. However, we can be thankful to God for His words of encouragement. Nothing encourages the people of God more than the Word of God! Therefore, whenever you start to feel that fear is immobilizing your faith, don't run and hide. Instead, read and be fortified in your faith. Christian, let God's Word remind you of God's faithfulness; let God's Word remind you of God's power and protection; let God's Word replace your fear with faith; let God's Word replace your panic with peace; and let God's Word replace your worry with worship!

Is Anything Too Hard for the Lord?

(stress, trust)

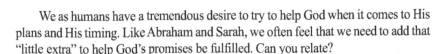

We as humans have a tremendous desire to try to help God when it comes to His plans and His timing. Like Abraham and Sarah, we often feel that we need to add that "little extra" to help God's promises be fulfilled. Can you relate?

"Abram said, 'You have given me no children; so a servant in my household will be my Heir.' Then the word of the Lord came to him: 'This man will not be your heir, but a son coming from your own body will be your heir.'" (Genesis 15:3-4)

God promised Abraham that nothing was impossible, and that he and Sarah would indeed be blessed with offspring. In spite of the fact that both were past the accepted age of childbearing, God made a promise that their offspring would be as numerous as the stars in the sky.

"Abraham believed the Lord, and he credited it to him as righteousness." (Genesis 15:6)

Abraham's faith is amazing in that he trusted that God could and would do what He graciously promised. By the way, verse 6 is a key verse in showing that Abraham and others in the Old Testament were saved by faith, and not by works (see Romans 4 for further explanation). However, as God's promise of an heir seemed to be taking much longer than both Abraham and Sarah had anticipated, they decided that perhaps God needed their help.

"So after Abram had been living in Canaan ten years, Sarah his wife took her Egyptian maidservant Hagar and gave her to her husband to be his wife. He slept with Hagar, and she conceived. When she knew she was pregnant, she began to despise her mistress." (Genesis 16:3-4)

In spite of his faith, Abraham grew impatient and decided that God needed some help to fulfill His purposes and promises. Big mistake! Big mistake for Abraham, and a big mistake for us when we attempt to do the same thing. Can you relate? Is there a situation in your life right now where you're running out of patience? Are you finding that you're trying to give that "little extra" to help God along?

" 'Is there anything too hard for the Lord? I will return to you at the appointed time next year and Sarah will have a son.'" (Genesis 18:14)

God did in fact fulfill His promise at the appointed time. The same faithful God will fulfill His promise at the appointed time for us as well. How can we be so certain? Is anything too hard for the Lord?

Are You Struggling with Fear and Worry?

(fear, worry, stress)

The Bible continually encourages us to be people of courage. We are to trust God and step forward in faith looking to fulfill the plan of God. However, when faced with difficult people or difficult circumstances, it's very easy to lose our courage. The result is that we are frozen in our faith, we become people of fear, and we fail to step forward in faith. Can you relate? Are you facing some difficult people or difficult circumstances right now?

"The righteous cry out, and the Lord hears them; he delivers them from all their troubles. The Lord is close to the brokenhearted and saves those who are crushed in spirit." (Psalm 34:17-18)

A wise person once said: "Courage is fear that said its prayers." In fact, courage is not the absence of fear—it's the conquest of it. How do we find the courage that can conquer our fears? By striving to get alone with the Lord, the One who can give us all that we need to be able to accomplish all that He has planned for us. However, that is not always so simple, is it? We get discouraged and distracted, forgetting to slow down and find our much needed time with the Lord. Once again, can you relate?

"I sought the Lord, and he answered me; he delivered me from all my fears. Those who look to him are radiant; their faces are never covered with shame. This poor man called, and the Lord heard him; he saved him out of all his troubles." (Psalm 34:4-6)

Fear can be looked at as a warning light. It can be a light that reminds us to stop what we are doing (or even thinking) and get alone with the Lord. This is what King David did when he was frozen in fear. He didn't run away from his fears, nor did he try to deny them. Instead, he sought the Lord—and he kept seeking the Lord until his fears were replaced with courage. Remember, courage is fear that said its prayers. Are you struggling with fear and worry? How much time are you spending with the Lord? Perhaps you need to look at the warning light and slow yourself down so you can get alone with the Lord. Or maybe you feel you have been seeking the Lord, and maybe you have experienced moments of courage. However, you are finding that your courage will only last for a day or so. Now are you wondering what you should do?

"Taste and see how that the Lord is good; blessed is the man who takes refuge in him. Fear the Lord, you his saints, for those who fear him lack nothing. The lions may grow weak and hungry, but those who seek the Lord lack no good thing." (Psalm 34:8-10)

Rely on the Power and Wisdom of God
(evangelism, trust)

Are you having trouble when it comes to sharing your faith with others? Are you finding yourself feeling afraid and intimidated when it comes to giving a reason for the hope you have in Christ? If so, understand that you're not alone.

"When I came to you, brothers, I did not come with eloquence or superior wisdom as I proclaimed to you the testimony about God. For I resolved to know nothing while I was with you except Jesus Christ and him crucified. I came to you in weakness and fear, and with much trembling." (1 Corinthians 2:1-3)

Can you believe it? The great Apostle Paul, called by God to spread the gospel of God, was nervous and in fear when he went to share the gospel with the people of Corinth. Yet, this shouldn't be surprising to any of us. Why? He was a human like us—he experienced the same emotions that we do, including the feelings of fear and intimidation. However, his weakness didn't disqualify him from being used by God; it actually qualified him to be greatly used by God.

"My message and my preaching were not with wise and persuasive words, but with a demonstration of the Spirit's power, so that your faith might not rest on men's wisdom, but on God's power." (1 Corinthians 2:4-5)

Paul saw his weakness and fear as a blessing. Why? It caused him to rely solely on the power and wisdom of God. It also allowed him to be confident that those who trusted in Jesus as their Savior, truly trusted in Jesus alone as their Savior—not in Paul and his great abilities of persuasion. Christian, it's the same with us. Our weakness and fear does not disqualify us from being used by God, it actually qualifies us to be greatly used by God! That's why He gets all the glory. This does not mean we shouldn't pray and properly prepare ourselves to share our faith. The Lord does not condone laziness. But it is okay to feel a bit nervous and apprehensive when it comes to sharing our faith. Like Paul, our weakness can actually be a blessing, because it causes us to rely solely on the power and wisdom of God. And, like Paul, we can be confident that those who trust in Jesus as their Savior truly trust in Him alone—not in our great abilities of persuasion. Once again, that's why God gets the glory.

Sin Is the Most Dangerous Disease

(thankfulness, prayer, sin)

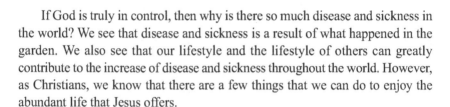

If God is truly in control, then why is there so much disease and sickness in the world? We see that disease and sickness is a result of what happened in the garden. We also see that our lifestyle and the lifestyle of others can greatly contribute to the increase of disease and sickness throughout the world. However, as Christians, we know that there are a few things that we can do to enjoy the abundant life that Jesus offers.

Live gratefully.

Pray faithfully.

Rejoice immensely.

1) We need to pray faithfully and trust that God has the power to heal.

"Is any one of you in trouble? He should pray. Is anyone happy? Let him sing songs of praise. Is any one of you sick? He should call the elders of the church to pray over him and anoint him with oil in the name of the Lord. And the prayer offered in faith will make the sick person well; the Lord will raise him up. If he has sinned, he will be forgiven. Therefore confess your sins to each other and pray for each other so that you may be healed. The prayer of a righteous man is powerful and effective." (James 5:13-16)

Our great God has the power to heal sickness and disease. God cares for His children. That is why we pray in faith, trusting in His perfect will to be done. Interestingly, as we faithfully pray and wait for God's will, we often receive immediate emotional healing as God pours His perfect peace into our hearts. Are you struggling with some sort of illness right now? Is the outlook causing you stress? Try to look up, for the prayers of God's children are powerful and effective!

2) We need to rejoice immensely because our Savior is the victorious King!

"Surely he took up our infirmities and carried our sorrows, yet we considered him stricken by God, smitten by him, and afflicted. But he was pierced for our transgressions, he was crushed for our iniquities; the punishment that brought us

265

peace was upon him, and by his wounds we are healed." (Isaiah 53:4-5)

The biggest and most dangerous disease we all face is our sin virus. This is a killer, and it's a virus that we inherited from Adam and Eve. The bad news is that no matter how hard we try to heal ourselves of this deadly disease, we cannot do so. However, the good news is that through Jesus we are healed: Forever! As Jesus hung on the cross, our infirmities and iniquities were put upon him, and He was punished in our place as our substitute. He died the death we deserve, but three days later He rose from the dead, overcoming sin, death, and disease for us. Although we still are vulnerable to sickness and disease for the time being here on earth, nevertheless we are truly healed through Jesus. We are healed spiritually, as we are now connected to God through Jesus. One day we will be completely healed physically, as we will spend eternity with our great God. How can this be? It's by His wounds that we are healed—forever!

"And I heard a loud voice from the throne saying, "Now the dwelling of God is with men, and he will live with them. They will be his people, and he will be with them, and be their God. He will wipe every tear from their eyes. There will be no more death or mourning or crying or pain, for the old order of things has passed away." (Revelation 21:3-4)

God Is Abundantly Able

(trust, future, faith)

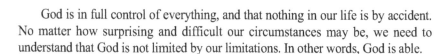

God is in full control of everything, and that nothing in our life is by accident. No matter how surprising and difficult our circumstances may be, we need to understand that God is not limited by our limitations. In other words, God is able.

God is able to establish us.

"Now to him who is able to establish you by my gospel and the proclamation of Jesus Christ, according to the revelation of the mystery hidden for long ages past, but now revealed and made known through the prophetic writings by the command of the eternal God, so that all nations might believe and obey him—to the only wise God be glory forever through Jesus Christ! Amen." (Romans 16:25-27)

God is able to keep us from falling.

"To him who is able to keep you from falling and to present you before his glorious presence without fault and with great joy—to the only God our Savior be glory, majesty, power and authority, through Jesus Christ our Lord, before all ages, now and forevermore! Amen." (Jude 24-25)

God is able to do abundantly more than we expect.

"Now to him who is able to do immeasurably more than all we ask or imagine, according to his power that is at work in us, to him be the glory in the church and in Christ Jesus throughout all generations, forever and ever! Amen." (Ephesians 3:20-21)

Did you notice that a proper perspective of God's power and control inevitably leads to a proclamation of praise? In all three verses, recognizing the fact that God is able causes the writer to pour forth in praise and worship. Shouldn't it be the same for us? Is God able to establish you in His family through Jesus Christ, blessing you with abundant life now and forever? Then praise Him! Is God able to keep you from falling, protecting you and providing for you all that you need to live the life He has for you? Then praise Him! Is God able to do not only what you ask, but is He able to do abundantly more than you can ask or imagine? Then praise Him! Although you may currently be struggling with some circumstances that you're unable to overcome, you have a God who has all power and control. Your God is the only true living God, and His Word assures us that He is able to overcome anything and everything you're facing. So praise Him!

The Blessing of the Lord Brings Wealth

(finances, contentment, peace)

"The blessing of the Lord brings wealth, and he adds no trouble to it." (Proverbs 10:22)

The blessing of the Lord brings wealth. Wealth is not limited to material blessings. Rather, wealth includes spiritual and emotional blessings as well. In other words, when the Lord brings the blessings, He enriches us with an abundance of blessings that far exceed anything we could gain on our own.

The blessing of the Lord doesn't bring baggage and burdens. When the Lord brings the blessings, He also provides the peace for us to enjoy the blessings. In other words, the blessings of the Lord allow us to have joy in the day, as well as to be able to sleep peacefully at night.

"Better a little with fear of the Lord than great wealth with turmoil." (Proverbs 15:16)

How would you characterize your feelings right now? Are you feeling enriched and at peace for the blessings the Lord has provided? Or are you feeling troubled and in turmoil? When the Lord brings the blessings, it doesn't matter the size of the blessings. What matters is the size of the peace and contentment that comes along with those blessings. This also is a gift from God.

"Moreover, when God gives any man wealth and possessions, and enables him to enjoy them, to accept his lot and be happy—this is a gift from God. He seldom reflects on the days of his life, because God keeps him occupied with gladness in his heart." (Ecclesiastes 5:19-20)

Contentment is an important key to a life filled with joy and peace. When the Lord provides blessings, He also provides contentment to accept and enjoy those blessings. After reviewing the above verses, where would you say that you rank on the contentment scale—one being very miserable, ten being truly content? Take some time with the Lord right now and think about the blessings He has provided you. Ask Him for the gift to be able to recognize and enjoy all that He has given you. In other words, ask Him to make you a person of peace and contentment.

What Nickname Would You Be Given?

(legacy, character)

If someone were to give you a nickname that describes your character, would you be proud of that name? That is a very challenging thought, isn't it? The Scriptures encourage us to live a life that reflects the character and conduct of Christ. We are not told to be perfect like Christ, for that is truly impossible on this side of heaven. However, we are told to live a life worthy of the "nickname" we have been given. What is the nickname for those who are followers of Christ? The nickname is "Christian."

What is a Christian?

A Christian is one who has trusted his or her eternal destiny to Jesus Christ alone.

" 'Salvation is found in no one else, for there is no other name under heaven given to men by which we must be saved.' " (Acts 4:12)

A Christian is one who desires to obey and follow Jesus Christ alone as Lord and Leader.

"Then he called the crowd to him along with his disciples and said: 'If anyone would come after me, he must deny himself and take up his cross and follow me.' " (Mark 8:34)

A Christian is one who desires to bring glory to Jesus Christ alone by living a life worthy of the calling that he or she has received.

"As a prisoner for the Lord, then, I urge you to live a life worthy of the calling you have received. Be completely gentle; be patient, bearing with one another in love." (Ephesians 4:1-2)

Have you trusted in the finished work of Jesus for your salvation? Are you following Him, looking to obey Him and live a life that brings glory to Him? Remember, a nickname very often describes something about a person. It often describes the character and conduct of that person. For example, a person with a quick temper may be given the nickname, "Hot Head." A person who is trustworthy and dependable may be given the nickname, "Mr. or Ms. Reliable." If someone were to give you a nickname describing your character and conduct as a Christian, what nickname would you be given? Would you be proud of that name? Better yet, would Christ be proud of that name?

Let Our Lives Bring Glory to God
(worship, thankfulness)

As Christians, our primary purpose is to give God glory. We are to love God, walk humbly with the Lord our God, using our lips and our lives to bring glory to our great God. Why? Because of who God is and because of what God has done for us through Jesus Christ.

"Not to us, O LORD, not to us but to your name be the glory, because of your love and faithfulness." (Psalm 115:1)

We are also to let our lips and lives bring glory to God because all that we are, and all that we have, is all because of God's love and faithfulness. There's no room for us to boast or brag about ourselves. Rather, we are to acknowledge and be thankful to God, remembering that all we are and all we have is solely because of God's grace working in and through us.

" 'You may say to yourself, "My power and the strength of my hands have produced this wealth for me." But remember the LORD your God, for it is he who gives you the ability to produce wealth, and so confirms his covenant, which he swore to your forefathers, as it is today.' " (Deuteronomy 8:17-18)

Christian, over the past week, have you been praising God and thanking Him for his continual grace in your life? Or, have you been complaining to God and telling Him everything that is wrong with your life? Pretty challenging questions, aren't they? Please understand, it's not wrong to bring our complaints and concerns to God. The Bible is very clear that we are to cast our anxieties upon the Lord, trusting in His care for us. But we all can sometimes slip into a form of "spiritual amnesia," where we forget to thank God for who He is and all He has graciously done for us. If you feel that you've been suffering from "spiritual amnesia" lately, take some time now to refresh your memory and praise God for His grace in your life over the past week. Review one day at a time and think of all that God has done for you. You'll be amazed at how much you actually have to praise God for! Our God is an awesome God, He is awesome for who He is and He is awesome for how He is towards us!

"The LORD is the great God, the great King above all gods. In his hand are the depths of the earth, and the mountain peaks belong to him. The sea is his, for he made it, and his hands formed the dry land. Come, let us bow down in worship, let us kneel before the LORD our Maker; for he is our God and we are the people of his pasture, the flock under his care." (Psalm 95:3-7)

Do You Believe In Eternal Life?

(resurrection, eternal life)

"If Christ has not been raised, your faith is futile; you are still dead in your sins." (1 Corinthians 15:17)

The Apostle Paul was basically saying, "Listen, if Christ hasn't been raised from the dead, we are all helpless and hopeless. We're all dead in our sins and we will all be eternally damned because of our sins." Do you believe that Christ was raised from the dead? Better yet, do you believe that Christ was raised from the dead after paying for your sins? Have you trusted in Him for salvation and life with God forever?

"Then those who have fallen asleep in Christ are lost. If only for this life we have hope in Christ, we are to be pitied more than all men." (1 Corinthians 15:18-19)

The Apostle Paul was basically saying, "Listen, if Christ hasn't been raised from the dead, then those who have died are dead forever. They are hopeless and helpless forever. They will never be resurrected, they are lost and lifeless forever—what a waste. Also, if Christ has not been raised from the dead, then we who are currently alive have no hope for eternal life. This means that our only life is down here on earth. We die and that's it—what a waste." Do you believe that Christ has been raised from the dead? Better yet, do you believe that because Christ has been raised from the dead, He is able to raise you and your loved ones from the dead? In other words, do you believe that there is life eternal through Jesus Christ?

"Jesus said to her, 'I am the resurrection and the life. He who believes in me will live, even though he dies; and whoever lives and believes in me will never die. Do you believe this?'" (John 11:25-26)

This is a very bold proclamation from Jesus. He makes it very clear that through Him there is life eternal. Why? He is the only one who can say (and prove!) that He is the resurrection and life. Do you believe that your sins were placed on Jesus and that He was punished in your place, as your substitute? Do you believe that the Perfect One of heaven was cursed on that cross in your place, dying the death you deserve? Do you believe that Jesus rose from the dead three days later, overcoming sin and death for you? Finally, do you believe that what Jesus did 2,000 years ago was completely sufficient for your salvation—to the point that you have placed your complete faith and trust in Him alone for that salvation? The evidence demands a verdict, Jesus is the only Savior, the ONLY ONE who can claim and prove that He has been raised from the dead. Do you believe this?

The Beginning of Birth Pains

(end times, Jesus' return)

It seems that daily we are hearing of various natural disasters throughout the world. We have seen an unprecedented increase of earthquakes, tsunamis and hurricanes. It also seems that daily we are hearing of an increase of wars and conflicts throughout the world. Additionally, we have seen an unprecedented increase of various world religions and religious gurus, claiming that they have the secrets to eternal bliss. What is happening? Better yet, why is all of this happening?

"Jesus answered, 'Watch out that no one deceives you. For many will come in my name, claiming, 'I am the Christ,' and will deceive many. You will hear of wars and rumors of wars, but see to it that you are not alarmed. Such things must happen, but the end is still to come. Nation will rise against nation, and kingdom against kingdom. There will be famines and earthquakes in various places. All these are the beginning of birth pains.' " (Matthew 24:4-8)

Why is all of this happening? Jesus said it would happen as a sign that He was returning. We need to be careful in saying that all that is happening is proof that Jesus is returning tomorrow. He made it clear that He is returning, but He also made it clear that we should not try to predict the time and date. Instead, we should make sure that we are prepared for His return.

" 'Therefore keep watch, because you do not know on what day your Lord will come. But understand this: If the owner of the house had known at what time of night the thief was coming, he would have kept watch and would not have let his house be broken into. So you also must be ready, because the Son of Man will come at an hour when you do not expect him.' " (Matthew 24:42-44)

How can we be ready for the return of our Lord? By staying focused and staying busy showing the love of our Lord, and sharing the truth about our Lord, all for the glory of our Lord. Christian, how focused and how busy have you been of late? Not how focused and how busy you have been when it comes to your career or your workouts at the gym. Rather, how focused and how busy have you been when it comes to showing and sharing the love of Christ, all for the glory of Christ?

" 'Who then is the faithful and wise servant, whom the master has put in charge of the servants in his household to give them their food at the proper time? It will be good for that servant whose master finds him doing so when he returns. I tell you the truth, he will put him in charge of all his possessions.' " (Matthew 24:45-47)

Live by Faith in God
(faith)

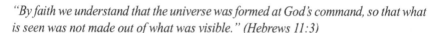

"By faith we understand that the universe was formed at God's command, so that what is seen was not made out of what was visible." (Hebrews 11:3)

This may be a bit surprising, but everybody exercises some form of faith. For example, it takes faith to go to the doctor. Why? Did you do extensive research on the doctor prior to visiting the doctor? If so, then you are trusting by faith that your research is accurate. If not, well, you're really exercising faith! It also takes faith to trust in the diagnosis and recommendation of the doctor. Why? How do you know that the doctor is correct? Have you first researched your problem and become an expert on it? Or, do you simply trust the doctor because he or she has a diploma on the wall and a name tag that says "MD"? Please understand, doctors are wonderful. But we exercise faith in them. It also takes faith to take prescribed medication. Why? Did you first research the medication to make sure it is the correct one? Did you first do all kinds of tests on the medication to make sure that it has no poison in it? Once again, please understand, medication is wonderful. But we exercise faith when we use it. Finally, it takes faith to start your car. Why? How do you know it will start? Or, how do you know that it will not explode when you try to start it? It sounds horrible, but you get the point.

"Without faith it is impossible to please God, because anyone who comes to him must believe that he exists and that he rewards those who earnestly seek him." (Hebrews 11:6)

The question is not, "Do we exercise faith?" Rather, the question is, "In whom or in what do we exercise faith?" In other words, are we exercising our faith in God, man, or ourselves? When it comes to your family, in whom are you placing your faith? When it comes to your employment or finances, in whom are you placing your faith? How about in your ministry? The verse above tells us that God is pleased when we place our faith in Him—for eternal salvation, as well as for our daily lives here on earth. When we live by faith in God:

1) We trust that He exists.
2) We trust that He is able to act in our lives.
3) We trust that He cares for us.
4) We trust that He knows what is best for us.
5) We trust that He is able to bring about what is best for us and for His glory.

"Now faith is being sure of what we hope for and certain of what we do not see. This is what the ancients were commended for." (Hebrews 11:1-2)

The Grace of God Sustains You

(grace, spiritual warfare)

In Matthew chapter 4, Matthew describes for us two incredible events that occurred at the very beginning of Jesus' earthly ministry. The first is the baptism of Jesus, the other is the three temptations in the wilderness that Jesus faced and overcame.

The Baptism of Jesus.

"As soon as Jesus was baptized, He went up out of the water. At that moment heaven was opened, and he saw the Spirit of God descending like a dove and lighting on him. And a voice from heaven said, 'This is my Son, whom I love; with him I am well pleased.'" (Matthew 3:16-17)

These words must have been a tremendous source of comfort for Jesus as He was about to face the upcoming challenges of His ministry. These words should also be a tremendous source of comfort for us as well. Why? Because these are the words that God the Father says about us as Christians. When He looks at us, He looks at us through the eyes of grace—He sees us covered by the precious blood of His Son—and as a result God says of us, "You're My child, My son or My daughter, whom I love, and with whom I am well pleased." However, it's at this very truth that Satan will shoot his fiery darts of doubt. After His baptism, we are told that Jesus was led into the desert to do battle with Satan.

The Temptations of Jesus.

"Then Jesus was led by the Spirit into the desert to be tempted by the devil." (Matthew 4:1)

Notice that this confrontation did not come about by Satan's will, but by the will of God. Jesus went into the desert on the offensive, not on the defensive. He went in there to conquer and to demonstrate His supreme authority. As our representative, Jesus went in there to be victorious where Adam and Eve had failed. Jesus went into the desert to be victorious where the nation of Israel had failed. Jesus went into the desert to give us a prelude to His ultimate victory over Satan at the cross. It's the same with us. If you feel that you're now being led into the desert or feel that you have been battling in the desert for a while; try to remember that the Spirit of God will never lead you where the grace of God cannot sustain you. If God brings you to something, He is faithful to bring you victoriously through that something. How can we be so certain of this?

"Because the one who is in you is greater than the one who is in the world." (1 John 4:4)

Overcoming the Darts of Doubt

(doubt, spiritual warfare)

As we continue to look at the temptations of Jesus in the wilderness, it's encouraging to see that through Jesus we too can overcome those "Darts of Doubt" that Satan fires our way. Today we will look at how Jesus faced and overcame the first temptation He faced.

Dart of Doubt #1

"After fasting forty days and forty nights, He was hungry. The tempter came to him and said, 'If you're the Son of God, tell these stones to become bread.'" (Matthew 4:2-3)

This "Dart of Doubt" was aimed at questioning the Father's care and provision for Jesus. The intent was to try to get Jesus to act independently of the Father, which then of course would be sin.

"Jesus answered, 'It is written: "Man does not live on bread alone, but on every word that comes from the mouth of God."'" (Matthew 4:4)

In other words, Jesus was saying that He was going to trust in the Father's care and provision, no matter what the circumstances. Are you dealing with this same dart of doubt? Have you been waiting for God to provide you with something that is a very legitimate need and all you have received up to this point is silence from heaven? Suddenly here comes the dart of doubt: "Are you sure God can be trusted?" Like Jesus, we must try to understand that God has a greater purpose for us. Silence from heaven does not necessarily mean no, it may simply mean slow. Why? Because God wants us to grow—to grow in faith, to grow in trust, and to grow in our understanding that when God guides, He always provides.

Three things Jesus did to defeat the darts of doubt:

1) Jesus countered immediately.

2) Jesus countered with Scripture.

3) Jesus countered with authority.

As you deal with your darts of doubt today, take some time to think about how Jesus countered immediately and did not let lies or negative thoughts penetrate His thinking.

"We demolish arguments and every pretension that sets itself up against the knowledge of God, and we take captive every thought to make it obedient to Christ." (2 Corinthians 10:5)

Am I Following God's Plan ?

(God's will, intimacy with God)

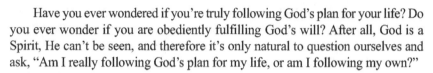

Have you ever wondered if you're truly following God's plan for your life? Do you ever wonder if you are obediently fulfilling God's will? After all, God is a Spirit, He can't be seen, and therefore it's only natural to question ourselves and ask, "Am I really following God's plan for my life, or am I following my own?"

"For it is God who works in you to will and to act according to his good purpose."
(Philippians 2:13)

Christian, relax and rejoice. God is working in you to bring about his perfect will and plan for your life; and He is doing it right now! By God's grace and through the Holy Spirit, God is moving in and through your life. By God's grace and through the Holy Spirit, God is bringing about His good purpose in your life. Our job is to stay close and connected to the Lord, asking Him to help us obediently (and patiently!) to follow His promptings.

" 'I am the vine; you are the branches. If a man remains in me and I in him, he will bear much fruit; apart from me you can do nothing.' " (John 15:5)

Christian, if you want to abound for Christ, then you must abide in Christ. In other words, the more time you spend talking to the Lord in prayer and listening to the Lord through His Word, the more you will start to see Him acting in and through your life. Why? You will be open and attentive to His promptings; you will be more aware and fervent to follow His guidance, and you will see the Lord working in you to will and act according to His good purpose. That is when it starts to get really exciting!

" 'If you remain in me and my words remain in you, ask whatever you wish, and it will be given to you. This is to my Father's glory, that you bear much fruit, showing yourselves to be my disciples.' " (John 15:7-8)

Once again, if you want to abound for Christ, then you must abide in Christ. Jesus promises that it is the Father's will and desire that we bear a ton of Christ-like fruit in our lives. Why? It brings glory to our great God. This means that God actually wants there to be a bunch of Christ-like fruit in and through your life. Christian, God is working in you to bring about His perfect will and plan for your life; and He is doing it right now! Always remember, faithfulness leads to fruitfulness. Stay faithful, and watch how your life will become fruitful!

"I can do everything through him who gives me strength." (Philippians 4:13)